In memory of Sally Philp

1960 to 2003

Chapter 1

The Hidden Village

I was born in a village near Oxford, called Kingston Bagpuize. I called it Kingston Bagpipes because it is difficult to say Bagpuize when you are under five.

In fact I was born in the Nuffield Maternity Home, Oxford. Does anyone say where they were actually born? So Kingston Bagpipes it is.

I was born on 6th January 1955. I only mention that as it is exactly the same date as Rowan Atkinson. If we had been switched at birth things would be much different now.

This year I reached my state pension age. I claimed mine – I wonder if Rowan claimed his?

My family lived in a 'transit' camp on the edge of the village. This camp consisted of a series of Nissen huts, which were metal structures thrown up to house families whilst the council looked for more permanent places for them to live.

I was five when my Dad took my Mum, brother and me to a nearby village called Sutton Courtenay. A brand new housing estate had been built on the outskirts of the village.

Many people lived on council housing estates in those days. Home ownership was mostly reserved for the middle classes.

I don't remember much, if anything, about my time in Kingston Bagpipes.

I remember the first time I saw the houses in Sutton Courtenay. Brand, spanking new they smelt of fresh paint and seemed huge. Huge rooms, huge gardens. I wanted to move in there and then.

Dad was not entirely satisfied with the first house we saw. I remember I was mortified when we left. I thought my dream was gone.

However, a couple of weeks later we moved into the house across the road. I have no idea why, but I guess Dad had his reasons. I remember being so happy. Room to run around and play. Space, not being hemmed in by other people

Old people reminisce about the good old days when you could leave your doors unlocked, safe in the knowledge that no-one would come in and steal your possessions.

That was certainly true of our estate. We never locked our doors. At least until we had something worth stealing.

Over time, it became evident the house wasn't perfect. It was cold because it had no central heating. It didn't have double glazing either. This was largely because they hadn't been invented.

The aforementioned old people will remember those days. In the Winter ice would form inside the galvanised metal, single pane windows. Breathing out would cause clouds of vapour.

It is said that modern, centrally heated houses harbour germs more easily, which leads to more colds. Some blame it for the increase in asthma amongst children too.

I would still rather have been warm. I remember sitting in bed, teeth chattering, talking to my brother to distract ourselves from the biting cold.

I had to share a bedroom with my brother. I don't know why, as it was a three bedroomed house. Perhaps it was so our parents could more easily keep an eye on us.

We used to get up to some strange activities in that bedroom, to avoid thinking about the cold and our parents.

Our bedroom was at the back of the house. There was a large garden with a chain link fence at the end. All council houses seemed to have chain link fences. Their replacement by wooden fencing is a sure sign that the occupants have purchased the house.

Beyond the fence was a huge field, where the farmer kept cows. As there was nothing between us and the outside, when the curtains were drawn open, the window glass was totally black and acted like a mirror.

My brother and I put on little acts to amuse ourselves. I remember one thing in particular. It might have been the only thing.

We would wrap ourselves in a blanket and stand to the side of the window. Individually we would leap out in front of the window and shout 'Dominyoor'

I don't know if that is how it's spelt, but it doesn't matter as I don't think it's a word.

I don't know what that was about, but we found it funny. This was a time when we had no TV.

Sometimes we would throw open the blanket as we landed in front of the window.

In order to get a good reflection, we needed the light on. I later discovered that with the light on everything in the room could be seen. It's a good job there were no houses behind us.

I don't know what the cows thought of it though.

I was very happy to be living in Sutton Courtenay on the New Estate as everyone called it, for obvious reasons.

The New Estate was made up of a series of roads, ways and cul-de-sacs. We lived in Bradstock's Way. There was a Tyrell's Way and a Barret's Way. Most councils seem to name the roads on their new estates after famous people. I have no idea who this trio were.

I soon discovered that Sutton Courtenay was made up of two distinctly separate parts divided by land, history and wealth.

There was our estate, built in the early sixties and housing a disparate range of people brought together by circumstance, that is the need for housing.

We had a Canadian guy. Everyone called him Canada and he had a maple leaf flag sewn onto the parka-like coat he always wore. I took that as proof that he was Canadian. He never told me himself. I never heard him speak

Canada was an impressive man. I would see him strolling through the estate, head held high. He looked like an indigenous Canadian. I thought he looked like a Red Indian, a term which is frowned upon today. At the time I knew no better. For no real reason he frightened me. Maybe I thought he would start firing arrows at me. I got out of the way when I saw him approach.

Next door to us was a rather large number of what we would call travellers today. We called them gypsies in a non-PC way. They were very noisy but friendly enough.

We had all sorts of nationalities. It was like a league of nations. Everyone got on in the main, although sometimes there were ructions, usually when people were returning from The Plough late at night on a weekend. It was the one pub fairly close to the estate and played an integral part in my family's history.

My Mums' family, that is. There were quite a few living in the village. My Dads' family lived in Reading and were doing well in the construction business. There was still a great deal of housing to be built after the war. This was a time of economic growth in the country

The other part of the village was completely different and there was little communication between the two. The only time was when one of the people from the other, more affluent end of the village wanted someone to paint their houses, maintain their gardens or do any manual work that they did not want to do themselves. In other words, we were a new source of labour for them. It was to everyone's mutual benefit.

I remember my Dad painted a sundial on one of the grand houses that faced onto the main road. He actually gilded it with gold leaf. It did look superb, even if he said so himself.

Many of those living in the older part of Sutton Courtenay were well off. Very well off. I don't say that with any sense of jealousy. In fact I spent most of my time in that part of the village which I found fascinating and still do.

As a young person, my very best friend came from that end of the village. His name was Martin Shepherd. Everyone called him Fatty Shepherd, which was unfair as he was not fat at all. Well built, but not fat.

This older part of the village was actually very much older. I found out that many of the buildings including the church are mentioned in the Domesday Book.

The River Thames flows behind the far end of the village on its way from Oxford to London. It doesn't start in Oxford but it ends in London. From its source in the Cotswolds to the town of Dorchester in Oxfordshire it has an alternative name, the Isis. The river Isis is best known as being the river that runs through Oxford. Many people don't know that it is the Thames. I used to think that the Thames became the Isis only when passing through Oxford. It is referenced in the history of the University. For example the second team of the Oxford rowing club is called the Isis.

I used to think it very arrogant of them to rename our national river just because it went through their territory. I considered myself to be an honorary member of the Town part of Town and Gown. That phrase has been around for centuries and represents the difference between the students of the colleges of Oxford University. and the locals. There can sometimes be a rivalry between the two.

Every year, on May day students of the University gather on the banks of the Isis, many around Magdalen Bridge. They eat strawberries and drink Champagne from the early hours. Many are inebriated by mid morning.

Every year the Oxford Times would report that some of the 'madcap students' had jumped off Magdalen Bridge in their state of inebriation. Most years the odd student fell into the river, mucking about with friends. If anyone had jumped off Magdalen Bridge which sits quite high above the Isis, they would probably have incurred quite serious injuries. The Isis is very shallow by Magdalen Bridge.

I used to say that the students didn't jump in, we locals pushed them in. It wasn't true but it was an interesting anecdote.

In Sutton Courtenay we used to have some great times down by the River Thames. We could have called it the Isis as we were situated very much before Dorchester, but we weren't that arrogant. We didn't know either.

I remember there was a small patch of sand at the edge of the river below the weirs. It was called Sandy Beach by the locals which was a bit of a stretch.

We went there often in the Summer, taking our swimming kits and small picnics with us. Great times.

I nearly drowned there once. Luckily my Uncle Richard dived in and saved me.

He was there again when I nearly drowned in the Abingdon open air pool one hot Summer. He was probably a bit tired of playing the hero to his non-swimming nephew.

At that end of the village there's a big old house called The Wharf. It's situated by the path that takes you to the river and backs onto the Thames. The house used to be owned by Herbert Henry Asquith. He was the 1st Earl of Oxford and Prime Minister at the start of the first world war. That is one of the facts that fascinates me about the village.

I was amazed to be told that he had made the declaration of war against Germany from the garden of The Wharf in 1914.

Unfortunately I recently found out that this is probably not true. Asquith was in London for all of that period. Many people still believe this urban myth.

It is true however that his wife Margot, a well known socialite, liked to host parties in the house and gardens on weekends. Apparently they were called weekenders.

Visitors included Winston Churchill, Lloyd George and other world dignitaries, such as the Aga Khan. It's unlikely that they would not have discussed the developing world crisis whilst at the Wharf even if the declaration wasn't made from there.

I still find it hard to believe that these legends of history were having discussions about Britain entering into a war that would result in the most horrific carnage ever seen in the world in my small village that few people have even heard about.

Churchill would definitely be talking about the possible military actions that could be taken. Winston was into war and would come into his own 25 years later.

Asquith and his wife Margot are buried in All Saints Church which is on the village green.

My interest in the village's history probably started when I first saw the large tomb and grave of Asquith and learned that he had been the Prime Minister at the start of the First World War.

I found out that Eric Arthur Blair is also buried in that churchyard. More famous as George Orwell, I could never find out why he is there. I knew his burial was organised by his great friend David Astor.

Different explanations are offered. Some have said he was refused burial in London because of his political views. That seems a bit unlikely as Karl Marx is buried in Highgate cemetery

Another idea is that Orwell said he wanted to be buried in the cemetery closest to where he died. He died in London and at the time all the cemeteries were full. His wife Sonia asked amongst his friends if any of them could find a burial site for him in a church that would observe Anglican rites as was his wish

Some say it is because of his love for the English countryside, which seems a bit vague to me. There's a lot of English countryside between University College Hospital in London where he died and Sutton Courtenay.

Whatever the reason, David Astor agreed to organise Orwell's burial in All Saints Church, Sutton Courtenay.

It is a rule that you can only be buried in the parish where you lived. Although I lived in Sutton Courtenay for many years, I don't live there now. When I die, I will not be able to be buried alongside my Mum and many of my family and friends.

How come Orwell who had no connection with the village and certainly didn't live within the parish was able to be buried there?

There is a note on the church which says Astor and the vicar came to 'an arrangement'

I was told that this arrangement involved Astor donating the yew trees that are on either side of the path that leads into the church. I don't know if this is true, but it's as good an explanation as any.

I always found it interesting that Eric Arthur Blair was buried with a small insignificant headstone that makes no mention of his pen name. It just states his real name, date of birth and death.

It's tucked away at the back of the churchyard and even though I have been to visit it many times, I still have to search to find it.

One day I found a note on the church door headed 'The Grave of George Orwell' with a map of how to find it. I ripped it down. I felt strongly that Eric did not want to become a local attraction. I still feel that way, as do some of the people who have lived in the village for a long time. I think we feel some sort of affinity and also want to see his wishes fulfilled.

Recently I have seen newly built houses for sale in Sutton Courtenay in Orwell Park and Orwell Gardens. I don't know if the great man would have liked that. Even George Orwell didn't want to be called George Orwell in Sutton Courtenay

In 2001, David Astor died and was buried behind his friend Eric. Astor's headstone is also plain and contains only his name, date of birth and death. Perhaps it was David Astor who decided how the headstones should look. At the time Eric wouldn't have had much say in the matter.

I would prefer to think that the socialist Eric Arthur Blair did not want his grave to be recognised as that of the world famous George Orwell and told his friend so. Then when David's time came, he followed suit.

Recently, in 2019, Astor's wife Bridget died. I don't know if she is buried with David. If she is, Orwell is the eternal gooseberry.

I returned to All Saints church the other day, having not been there for fifteen years. I don't know why I had not visited sooner, it's not that far away from where I live now. Maybe writing this was why I felt compelled to go there.

I went to the local florist, Richard Mathews and Son. I needed flowers for Mum's grave. I remembered them well from my childhood. I walked past the shop most days on my way to the big school. I was surprised to find that it was still there. The son served me. I said I was pleased to see they were still there.

I was, they were one of the few things that were still as I remember. He said they had been there on the same site for 120 years. I told him that I wanted some flowers. He made me a nice bouquet.

Somehow I started talking about Orwell. I said about all these roads and estates being named after Orwell. Did they ask his permission? Without my prompting he said 'He would have hated that' I was surprised but pleased that someone who had lived in the village all his life felt the same way as me. After I had left the shop, I wondered how he knew.

I drove back and asked him if he had any proof that Eric Blair wanted to remain anonymous. Had he spoken to Astor perhaps when he was buying flowers. Perhaps his Dad had provided him with flowers for Blairs funeral. That would have been great. Stranger things have happened. His Dad was well over eighty so it was entirely possible.

He said that he didn't have any concrete proof but that anyone who had read his books and was aware of his politics should know. His headstone is final proof. Why would a world famous author want his pen name left off his headstone if not for anonymity.

His Dad appeared after a while. He was able to recall the past in great detail. My Mum's family were large and still are in the village from what I can gather. My Mum's family name is Dodd. I told Richard this. The florist is named after him. He told me he hated school and left as soon as he could to work for his Dad. I could relate to that.

Richard Mathews told me tales about my family that I never knew. Some of it was quite rude. He told me about my Grandmother on my Mum's side. He said she was quite a character. I was fascinated by this. I never met either my Grandmother or Grandfather. They were dead before I was born. It made me feel closer to them in some way, to meet a person who knew them

He talked about some members of my family that I didn't know had existed. He told me about a 'poem' that hung up in the Plough, the pub so many of the Dodds went in. Practically lived in.

It had been written by Ted Blinman a lovely man who lived in a big old house next to the pub. He had an open house for my Mum. He seemed to understand her illness. Her name was Nettie. Some people called her Nutty Nettie. Not to me they didn't.

Ted collected all sorts of ancient artefacts. He gave me a small Roman coin once. And a microscope with lots of ancient slides.

The poem was titled Dodds, Dossers and Didicoys. Richard told me it went through all of my Uncles giving an individual description of each and then did the same for the Dossers and Didicoys. The latter is one of many names for travellers with either mixed or no Romany blood.

He has been trying to find it for years, he told me. He took my number so he could get in touch if he ever finds it. I hope he does. He also told me that his Mum had died two weeks previously. She was 102

Orwell said in his will that he did not want a biography written about him after his death. That seems to confirm his humility.

I went to All Saints church after the florists. I parked up and went in. I went to my Mum's grave. It took me ages to find it. When I did, it was in the area I had been searching. The headstone was covered in lichen and moss. I couldn't make her name out.

My brother had said he was maintaining it. That was a while ago admittedly, but he clearly wasn't. I will be going back soon to sort it out. I didn't have time this trip, but there are many things I want to see again. The walk down to the river is a big one.

I went back today. I scrubbed my Mum's headstone clean. Her name is now clear as is the quote that I asked to be inscribed on the stone 33 years ago. I had completely forgotten what it was and could not see it until the moss and lichen was gone. 'How blest are those whose hearts are pure they shall see God' I had made a good choice, I decided. If there is a God, Mum will be with her/him now.

I won't be leaving my Mums grave for another fifteen years.

I had a look at the graves in the area where my Mum is. There were no new family members, thankfully. I did find one in a new cemetery that had been started elsewhere in the village. It was for Mick Dodd. He was my cousin and a really nice guy. He died of cancer.

He died in 2006. That was the last time I had visited Sutton and I met him in a local shop. He told me he had cancer, but shrugged it off. He was smiling and chatting. That was the last time I saw him.

I finally decided to go and say a quick hello to Mr. Blair. I could not believe what I saw.

I had taken a photo of his grave in 2006. It shows a small curved headstone with no fancy scrolls, angels, lettering. Nothing. Just a plain headstone with a small rose bush in front.

I always feel calm standing in this serene and ancient churchyard. I go there whenever in the area. I used to go all the time when I was a chorister in the choir there in the mid 60's I would frequently go and stand in front of his grave.

I have enjoyed Orwell's books since I was a child. Along with Aldous Huxley he is one of my favourite writers.

I was surprised and disgusted with the state of his grave. It was covered in flowers, many of them plastic. There were dead flowers still in cellophane wrappers. In time these would blow around the churchyard. They certainly are not biodegradable.

On top of his headstone was a line of coins. Pound and two pound coins and a lot more twopenny and fivepenny pieces. I could not see the significance of these coins.

On top of the stone was a small plastic pig. Someone had written 'All animals are equal, but some' There obviously wasn't enough room to complete the quotation from Animal Farm. They had run out of pig.

The rose trees had gone totally wild. There was a pink as well as a red one. I didn't remember that.

With this taken altogether, it was almost impossible to read his name.

Whoever is doing this might know his books, but they clearly don't care enough about the man.

Since writing this, I have been contacted by the Orwell Society. They have been very helpful and have cleared up one of my main questions regarding the grave. They quoted me directly from his will: **"I direct that my body be buried (not cremated) according to the rites of the Church of England in the** nearest convenient cemetery, and that there shall be placed over my grave a plain brown stone bearing the inscription "Here lies Eric Arthur Blair born June 26th 1903, died ___"; in case any suggestion should arise I request that no memorial service be held for me after my death and that no biography shall be written."

So Orwell himself decided on his gravestone. The nearest convenient cemetery turned out to be the most convenient for David Astor. A good choice, it is a beautiful place.

I thanked the society saying that I still don't know his motivation for these requests. They felt the same, but did say that he was a very private man, who referred to himself as Eric Blair throughout his life, other than when it was necessary to be Orwell. Personally I think taken together, this strengthens my belief that he did not want to be disturbed once he was 'Resting in Peace'

Every year the Orwell Society meets up at All Saints church on the Sunday nearest to his birthday. They spend a brief time at Orwell's graveside. Orwell's son Richard Blair who is patron of the society reads a passage from his Fathers' work. This sounds like a dignified ceremony to me. I am planning to go to the next one.

There is an aerial photograph showing the location of both Blair and Asquith in the churchyard. It is locked into a glass display case right next to the gate at the entrance to the church. If it wasn't I would have ripped it down as I did 56 years ago.They are alongside details of the next church bazaar and coffee mornings.

Of course Blair is identified as George Orwell. If the church used the name that is carved onto the gravestone, most people would not know who he is. Which I think is exactly what Orwell wanted.

In my latest visit I took a walk down to the river as I planned. I passed by Wharf House heading towards the river. Margot Asquith had bought three properties and ran them together. There is Mill House and Walton House as well as the Wharf. They are all big, Mill House also has massive gardens. They extend right along the river where we walked as children. I have never been inside the gardens, but there must be many acres. Mill House is detached from the other two, fronting onto the main road and across from the Fish pub, now Bistro.

I would imagine it would have actually been Mill House where Margot put on her celebrated 'weekenders'

In 2006 Mill House was purchased by Helena Bonham-Carter and Tim Burton. They are now separated so I don't know what is happening to the place. Helena is the great granddaughter of Asquith which might be the reason why they chose to buy it. She would probably have not heard of the village but for the family connection.

She and Burton annoyed many of the residents of the village by erecting a seven foot fence around the property. There were complaints about this at the time. When I lived in the village all those years ago, there was a fence that ran along the weir pool at the top of the river. Probably about 30 feet in length.

I thought what is wrong with them putting up a fence? They are internationally famous and need a greater level of privacy than us mere mortals. Apparently Johnny Depp visited when he parted from his wife. He wouldn't want the locals spying on him when he was walking in the garden.

So I thought it was perfectly reasonable for them to put up a fence. Until I went for a walk today. The fence runs along the weir pool as it did before. It then continues for what seems like miles. There is no view of that side of the river at all. I used to love looking out across the river whilst walking down to Sandy Beach with my swimming gear and picnic.

This monstrous fence runs almost to the small copse that leads down to Sandy Beach. That is also blocked off, but by a locked gate. I would have easily been able to climb over that gate in order to get to Sandy Beach. I'm sure local children do now.

This fence ruined my long anticipated walk. I couldn't picture where I had stood for a photograph with my Mum. The last picture I had of her before she died. There must be many memories throughout our community taken away by these vain actors.

I ended my walk long before I planned to. Centuries of villagers have walked along this path. They can still do that. They just can't see anything.

These people are so rich they could live anywhere in the world. They do have other properties apart from this one. Unfortunately, they have chosen my village as a rural retreat.

There is a third world famous person that I saw in the village. He was very much alive. I was in the Swan pub, which is on the village green. The Swan was a proper drinking pub in those days. Now it's a swanky bistro serving international cuisine.

Same as the Fish around the corner. It advertises that it serves the finest European cuisine. The council have recently shut down the Plough, the only remaining pub in the village.

Anyway, I was in the Swan. This was in 1973 when I was 18 and actually in a pub drinking legally. I had been drinking in the village pubs for a couple of years, but nobody asked your age, or was bothered as long as you didn't cause trouble.

I was playing bar billiards with some friends when we saw a group of monks coming out of the Abbey, which is adjacent to the pub.

David Astor had bought the Abbey in 1958 and leased it to the Ockenden Venture, an organisation which offered sanctuary to refugees and displaced children . In the 70s the Abbey was lent to the Namibia International Peace Centre. So that was the organisation based in the Abbey at that time.

The group emerging from the Abbey were Tibetan monks. Occasionally one or two of them would come to the Swan to show us carvings they had made out of ivory. Another thing you could not do now. There were tiny figures carved inside the ivory, so intricate it was difficult to see how they had done it.

That is how I knew they were Tibetan monks. Amongst the group there was one man who stood out. He was not dressed differently, they all wore purple robes. He just projected from the group somehow.

I had come out to see what was going on. Standing in front of the large bay window of the pub and being the only person around, I must have been quite visible.

I was staring at this very impressive man when he looked in my direction. He must have seen me because he gave me a warm smile. I smiled back. I felt a wave of love coming in my direction. Then they turned and went back into the Abbey. The Dalai Lama had just exchanged smiles with me.

When I was younger, I joined the Cubs (junior boy scouts). I was 'bob a jobbing' round the church end of the village. (Offering my services for one shilling, called a bob) My rationale was that there were far more bob's around in that area.

I have always been competitive. I had raised the most money the previous year and wanted to beat my own target.

I picked the biggest house, built up courage and went through the imposing gates and across the driveway that led to the massive front door of Manor House (it said on the sign). I had no clue that this was David Astor's mansion. In fact, I had no clue who David Astor was.

The mansion is near All Saints Church where he would eventually end up. I guessed there would be more than a bob or two here.

I knocked on the door and an imposing gentleman answered. He asked me what I wanted, rather gruffly I thought.

I asked him if he had any jobs I could do, for a bob. He said he didn't so I left.

A brief meeting, it is true. Nonetheless, it would always be the case that I had met the editor of the Observer, general newspaper magnate, philanthropist and great friend of George Orwell.

At the time I was more concerned that he had set me back in my bob a job quest

Slightly disheartened, I crossed the road to yet another mansion, this one called Norman Hall. I knocked on the door and was greeted by a man called Heinz. He appeared to be an American. I didn't know if Heinz was his first or last name. Of course I immediately thought about baked beans.

He was charming and told me he was a film producer. I gave him my bob a job spiel.

He said he didn't have any jobs that needed doing but he would see what he could find for me. He went off, and came back a while later with a box full of stuff. One thing I remember distinctly was an e.p. by the Beatles.

An e.p. was an elongated player, the same size as a 45 but with 2 tracks either side. This would have been the early sixties. One of the songs was 'I'll follow the Sun'.

I gave it to my cubmaster to put into the next jumble sale. Then I bought it and kept it. It didn't count towards my bob a job fund which was growing, but slowly.

I lost that e.p. a long time ago. I wonder whether it was worth anything? I have lost many things that might have had some value over the years.

In the 70's I went to a book signing put on by Eric Idle and Neil Innes. It was in the Randolph Hotel in Oxford. I was accompanying my girlfriend at the time who wanted a signed copy of the book. I can't remember its name. Something to do with Rutland.

My girlfriend was a very attractive young blonde. Eric Idle was impressed and Neil Innes wrote a little ditty in the book for her.

While they were talking to her, I found a Chinese takeaway menu in my pocket. I wrote on it I owe you £1,000,000. I added Eric Idle's name underneath with a line of dots for his signature.

When they finished chatting up my girlfriend, I thrust the menu under Eric Idle's nose and said 'could you sign this please'. He had a little chuckle and signed it adding the phrase 'in hot meals'

A million pounds worth of Chinese meals would last a long time. But I lost it.

I still have one thing left that could have some value. I don't know. I used to do some business with the UK sales manager of a US components manufacturer. One of their major customers was NASA.

He had a paperweight on his desk. It was a clear plastic prism which had a small component embedded in it. I found it fascinating. You could see the component from all angles. It looked like a miniature circuit board. Every small detail was clear, even the minute gold connections between the individual circuits.

The sales manager was called Neil. He told me that it was indeed a miniaturised circuit board. He further said that it had been quality tested and was fully functional for its intended purpose. Not now, obviously. But it was not a reject before being encased in plastic.

Also inside the prism is a small but clear picture of a man in a spacesuit. The tiny circuit board would have been inside the spacesuit of an Apollo astronaut had it not been sunk into the prism in front of me. Miniature electronic components are in everything nowadays and nothing special. This was the 70's when a mainframe computer at Harwell filled a building the size of a warehouse.

Neil said I could borrow it as I was clearly taken by it. I thanked him and have borrowed it for the last 40 years.

One day, about 20 years ago I was interviewing a sixth former in my office at school. I am a Careers Adviser now. He was a bit of an oddball it has to be said. Charming and very intelligent though.

I first met him in year 9, when we were to talk about his GCSE choices. He came into my room. He was very striking with a huge explosion of hair. I remember he had a permanent quizzical look on his face. I thought he looked like Mozart. He told me he was only going to take music as he was going to be an internationally famous pianist.

I thought that's a first. But I believed him.

He was an outstanding pianist and we went to see him many times. I am not really into classical music, but I loved watching and listening to him play. Becoming an Internationally famous pianist is not easy. I last saw him working in Morrisons. I hope he makes it in the end.

He was looking at this prism, which I had on the shelf. He asked what it was and I told him. He said 'that is worth a lot of money'. I wonder if it is.

Just in case, the company name on the prism is DDC ILC Data Device Corporation if anyone wants to make me an offer.

Returning to the bob a job theme and to conclude it. Although it was called bob a job, most people gave us more. Once I got five shillings and frequently got half a crown (two shillings and sixpence)

Towards the end of bob a job week in the year when I met David Astor and Heinz, I was close to my previous years takings. It was Friday, the last day and I had all afternoon. I was confident that I could beat my target.

There was a big pink house in the middle of the village. It had massive gardens and a thatched roof. I thought this must be a good prospect.

I went through the gate and approached the house. I had no fear in those days. Or maybe things were just less dangerous. Would an eight-year-old be allowed to wander around today, alone, asking complete strangers for money in their own homes?

This kindly old man answered the door and said yes, he had a job that needed doing. He took me to the back garden that was the size of a football pitch. It was covered in leaves. He said that the leaves needed raking up and putting into a pile.

I thought this'll be worth at least five shillings, maybe even a ten-bob note. That would easily beat last year.

It took me all afternoon to complete the task.

After I had finished I went to the back door and knocked. The old man came out to look and was clearly impressed.

He congratulated me on my efforts and pulled a one shilling piece from his cardigan pocket. He smiled and looked as though he felt he was giving me a great reward for my efforts.

I took the coin, totally speechless. I did manage to mumble thankyou, being a well mannered boy. It was not what I was thinking. I walked out of the garden. My hands were blistered and I was very tired.

All I could think of was that this was the end of the day. I had failed to beat my target because I had done at least 10 shillings worth of work for a single, solitary bob.

That taught me a lifelong lesson. Always get the price agreed before you start the job.

My friend Martin was both an Ornithologist and a Lepidopterist. I didn't know that at the time. I just knew he liked birds and butterflies. He got me interested too, but I was never as knowledgeable as him.

We used to collect bird's eggs and butterflies. Both of these things are no longer allowed.

We went bird's egg collecting. Known as birds nesting. When we found a nest with eggs, we would take an egg, take it home and prepare it for display. This was always at Martin's house. We made a hole at one end, a bigger hole at the other end and blew out the contents.

I invariably broke the egg, so Martin took charge of this.

Martin had specially made display cases, lined with sawdust. The eggs were labelled and placed in the case.

As mentioned, this is illegal nowadays. In our defence, we never took more than one egg from any one nest. We would not take an egg if there was a parent bird nearby. We returned to make sure all was OK after the removal of the egg.

These were Martin's rules, although I totally agreed.

We also collected butterflies. This was a bit more barbaric. We would catch a butterfly in a net. We would then take it to Martin's house (everything was taken to Martin's house)

He had Kilner jars with foam rubber in the bottom. He would put a few drops of carbon tetrachloride in. Then the butterfly went in and the top was sealed. The butterfly would flutter about feebly, then die.

I have to say I was not keen on this at all, and never did it myself. Martin was totally scientific about it.

The dead butterfly was pinned to a piece of balsa wood, and it's wings were spread out and fixed with tissue. When it had dried out, the butterfly was put into another display case, pinned to a cork lining. The type of butterfly was written on a piece of card, and fixed beneath each specimen. I'm sure he included the English and Latin names.

Martin's collection was impressive and quite extensive.

I tried building my own bird's egg collection. Uncle Richard who apart from occasionally saving me from drowning made random things for us boys. He made me a very handsome display case with a glass front.

I collected some eggs. Pretty common stuff like starlings, sparrows and blackbirds.

I kept the case under my bed as I didn't have a spare room like my friend Martin. After my brother had jumped on my bed and smashed the case I decided not to collect my own, but admire Martin's far better collection

Uncle Richard lived close to us on Bradstocks Way. He was the youngest of my Mums many brothers and the only one who lived on the estate. He lived at one end of Bradstocks Way, we were in the middle. Mum had 3 other brothers living in the village towards the older end in a place called Frilsham Street.

There were stories about all of my Uncle's. Some I knew to be true, others I am not too sure about.

It was a fact that Richard was a clever man. I was told that he was very good in school. So much so that he was offered a scholarship to Oxford University. For some reason he did not take it up.

One Christmas, I think the first Christmas in our new house, my Dad bought Tim and me a pedal car each. I had a yellow jeep. It had working front lights with a switch on the dashboard to turn them on. I loved it. Tim had a police car with a revolving light on the roof.

Tim started whingeing. That wouldn't be the last time. He wanted front lights like mine. Dad sent for Uncle Richard who quickly fitted lights to the front of the police car. He did an excellent job cutting out the metal and properly inserting a set of lights. He was a very clever man in more ways than one.

I did make the point before Uncle Richard started work that it was not fair as I could not have a revolving light on the roof of my car because it didn't have a roof. My brother kept whining until he got his way. I was 5 and Tim was 7. He was the elder son and should have been more adult about it.

Richard liked to go to the plough. Every day, later in his life. He wasn't a drunk, he had a specific set of friends and that was their meeting place. Later he had a good reason to drink. I only remember one of his friends, an Irish man called Jimmy Lyons. In those days everyone was a character or seemed to be.

My Uncle Phil for example was purported to have a metal plate in his head from the war. He claimed he could get Radio Caroline on it.

Jimmy found out I was joining the Army Catering Corps. He told me I would never go hungry with a frying pan in my hand. I did think, only if I have got some food to fry in it. I was only 15 and not prepared to debate this with my Uncle Richard's drinking partner.

For a long time I thought Richard was unemployed. I never saw him working and he seemed to be in the pub from mid morning. I found out that he had a job on the bins. This was so he could finish work and then get to the pub to meet up with his friends. I am certain Jimmy Lyons did not have a job.

Richard had four children. A boy and a girl, and young twins, also a boy and a girl I think. Derek was his son, and the oldest child. He was turning into a lovely boy the last time I saw him, which was a very long time ago. His eldest daughter was Tangie, a beautiful young girl.

I have vivid memories of an incident I wish had never happened. I was living in my small terraced house in Abingdon. It was the first house I owned. I bought it as I was about to leave the employment of a recruitment company called Coates Johnson.

One night there was a knock on the door. I opened it to find a policeman standing there. He told me there had been a traffic accident nearby and asked if I had heard anything. I hadn't and said so.

I don't know how it came out, but he mentioned the name Tangie. That is a very uncommon name. It suited Tangie, but I have never met anyone with it then or since. I told him she was my cousin. He told me to sit down. I did.

He then told me that Tangie had been hit by a speeding car that had mounted the pavement and was driven deliberately straight at her. She was killed instantly.

It later came out that she was killed by her ex boyfriend. She had ended their relationship. He found out that she was going out on the night he murdered her. He waited for her to walk past with her friend and then ran into them. Her friend survived.

This excuse for a human being will be out by now, probably some time ago. This destroyed Richard understandably. He adored Tangie.

Last time I went to All Saints church to see my Mum and have a quick word with Eric and Herbert, I saw a new headstone a couple of rows behind her against the church wall. It was my Uncle Richard. He was buried next to Tangie. I know he would be happy about that.

I used to love spending time in the extensive countryside that surrounded the village. I would explore with Martin and on my own.

I remember there was a lane that started across the road from the Plough pub. I think it was called Mill Lane.

If you walked to the end of that lane, which was quite a way, there was a field with a gate. The gate was always locked, so you had to climb over. Once in the field there was a path, created by the feet of many children like us over the years. It led to a shallow stream which we would paddle in during the warmer months.

Further on the stream went under the mill house. If we were lucky, we sometimes saw trout appearing to hover around the edge of the mill pool.

In the lane before reaching the gate on the left hand side we had a special place that we thought no-one else knew about. It was a small copse, fenced off with no gate or obvious means of entry. We got in through the fence out of view.

The reason this place was so important to us is that it was the location of our headquarters. When we first found our way in, we explored and found this big old tree that must have been struck by lightning in the distant past. It was split in two, down to about three feet from the ground. Both sides bent towards the ground forming a shape like a pair of cupped hands.

It was like a perfect pair of seats, one for each of us. It was even covered in moss and was very comfortable to sit on.

There were places within the tree – little nooks and crannies – where we could hide stuff. We created a concoction from dock leaves and nettles that we believed would alleviate the pain caused by stinging nettles, put it in one of Martin's Kilner jars and hid that.

Some people do believe that dock leaves rubbed on the site of the sting can take away the pain. I think that the cool feel of the dock leaf does make it feel better, but not for long. Our potion was not cool, so of no use at all.

Somehow, we found out that this small copse was owned by our old primary school teacher Mrs. Skinner. Everybody loved Mrs. Skinner and we were no exception.

We had a meeting at our headquarters in the tree and decided to go to Mrs. Skinner's house. I being the least afraid, was the spokesperson.

I must admit I was a bit tongue tied initially when Mrs. Skinner answered the door. But she really was an exceptionally lovely person and instantly put me at ease. She knew who I was, and Martin. It must have been a couple of years since we were in her class, but she remembered everyone.

I explained about the tree and requested, as per our meeting, that we be allowed to treat it as our headquarters

She asked us to wait, and after a while came back with a piece of paper which bestowed ownership of the tree on myself and Martin. She had signed it and we had to sign it too.

What an extraordinary person Mrs. Skinner was. We took the document and immediately hid it in our tree.

It might still be there. But the copse has probably been bulldozed to make way for Orwell Gardens.

Remembering Mrs. Skinner (bless her) makes me think of school.

There were two schools in Sutton Courtenay. The little school and the big school. Little school was on our estate. It is still there.

Big school was towards the end of the old village and has been closed for a long time.

It's now a private residence. I remember my Father agreed that I would produce a sign for the people who first bought the old school. He thought I was artistic, which I was a bit.

They imaginatively named it the old school house, and that was the sign I produced in a kind of lopsided old English style. They must have been happy as it was there for many years.

In those days, you started school at 5 years old. As the little school was on our estate and about a 5 minute walk away, I was left to go to and from on my own. I don't remember that being a problem. Perhaps that's where my independence started.

I don't really remember a lot about the little school. My memories really kick in when I get to big school.

Big school was about a mile from where I lived. But I walked quite happily there and back every day.

On my walk I passed a couple of shops. One was called Ted's owned by a couple of brothers called Bill and Ted Davidge. I often wondered why it wasn't called Bill and Ted's. It was largely a hardware shop.

Further on was a shop where they sold several things, but most notably sweets. The shop had an odd name which I vaguely remember but can't spell.

One day I was walking to school with a couple of friends from the estate. We went into the sweet shop and were having a look around. For some inexplicable reason, I stuck a Sherbet Dib Dab in my pocket and walked out. Of course, I was caught.

Subsequently my parents had a visit from the village bobby, Mr. Nobby Nobes.

People who lived in the village at that time will remember Nobby Nobes. He was the sole representative of the constabulary in our village.

Nobby had a set routine. He lived in a police house in the middle of the village and every day would set out on his bicycle to go up the village and back.

His routine was always the same, so if you were intent on criminal behaviour you could easily avoid him.

But I didn't. Nobby told my dad that I had stolen the sherbet dib dab. Dad said he would deal with me and did. Nobby was OK with that

I had other run-ins with Nobby Nobes. As I have mentioned there was a large field behind our house where the local farmer kept cows. At this time there was a programme on TV called Rawhide. One of the main characters was Rowdy Yates, played by Clint Eastwood. I think it was his first acting role.

Martin and I were fans of Rawhide. We would climb over the fence at the end of my garden and go in search of the herd of cows. When we found them, we began to re-enact scenes from Rawhide, which invariably involved rounding up and moving cattle.

The song was 'head 'em up, move 'em out' so we did. We chased the poor cows around the field shouting the theme, ending with 'RAWHIDE'

That was the first time my parents met Nobby Nobes. He told them that the farmer was complaining that our activities were causing the cows to stop giving milk.

We were told to desist and did. We were both concerned that we had upset the cows.

I might as well confess to my last act of criminal behaviour. Again, one morning walking to school (If only my mum had taken me in a Mitsubishi Shogun I would never have done these things) I stopped by Ted's.

In the shop window was the most wondrous thing. It was a silver torch, but it was no ordinary torch. On the side of the torch was a slide that changed a filter over the bulb so you could have a red, blue or green light as well as the normal one.

The sign said it was five shillings. That was a lot when you had no income. I got the odd thruppenny bit or tanner, but that would take ages to save.

So I did probably the most stupid thing ever. When I got home I went into my Dad's coat and took out his wallet. In it was a solitary 10 shilling note. My need was that strong that I took it. Clearly he would notice, but I wasn't thinking clearly. I had to have that torch.

Next day I went into Ted's. The torch was still in the window. I asked him for 2. Why? I don't know. Perhaps I wanted to get rid of the whole of the stolen money.

When I got them home, I tried to hide them in the bedroom. But my brother saw them and told Dad.

After a brief grilling from Dad, he judged me guilty and sent me up to the front bedroom to await my punishment. I had not been punished before so didn't know what to expect.

I realised when he appeared with a massive leather belt that I was about to find out. I had never seen my Dad wearing a belt, so perhaps this was for special occasions.

The pain was horrific. I could not sit down for a week. It was even worse than the caning I got from Derek Hurd, headmaster of John Mason High School, which I will come to later.

My Dad certainly put an end to my embryonic criminal career.

I'm still not certain about the use of corporal punishment. It might work, but it flippin' hurts.

I loved school. At least in the village. What came after is another story.

I loved reading, writing and spelling in particular. I am still a pedant when I see words mis-spelt. I see them all the time, even on BBC Broadcasts and constantly in my company management missives.

We had a spelling test every Friday. I always wanted to win and often did. There was no reward, just a feeling of smug satisfaction.

The English teacher was Mr. Davies. He was instrumental in developing my love of literature. Mr. Davies was Welsh and had a mop of ginger hair. I can still see him now.

When I was about 8, he introduced me to Aesop's Fables. He had a very big book, full of stories. I would listen spellbound while he read me stories of animals solving all sorts of moral conundrums.

He was the teacher in charge of the final year in Primary. There were three classes and you reached his around 10 years of age. In that year he gave me his copy of Aesop's Fables. He also gave me the Hobbit, Tolkien's first book that led him to go on and write Lord of The Rings

Nowadays I see more of the significance of Tolkien's books than then. As with Orwell, there are always underlying messages. To an eight year old, they were just highly entertaining books.

Mr. Davies was head of the third year. In charge of the second year was Mr. Vale. Like all of our primary teachers he was a nice enough man. However when he got annoyed with any particularly unruly pupil, he would often hurl a board rubber at them. That is another thing that is frowned upon nowadays.

Some would say to the detriment of school discipline. But not those pupils who had a board rubber hit them on the side of the head.

Of course, being a perfect pupil, I was not one of them. Not yet.

It was around this time that I recall a particularly harrowing experience. I was quite a sensitive child. One night my Dad had taken my Mum to the Plough. I was left at home. I don't remember if my brother was there, but he must have been.

Dad later claimed that he didn't drink alcohol. That was after he had run off with his tee-total secretary, who he later deferred to in all things. In fact, he was more than partial to the odd pint of bitter.

On that particular night I was fast asleep when something must have woken me up. I opened my eyes and could see nothing. The room was pitch black. I was afraid of the dark back then so Dad left the lights on for me. The electricity had run out. I was terrified.

My heart was pounding. I started to cry. I found my way downstairs, went outside and took my bike from the shed. I wasn't sure but made a fair guess that my parents would be at the pub. I pedalled as fast as I could towards the Plough. I was still in my pyjamas.

When I got there the pub was well lit up. I could see my Dad clearly. He was sitting with mum and a few of the brothers. Richard was there of course.

I went up close to the front window, staring in. I was not so terrified, seeing my family. Richard spotted me. He began talking to Dad, who turned and saw me. He was clearly not happy, but my relief was so intense I did not care.

Next thing my Dad was next to me. He looked annoyed but seeing me standing there in my pyjamas, crying and clearly frightened I think his annoyance turned to concern. He took me to the back of the pub and put me in the family car. He then got Mum and he drove me home.

Even now I can remember the sheer terror I felt that night.

When I was in Mr. Davies's class, I was sent up to the little school where with the rest of my class I was given a number of written tests.

The little school was in fact much bigger than the big school and easily accommodated all of us in one room. It was the dinner hall.

I remembered it well. One day when I was a pupil there I hadn't finished all of my dinner. A dinner lady told me that there were starving children in other countries that would love to have that leftover food.

In all innocence I said 'well send it to them'. I got into trouble for that, but I had genuinely not meant to cause offence. It just seemed logical to me.

Because the Dinner hall was so big, we could all be spread out so we could not spy on each other's answers.

As stated, I loved tests and always did my best.

If I had known this was the eleven plus, and the consequences of passing it I might not have tried so hard.

Our Headmaster in the big school was Fred Curd. He always seemed quite remote and fairly scary.

After the tests, he called me into his office. I had never been there before and entered with some trepidation

Mr. Curd told me that I had done very well in the 11 plus. What's that? I wondered. Honestly.

He said I came top in English but my maths had let me down. Not surprising, I hate maths. Adding up, taking away, fine. But the rest of it? I could see no purpose.

Apart from that, I had no clue what it was all about.

Then Mr. Curd made me an amazing offer. He told me that if I was prepared to come to his house and study maths over the Summer and if I reached a good enough standard I could pass the 11 plus and go to Grammar School.

I was so happy that Mr. Curd should be prepared to help me, that I gratefully accepted the offer. I later wished I hadn't.

It was a pretty rubbish Summer, but I stuck with it, passed my maths and went to Grammar School in September.

It was around this time that I got my first real job. I think I must have been around 10 years old and when I look back, it is difficult to believe that I actually did do this job. I remember I had left little school and had reached Mr. Davies's class in big school, so I must have been around that age.

The job was working on a farm. The farm was called Home Farm and the Farmer was called Farmer Allen. The older Farmer Allen who owned Home Farm was no longer active in running it. That was left to his son, Bob Allen. Through my own choice I did not call him Bob. I don't think he would have minded but to me it just seemed disrespectful.

So Farmer Allen Jr was my mentor and taught me a great deal in the first few weeks. I was a very quick learner, mostly because I really loved the job and wanted to know as much as possible. It was not too long before he began to trust me, and he gave me a ridiculous amount of responsibility for someone of my age, I still find it difficult to believe.

I worked every weekend and during the school holidays. My routine was always the same. It has to be with livestock farming because there are things that have to be done at set times for the animal's health and wellbeing. A big one is milking and that became my primary job.

Once I knew what I was doing, Farmer Allen left me in charge of milking. I had to get to the farm for 6am Saturday and Sunday morning. That meant getting up at 5.00 am, getting dressed, grabbing a quick breakfast, having a wash and leaving. I would do this on my own. Mum and Dad would still be in bed.

As would Farmer Allen. I'm sure he gave me the milking job so he could have a bit of a lie in on weekends. Why not? He did it all week. It took me about 10 minutes to get to the farm which was halfway between my house and big school. The shops were shut, so no temptation there.

The farmhouse fronted onto the main road. There were many acres of land behind it. When I got there I would go through the gate, making sure to shut the gate firmly behind me.

Old Farmer Allen had a Jack Russell that he let loose around the farmyard. Every morning it came at me barking and snarling. I knew if I just kept walking he would leave me alone. He was protecting his territory and Master, which was fair enough.

I would go to the milking parlour and go in the small back door. Putting on my overalls and wellies, I went outside and dipped my feet in the tin bath containing water and bleach. We always did this after foot and mouth.

I would pick up my stick - a small switch of witch hazel - and start to head out to get the herd. It was quite a way. I had to go through the top field and then through a large metal 5 bar gate to the bottom field.

When I reached the bottom field, I could see the herd. There was a stream at the bottom of the field and they would invariably be on the other side of it. They always seemed to think that the grass was greener on the other side. So I had to wade through the stream to get to them. The first time I did this I realised it was the stream that I had played in during the Summer holidays. I never realised I was playing in Farmer Allen's stream.

When I got to the cows, I walked to the rear of the herd. They would always start to move across the stream, heading in the direction of the farm. They knew they were going for milking. They did it twice a day. I was back at tea time too.

Cows want to be milked. A full udder becomes painful for them and they need to express it. So taking them up was no problem. Now and then one would stop to chew on some grass, which is when I used my hazel switch to give them a light tap on the rear. They would then realise where they were going and start off again.

When we reached the farmyard, they went into the holding pen. I left the gate open ready. There was more grass and hay, so they were happy. All cows do is eat and excrete. I would open up the milking parlour, go inside and get things ready. Switch on the milking machines, check everything was in order. There were 6 stalls, so I would bring in the first 6 cows.

Once in the stalls, I would put this brown liquid on each cows' teats, by hand. It was a treatment to prevent mastitis and such diseases. Once that was done, I could attach the 4 suction cups which drew up the milk. The milk travelled up rubber lines and into a large glass jar. I always liked to watch the milk squirting into the jar. By the time the cow was done, each jar was quite full, but never overfull.

The milk in the bottle was released into a large tank, prepared for the milk lorry to take it away. At the end of every morning milking, I would dip a mug into the fresh, warm milk. It was absolutely gorgeous. It was not pasteurised, homogenised or any type of ised. It didn't do me any harm. I was as fit as a butcher's dog.

Whilst being milked the cows chewed on a trough full of pellets. I had to keep them topped up too. As I said all cows do is eat. But all that eating has obvious consequences. At the time I was about 5 foot tall. At that height I was precariously in line with the cows' rear end at the point of ejection.

If you have ever seen a cow poo, you know it sometimes comes straight out. I had to have my wits about me to avoid getting an earful. Whilst I could see them, I was alright.

Sometimes when I was looking the other way I felt a sudden warm sensation on the back of my neck. Then I had to head out to one of the water troughs for a quick wash making sure it wasn't the one with bleach in

There were about fifty cows in the herd, so it didn't take that long to get all the cows milked. Once they were all done, it was back to the lower field. Sometimes they stopped before the stream, sometimes after.

I loved working on the farm. It gave me two things I needed. To be out in the countryside and money.

In the Summer I also worked on the farm in the grain store. This was hard work and again I still can't believe I was allowed to do it. It was a lot more dangerous than milking. When the wheat grains had been prepared, they were poured into a tipping lorry. That was driven to the grain store and the load was tipped onto a metal grid a bit like those you see in roads to stop cattle getting out.

There was a huge machine that sucked the grain down through this grid and up through a hopper depositing it into the grain store. That machine was extremely noisy but there was no PPE in those days. Health and Safety would have been appalled. That was not the worst of it.

As the machine sucked the grain down, the centre of the pile went down much more quickly than the outside. My job was to shovel the grain on the outside into the middle. It was constant, back breaking work. At the end of the Summer, I had arms like Popeye.

I got paid on Sunday evening. Five shillings a day, so ten shillings for the weekend. I could have paid my Dad back for the money I stole. I felt the walloping was payment enough.

I had to go to the back door of the farmhouse to collect my money. I got paid by old Farmer Allen. Every time I approached the Jack Russell would appear. Because I was too close to his Master, he always went for me and I had to dance around the yard to avoid him.

I am sure this was old Farmer Allen's idea of a joke. I never saw the funny side of it. I was sure that Terrier was going to bite a lump out of me, though he never did.

Eventually old Farmer Allen would appear with my ten shillings, but not too quickly. He handed me the money with a straight and sombre face, but I knew he was laughing inside.

I was there for about two years but had to stop when I was at Grammar school because of my studies. I would happily have stayed on the farm and not bothered with school, but that was not allowed at 11, even then. I still went back for the harvesting in the school holidays.

I am now approaching retirement. I work for the Welsh careers service. I have been here for 26 years. I can honestly say I did more, learned more and was far happier in those two years back on the farm.

Chapter 2

Mum

I have not mentioned my family much. When I was young, I was usually left to my own devices. That was not a deliberate choice of mine or my parents, it was just circumstance.

My Mother was a Paranoid Schizophrenic, according to the doctors. I'm not so sure, but nonetheless she was very unwell, mentally.

Because of her illness, Mum's moods were very erratic. In the early days, I remember she had jobs. She used to work for a company called Phonotas. She would go round the area on a moped that she called her 'pop pop' cleaning telephone boxes.

She also worked cleaning out students' accommodation in a nearby teaching college.

Unfortunately, her illness got worse and eventually she was not able to work, losing her independence in the process.

I remember her going in and out of Littlemore Hospital, which was a mental asylum located in Oxford. I have absolutely nothing good to say about that place.

Whilst there she was forced to undergo ECT (Electro Convulsive Therapy). This barbaric 'treatment' is still in use today. It did not make her any better and probably made her much worse.

There were other things that happened to her there that I don't want to think about, let alone talk about. Not even now.

My Dad did his best to take care of his wife and boys. I cannot say that he did not do a good job. He made certain that my brother and myself were well dressed and fed at all times.

He coped with his wife as best he could, but sometimes it was a real struggle.

I remember one time when he took me and Mum out to a local pub in Appleford. We were settled down, he had a pint and Mum had a port and lemon, her favourite drink.

Suddenly she stood up and announced at the top of her voice 'This is my husband and my son. They beat me and lock me up' I wanted the earth to swallow me up, but my Dad was so cool.

He just helped her up and put her coat gently around her shoulders. My mum was tiny, 4 feet and half an inch tall. She used to tell me that the half inch was important as it took her over 4 feet. She was funny when she was lucid. Unfortunately that was becoming less and less. Dad was very protective of her, but it was hard.

People stared, I tried to ignore them. Dad didn't, he stared right back, silently challenging anyone to say something. Nobody did. I was never more proud of my Dad than on that night.

Dad was a good man without question. He certainly did his best for me and my brother. He had to do everything at home as well as run his businesses. According to my birth certificate he was a house painter and decorator (journeyman) whatever a journeyman is. He had a number of jobs that I recall, many involving painting and decorating but not exclusively.

His work kept him very busy so he did not have any spare time for us. We were fed and watered and disciplined as necessary. I can't say that I remember much affection. I think he saw us as a duty that he had to fulfil.

He had to look after us as Mum was not capable, but to be honest he spent most of his effort trying to keep his businesses afloat over the years and help Mum as best he could.

We had a hot bath on a Sunday and our hair was washed with soap or fairy liquid. On Monday morning, we were lined up by the back door in our school uniforms.

We then had liberal amounts of Brylcreem slapped on our heads and our hair was combed into shape.

We had one bath a week, but got Brylcreemed every morning.

Then we were packed off to school and Dad went off to work. I guess Mum stayed at home, when she wasn't in Littlemore.

Dad tried his hardest to keep her out of that place, but sometimes he couldn't cope and needed respite.

When she was particularly bad, which became increasingly the case he had no option but to have her admitted.

We went and visited her now and then. As we left, she always sang 'Please Release Me' a popular song of the time. It always made me cry. Even now. I'll have to stop for a second. I can't see the page.

I loved my Mum dearly, but it was hard to bear living with her. People would say 'She can't help it' and I knew that was true.

But in the moment, it was impossible to be that objective.

Eventually my Dad had enough and left. As previously mentioned he ran off with his secretary. Or she ran off with him. To my eternal shame, I followed him and moved to Abingdon, leaving her on her own. I was 19. I just could not live with her alone.

Abingdon was a pretty little market town back then. Everything revolved around the market square. It was very large, and surfaced with cobblestones. On one side was the town hall and the other three sides had pubs and shops facing onto the square.

The side opposite the town hall led into a fairly new arcade. Woolworths was at the far end. Locals were annoyed as there was no Marks and Spencer. There was one in Oxford, but that was nearly nine miles away.

There was a unique event that took place when there was an important royal occasion like the wedding of Charles and Diana. It was called the bun throwing for reasons that will become evident.

The town council would decide which occasions warranted a bun throwing. I would imagine that this 400 year old tradition is still taking place. The event is pretty much what the name suggests. The Councillors would climb to the top of the town hall. There was always a large crowd gathered beneath them, filling the square.

The buns were specially baked for the occasion. They were currant buns, with a crown design on top. When ready, the councillors would start to throw the buns down onto the crowd gathered below. On every bun throwing occasion a bun would be kept and displayed in the museum inside the town hall. That is well worth a visit.

Underneath the town hall and to the rear used to be a cafe called the Mousehole. Dad took me to it whenever I had a tooth out at the nearby dentists. The dentist was Dr. Vivian. Oddly, our GP on the estate was called Dr. Vivian too. They were not related. Dentist Dr. Vivian was more like a butcher. He would rip your tooth out whether you needed it or not.

I was terrified of the dentist. Mostly because of the big rubber mask he would stick on your face to put you to sleep before he attacked your tooth. It had a particularly offensive taste and smell.

People called the stuff that put you under laughing gas. I never understood the joke.

If you stood in front of the town hall and looked right you would see the Roysse Rooms and the big archway through which you had to pass to get to the River Thames. There was a reasonably long drive or walk to the river. Just before the river was the Abingdon lido where I had nearly drowned.

When big school were taken swimming, we went in a coach. It wasn't far from the school to Abingdon pool, but far enough for a spot of pigtail pulling and cap stealing. As the coach went through the archway, everyone had to hold their breath until we got to the other side. It only took a few seconds so was not particularly arduous.

I was never sure what would happen if you didn't hold your breath. Maybe something bad would happen to you. Perhaps I hadn't done it the day I nearly drowned.

On the way to the river in a small wooded clearing there was a large stone. A boulder really. There was a hole in the stone. When you looked into it, there was a rusty cannon ball solidly embedded into the stone. We were told it had been fired on a bunch of cavaliers by some roundheads. There was some real, proven history there so we believed it and marvelled at the cannon ball in the stone.

It was quite recently that I found out it was a folly. Not real at all. I had believed that tale for more than half a century. Like George Orwell's grave, I would have preferred for that truth to have remained undiscovered.

Once Dad and I had left Mum seemed to improve in many ways. Perhaps it was because she had to start to look after herself. Dad's life appeared to get better but Mums definitely did. She started to go to All Saints church as she did in the early days and generally got out and about.

She got back in touch with Mary who was a local Romany Gypsy. Mary had been a good friend of hers in the past and now was again.

Mary lived down a back lane by the church. She lived in a Vardo which is an old, original Romany home. It was a waggon really and brightly painted in all colours. Mum told me it was really comfortable inside and nice and warm. She had hardly spoken to me for years. This made me feel a lot less guilty.

The council eventually made Mary move out of her Vardo and stuck her in a flat on the estate. She hated it, but at least she was a lot closer to Mum.

Chapter 3

Dad

My Dad seemed to be constantly setting up businesses. Initially they would do well and we would flourish. In those times he bought expensive cars, nice suits and we ate well. Still no love though. I guess you can't have everything.

I remember his cars. He had a Morris Oxford. It had a number plate Hot 4. I wonder what happened to that. If it is still about it would be worth a lot. It probably isn't though.

He also had a Ford Capri 3 Litre Ghia. Top of the range. It was stunning. It was also fast. I'm not sure how old we were, but one day Tim got the keys to the car and we went for a spin. We went up onto the bypass from Abingdon to Oxford. Tim let her rip. The speedometer was just above 120 mph when I told Tim to slow down. I didn't fancy getting wrapped around a tree like Marc Bolan.

Tim was not an experienced driver. I'm not sure whether he was old enough to drive. Probably not. Tim suddenly seemed to realise how fast he was going and slowed down. We went back home and he parked the car in exactly the same place. Dad never knew anything about it.

After the boom came the bust. I still have no idea why as he always seemed busy. I suspect it was that he was just no good with finances. I know he did not handle his tax affairs well. Perhaps it was that. Also he liked employing people and had a large wage bill. Quite a few people from the estate worked for him, which was awkward. One of them was my first girlfriend's father, which was more awkward.

I remember some of the more dubious of them coming to our house and asking Dad for a 'sub'. An advance on their wages.

More often than not he would give them it. Some never returned.

Maybe that was it. My Dad was too soft. But not with us!

Often when the good times had gone really bad the bailiffs would come knocking. I remember hiding behind the sofa with the lights out when they came. My Father would always deny that, but it was true. More than once.

In one of the good periods, dad decided to concrete over the large back garden. I used to have a little patch of ground where I grew radishes, lettuces and other salad plants. Sometimes they grew. Often they didn't. That was concreted over. It upset me.

Dad built an extension on the back of the house. We moved our black and white telly in there. This enabled me to watch Tales of Mystery and Imagination on my own, thereby scaring myself half to death.

He also built a triple garage at the end of the garden, if you could call it that now. It was massive and housed his car and plenty of other stuff easily. There was a gigantic chest freezer, in which he would place sides of beef, half and sometimes whole lambs and miriad vegetables. I have no idea why. Perhaps he was preparing for nuclear war.

The main thing this garage did was completely block my view of the fields beyond. It made the garden much smaller as well. In the end Dad parked his car on the concrete and kept his painting gear in the garage. Saves money he said.

This was the time when the tories started to allow people to buy their council houses. With all this time and money spent on it, why didn't Dad buy ours? I asked him. Not interested, he answered. I am pretty certain the real reason was that he couldn't get a mortgage.

Chapter 4

John Mason Grammar School

So back to my education and my progression from my lovely little primary school in my lovely village to the massive grammar school in the metropolis of Abingdon.

The grammar school was called John Mason High School and was to become a major turning point in my life. The turn was downwards.

In Sutton Courtenay Primary there was a football team, and I was the Captain. I played centre half, and was quite good.

Well, quite good at stopping the opposition getting past which I did with all the means at my disposal. I was quite big and strong for my age and whilst not as skilful as some, the other team couldn't go through me and seldom got past me.

I loved my football. The first thing I found out when I arrived at the school was that they played Rugby. I had no idea what rugby was.

That was the first thing I did not like about Grammar School.

I did not like the fact that all of my friends (except Martin) had failed the 11 plus and gone to secondary schools. They told me after that they played football and things were similar to our old school.

Also, most of the other students were from quite well to do homes. Posh, I called them. They spoke and looked differently to me. I felt like a fish out of water.

I began to wish I had failed the 11 plus. I thought I would have if it wasn't for Fred Curd. Why did he have to interfere?

There were two other kids from our estate. Stephen Wright and Keith Carter. I didn't know either of them and for some reason didn't really get to know them either.

And although Martin and I had been such close companions for so long, he now mixed with students closer to his own position in life and we had little to do with each other. That really was a shame.

I can't say I was particularly happy with my new circumstances.

I dealt with this by not getting involved and staying in the background.

I have still got the original copy of my school report. It is kept in an A4 size booklet so it is easy to see the progress, or lack of it over the terms.

On the front cover it says first to fifth forms. The last pages are blank, as I didn't make it to the fifth form.

It still makes interesting reading. The first report states that I was 11 years and 7 months. I had been absent for 1 day. I achieved a variety of grades, nothing lower than a B which was average.

My form master was Mr Vignoles who was young, and I would imagine a recently qualified teacher. He taught music and was an all round nice guy.

Each teacher gave a grade and comment. Mr Vignoles did a summary.

On the first report he summarises: 'Arthur has made a very satisfactory start. However, he must not be afraid to speak up for himself in class'

The Headmasters comment was 'A quiet beginning'

They didn't know what was to come!

Midway through the report, our form master changes to Mr. Winfield. He was not a nice man.

He looked like one of the gargoyles on the Radcliffe Camera in Oxford. He hated me from the off and the feeling was mutual.

His first report was when I was 13 years and 5 months and had been absent 13 times (home life was not so good) read:

'Clearly the retarding factor is his immature attitude and general lack of application. He is letting opportunities slip that will not be offered again '

The Head agrees:

'His behaviour is bad and he has been sent to me too often this term. I will not accept his present conduct and I expect an improvement in 1969'

Not so quiet now! They wished I would shut up in class. Bit of a change in less than 2 years. A combination of factors caused this, but in those days schools were not particularly interested in the pupils' home life situation.

Not that I am making excuses. I was what my Dad would refer to as a 'toe rag'

Looking through the report, towards the end of my school career, my favourite grade and comment by far was given by Mr. McIntyre the Art teacher. He gave me an A for the term grade and an A for the exam grade. His comment was 'An outstanding talent, excellent progress'.

I also like the comment made by Mr. Peters, who taught religion. He wrote 'A poor attitude' in very small, neat lettering.

Mr. Peters was an inoffensive man who looked like a dormouse. His lessons were always the same. He would give everyone a copy of the scriptures and tell us to read quietly. I suspect he knew that most of us weren't really interested in his subject.

Invariably, Mr. Peters would sit at his desk and quietly nod off. His room was on the ground floor of the school. One day, bored, I opened a window, climbed out and went home.

I think that is why he thought I had a poor attitude.

The Head mentions me having been sent to him several times in that term. That hadn't happened until Mr. Winfield took over my form.

The Head did not mention that on 2 of those occasions, he gave me the cane. The Headmaster at John Mason High School was one Mr. Derek Hurd. He was a big man, well over 6 feet and well built. As an aside he is or was the twin brother of Douglas Hurd a senior Minister in Margaret Thatcher's cabinet.

Both times that I got the cane I was given the maximum sentence, six of the best. Strange expression, although he definitely gave of his best. Derek Hurd had been an Oxford Blue and was a very strong man.

I swear that when he administered the cane he bent so far backwards that he touched the floor behind him with the tip of the cane.

Then it came down. Thwack. Six times. Afterwards it was not the done thing to cry. Not in public anyway.

I walked quickly to the boys toilets, went into a cubicle and had a quiet sob to myself.

Then I looked at his handiwork in the mirror, admiring the evenly spaced red welts on my backside.

Always when someone was caned a group of boys would form in the toilet and also admire his handiwork, comparing it to others who had suffered the same punishment. It was the general consensus that mine was up there with the best.

By the way the 2 canings were for smoking and for climbing out of the window during Mr. Peters' lesson.

I don't know why Mr Gargoyle Winfield took a dislike to me, but he did. Every morning when the class registration was called, he started with 'Outside the door then Hutt'. He left me there until it was time to go to lessons.

In time, as soon as he started to speak the whole class shouted 'Outside the door then Hutt'. I would traipse off, laughing. It amused me every time.

Clearly my school career was heading downhill. I know a lot of it was because of what was going on at home, but I make no excuse for that.

My grades were good in the main subjects. English, Art and towards the end, EPA (Economic and Public Affairs) I loved that last subject. The teacher was Mr. Jones.

Jonesy as we called him except to his face was an ex Miner from the Rhondda. He was a tough cookie.

He took no prisoners. If you asked him a stupid question, or if he felt like it he would take your tie, cut it off half way up and write the answer or some sarcastic comment on the bit that had been removed. This was only with the boys, even though there were girls in the class. That was an equal opportunity that I am sure they were happy to pass on.

Jonesy's last comment in my report was ' Arthur continues to develop in this subject. He is most helpful in school' There's quite a few that would not agree with that last bit.

So back to the Gargoyle, who was to prove to be my Nemesis.

Mr. Winfield had all sorts of petty rules that he liked to impose on us. One was that nobody except members of our form (4W) was allowed in our form room. This rule was not applied to any other form room in the school.

At this time I had a girlfriend (well she was a girl and a friend). Her name was Yvonne and I was very fond of her.

She was in 4H whose form room was next to ours. One lunch time she had come into our room to see me.

Unfortunately Winfield came in and saw her with me. What happened next will stay with me forever even though it was 52 years ago.

He marched up to her and told her to get out. He put his hand on her 'chest' and started to push her towards the door. She was 15 then, and a young woman.

I totally lost it. I grabbed him and threw him across his desk. I then stormed out of the room.

In the corridor there were wooden lockers for pupils to keep their school books in. They opened outwards. I ripped about 6 off the walls as I left. I went home and told my Dad.

He phoned the school and offered to repair the locker doors. The Head asked him to come in and see him. I was to go too.

The next day we went in. I was made to sit outside the Heads office while he talked with my Dad. As I sat there numerous lads walked past giving me the thumbs up which made me feel a bit better.

I was eventually ushered into the office. My Dad was sitting sombrely in a chair by Mr. Hurd's desk. The Head was sitting at his desk, staring at me.

He started to speak. He told me that what I had done in ripping off the locker doors was inexcusable. He didn't seem bothered about Winfield.

Given my recent reports and behaviour, he felt that I should not continue to be a pupil in his school. I was thinking that's OK with me.

He said he had discussed this with my Dad and they had reached an agreement. There were 2 ways in which someone in form 4 (year 10 nowadays) could leave school. One was expulsion. The other was to enlist into the British Army.

Dad had gone for the latter option to avoid family embarrassment, which was a laugh. I didn't mind the idea at all. It would get me out of school and home in one fell swoop.

Chapter 5

The Army and Aldershot

Next day I was in the army recruiting office in Oxford.

After initial discussions about which regiment I might like to join they gave me the Barb test. It's still used today, but not in the paper format we used.

Once again I love tests, so I did my absolute best. There were English and Maths questions, plus general logic tests. A series of cogs so when the top cog is turned left which way does the bottom cog go. I couldn't be bothered to waste time working it out. These were timed tests. It can only be one of 2, so I went right. Always right with me.

I ended up doing very well. The recruiting Sergeant told me I had my pick of the Regiments. He told me REME was the best one to go for. He said it stood for Royal Electrical and Mechanical Engineers. That involved maths didn't it? No thanks.

I worked out that the only ones that did not involve maths or science to some degree were the Infantry Regiments and the Catering Corps. I didn't fancy getting shot at, so I joined the Army Catering Corps.

The ACC was based at St. Omer Barracks in Aldershot. I arrived there in September 1970 at the age of 15.

There was a period of grace. You had a week to decide if this was right for you. If you were there after the week was up, they had you.

The first week was very relaxing. Nothing much to do, we collected our uniforms from the stores and got to know each other. We were shown to our barracks and allocated our bed spaces. There was the bed and a locker to keep your clothes in.

I remember there were lists put up detailing who was in each room. I was looking for my name when I saw a Mike Fluck just above me. I said to no one in particular 'Oh look there's a MIke Fluck here. Fluck me who would have Flucking thought it'

A deep voice immediately behind me said 'I'm Mike. You got a problem with that?' I looked at him. He was as wide as he was tall and had a broken nose which made him look exceptionally hard. 'No, no not at all. Hi Mike I'm Arthur' I said in a squeaky little voice. He looked at me, deciding whether to beat me to a pulp or let it go.

Luckily for me, he chose the latter option. We became friends after that. I never made fun of his name again.

There were eight of us in a room and a side room where the junior corporal lived. He was in charge of the room and was an apprentice like us.

This was an army training college. Apart from the normal NCO (Non Commissioned Officers) ranks, there were junior NCOs chosen from the apprentices. We found out that these junior NCOs were far worse than the regular ones.

The day after the week was up, we were woken about 6am by a lot of shouting and banging of beds. The junior NCOs were about. These guys had red stripes as opposed to the proper NCOs who had the standard white ones.

Now we could not escape, they showed their true colours. The junior sergeant was particularly nasty. His favourite thing was to get you at lights out, stand toe to toe and nose to nose with you and make disparaging comments about your Mother. He didn't do it to me, which was fortunate for both of us.

Apparently the Army was our Mother now. Sometimes he would get hold of a nipple and twist it whilst making these comments. I was told that it hurt.

The whole of the new intake was marched across the camp, ending up facing a row of barbers chairs, each with an accompanying barber. We were lined up with the longest haired recruit at the back. In our line, that was me.

Then they started to cut. Very short. As I got closer, I became more nervous. I had grown my hair long deliberately. I had bad acne, particularly on my forehead. My hair acted like a curtain, obscuring the spots. The curtain was about to open.

I sat in the chair. The barber took his hair clippers and placed them at the base of my neck. He started to deploy them. In one move he went up the back of my neck over the top and down the front. One bald furrow appeared on my head. An inverse mohican. I had no choice but to put up with it.

Although I wasn't the best pleased, I did and said nothing. I would not give anyone the pleasure of seeing me look upset. Especially the Junior NCOs. When he had finished I said thank you, very politely. The barber was pleased as he didn't often get that, especially from the last one in the queue. I might have imagined it, but the red stripes seemed to be impressed too.

I didn't mind taking orders from the regular NCOs, but I found it very hard to take orders from someone with a stripe who was often only a few months older than me. In the main I did, but sometimes when I was being told to do something particularly pointless I would rebel.

I was told that this was being insubordinate which is not acceptable in the Army. Sometimes I couldn't help myself and therefore ended up being given tasks to do that were even more pointless than the orders that made me insubordinate.

On a few occasions I was made to clean out all of the toilet bowls in the block with a toothbrush. At least they ended up cleaner, I suppose.

The worst was when I was told to take all of the large stones on one side of the path leading into our barracks and swap them with the stones on the other side. That really was pointless.

Generally, I enjoyed being a junior soldier. The bit I liked best was shooting. I found I had a talent for it.

They would take us in a troop carrier to Ash Ranges which was and probably still is a few miles out of Aldershot. It was a firing range, there to be used for soldiers to practice shooting.

They had cardboard targets with pictures of a soldier charging towards you with a rifle, looking aggressive.

Sometimes they were in a line of 10 or so. Sometimes they popped up all over the range. I preferred the latter as it required speed and accuracy. At that age I had both. Not so much now.

We were issued with the standard Army rifle at that time, the SLR (Self Loading Rifle). It was a superb weapon. There was a separate cartridge which you loaded individual bullets into. I think it was 12. Then you snapped the cartridge into the rifle stock and you were ready to go.

We would get into the prone position and get our rifles ready. When the targets appeared we would shoot as quickly and as accurately as we could.

Although I say so myself, I was good. In fact I was selected to represent the training regiment at inter-regimental contests. I am not sure how well I did. That suggests not too well or I would remember.

I even started to enjoy the parade ground. This activity involved marching up and down with the rest of your company whilst the Sergeant Major screamed at you. Anyone who stepped out of time got an individual roasting, designed to humiliate him in front of the whole company.

Initially it was hard keeping in step with the person in front and behind you. There was a lot of standing on heels and toes, which always attracted the Sergeant Major's attention.

There are two types of Sergeant Major, known as Warrant Officers. A WO 2 Is the Company Sergeant Major. A WO 1 is the Regimental Sergeant Major. The RSM shouts the loudest and is the most feared. When he is in charge of the parade ground it is best to keep in step.

Which is not always easy. It was left right, left right, left right HALT. Shoulder arms, bear arms, present arms. Left right, left right HALT. Attention. Stand at ease and so on.

It was all quite confusing, I suspect deliberately so. I realised that this was all part of the process of breaking an individual down and then building them back into a cohesive fighting unit that instantly responded to an officer's orders.

The proper corporal in our company slipped into human mode once, briefly. His name was Corporal Galloway and he was OK. He could bark and occasionally bite, but his heart was in the right place.

A few of us had been into town and ordered Corporal Galloway a new swagger stick. Because he was one of the few decent ones.

When we took delivery and gave it to him, he almost welled up. Almost. It was then he explained the Army ethos to us.

We were sitting on our beds in our barrack room. Dave Hodgson, Smelly Smith (he was and it wasn't nice in a small barrack room) and I can't recall the others. Corporal Galloway stood in front of us.

He said, 'boys the reason we have to treat you so harshly (I'm not sure these were the exact words, but it was along those lines with the odd swear word thrown in) is so that you will respond immediately when we give an order' (as I suspected).

He continued 'If you were walking along the Falls Road (the Army was in the middle of the conflict in Northern Ireland) and I saw a sniper taking aim at you and shouted DROP, you have been trained to do so immediately without question'.

If you turned to me and said 'I beg your pardon sir, what was that you wanted?' You would be dead.

But that was definitely not how Corporal Galloway put it. That made sense to us. It still does to me.

I didn't realise how things were going to develop for me in the Army Catering Corps. I guess the clue is in the title.

For the first 3 months it was all soldiering and I loved it. Even the punishments did not put me off. Not even the one day I spent in the Guard Room (A sort of on-site prison)

But after 3 months we were to spend half of our time soldiering and the other half in the kitchens. After 6 months, no soldiering, full-time kitchen.

I was in A company. We were going to be trained to cook in the Officers Mess. Our training would involve making fine cakes and pastries, preparing intricate and fancy meals for the officers. We were in fact going to be trained as chefs. Quite a few of the top chefs in Britain if not the world were trained in the Army Catering Corps.

B company on the other hand were being trained to cook for the common soldier in the private's mess. Their training consisted mostly of learning how to open huge sacks of spuds and tip them into a massive drum which turned them into chips. And also open equally massive tins of beans. Not sure how they did that, but then I wasn't in B company

That isn't actually true, but it's what we said in A company.

The first time I was in the kitchen, they taught us how to make filo pastry. I could not get the hang of it and frankly I did not like it one little bit. I wanted to get back on Ash Ranges.

I began to dread going into the kitchen. We seemed to be constantly making pastry. Choux pastry. Puff Pastry. Is this all these officers eat, I remember thinking.

I was happy for the 50% we were soldiering, but desperately unhappy for the rest of it. I realised that I did not want to become a chef.

I knew without doubt that I could not face working in the kitchens on a full time basis after six months. I decided I had to leave.

I told Corporal Galloway that I didn't think I was cut out for the Army and explained my reasoning. He seemed to understand and arranged for me to meet the Regiments Commanding Officer, Colonel something.

Colonel something was very kind. I guess he was dealing with a young boy and he was a high ranking officer. It's something I have noticed over the years, the guys at the top are invariably charming and considerate. It's the ones in the middle you have to watch out for.

He asked me why I wanted to leave. He didn't beg me to stay but he did say I had a bright future in his regiment. I wasn't sure if he actually knew anything about me. He also said he knew I had spirit (was insubordinate) and might attain junior NCO rank. The Army often promotes those with 'spirit' to shut them up. They can then take it out on the junior ranks beneath them.

I found out sometime later that my good friend David Hodgson ended up as the Junior Regimental Sergeant Major. The top slot. David and I were rivals and fairly equally matched. I wonder where I would have ended up had I stayed. I was certainly as spirited as David although I could not shout as loud so probably would not have got to RSM

My old regiment is not the Army Catering Corps any more. It's part of the much larger Logistic Corps.

2 Para were based next to our barracks in Aldershot. Hard men. Great regiment. I wondered whether I might transfer to them because I enjoyed soldiering so much. Then I remembered I didn't fancy getting shot at. Or jumping out of aeroplanes for that matter.

The soldiers of 2 Para called us Andy Capps Commandos. They can't now.

I turned 16 whilst I was in the Army. It was a lonely birthday and I think that also played a part in my decision to leave. I missed my home. By that I mean my beloved Sutton Courtenay.

Chapter 6

Burgess and Sons

So I returned home, not so much in triumph as in ignominy. Within weeks my Dad had got me an apprenticeship in a local printing factory.

He'd got rid of me once and was keen to see me out from home as much as possible.

The company was called Burgess and Son. It was a big factory and they printed many publications, the main one being the British Medical Journal. I was going to be an apprentice compositor. I remember clearly going with my father for an interview with the Managing Director. We were shown into his office. The MD was sat in a large chair behind a very large desk

He asked me a few questions, but I got the impression the apprenticeship was mine. When he offered it to me it, I agreed. I think Dad had already got it in the bag. The MD said he was going to draw up a contract. An indenture he called it.

We came back a couple of days later, signed the indenture and I started the following Monday.

Printing then was nothing like today. It was all hot metal type which was moulded into metal slugs with letters on. For the British Medical Journal whole pages were put together and set on Heidelbergs or something like that. I did not enjoy printing anything like as much as soldiering so my memory is not quite so clear.

There were other apprentices there already. They were all much more senior than me. There was a big, burly guy called Frank Clegg. He was in year 3. There were 2 more, senior to him. One of them was called Steve Eagles. He was quite tall, very skinny and had bright ginger hair. I don't remember the other one. I did feel quite intimidated by them all.

They didn't really bother with me as the Welsh say. I tried to get on with them, but they stuck together and froze me out. I have no idea why, it must have been because I was so much younger and less experienced than them.

You would expect that over time, that would change. It didn't. As an apprentice I was assigned to an experienced compositor. His name was something Brett. His surname was Brett and I can't remember his first name. John maybe? Yes I think it was John.

John was a nice guy. He tried to teach me well and succeeded to some extent. To put a print job together then was quite interesting. Apprentices as new as me were not allowed anywhere near the huge machines that churned out the BMJ.

I was given a compositor's stick. It was an angled piece of metal with a sliding bit at the end. It was divided up into something called emms. The idea was to drop individual slugs in with the letters needed to make up words and measure them to so many emms. Typically we would make business cards, or wedding invitations. That sort of thing.

When you had created a line, you put it into a frame. You continued this until the print job was finished.

Once complete, the whole thing was locked into the frame. It was inked with a roller and then the printing was done on card or whatever. The slugs were kept in galleys. Big cases that were stored in the desks we worked on.

There were all different sizes, denoted by points. 8 point, 10 point etc. The higher the number, the bigger the type. And there were all types of font. Comic Sans, Garibaldi and so on. In fact what you find on a modern computer. They've been around for centuries, some of these typefaces.

Setting up the small jobs we did was quite enjoyable. It was creative to some extent and I had always been pretty good at that.

Obviously in order to set up a job you had to get the required slugs from wherever they were in the compositor's section. Mostly you could find what was needed in your own galleys. Sometimes however, you had to go to other sections.

About 2 rows over from us was Eddie Jones's work area. He had some quite rare type faces, seldom used. And also some huge ones, like 62 point or something mad.

Some of these were stored in galleys quite low down. I mention that for a very good reason. Eddie Jones had extremely smelly feet. It was like there was a gaseous fog around his ankles. Everyone dreaded having to look for type at low level in Eddie's section.

So of course, I was usually sent. The typefaces I was sent to fetch were , as I said, quite rare and not easy to find. I could only hold my breath for so long and at some point if I had not found the correct type, I would have to come up for air. It was disgusting. Like sticking your face in a two year old piece of Gorgonzola. Probably worse.

Unfortunately Eddie was a really nice guy. Nobody was able to tell him that his feet stank. So it just continued. Talking about it now, it seems quite funny. But it wasn't. It was bad in Winter so you can imagine what it was like in the hot Summer.

The first few months at Burgesses were quite pleasant, making up small pieces of print work with my setting stick. Most were Times New Roman so I didn't have to go near Eddie's feet too often.

Then, when I was approaching almost a year with them, I was given a different, full time job.

I was put in the melting room. This was a smallish room where the used type was melted down for re-use. Most of the room was a furnace, constantly lit and chucking out a blistering level of heat.

My job was simple. I had to shovel the old type in and keep the furnace fed. Molten lead came out via a spout, into moulds. When the moulds were full, I carried them out to the stores ready to be turned back into type.

That was my only respite, a chance to taste clean air. I almost longed for the chance to smell Eddie's feet. It was like working in Dante's Inferno. If an apprentice had to work in those conditions today, the company would probably be closed down.

I was in there for what seemed an age. I could not see what this had to do with learning how to become a compositor. I talked to my Dad about it and I was surprised when he agreed that I should resign. Do apprentices resign? Anyway I left, After one year. Which was twice as long as I lasted in the Army, but not half as enjoyable.

It became evident why my Dad had so readily agreed to my leaving Burgess and Son. He was going to employ me as an apprentice painter and decorator.

Chapter 7

Arron Decorations

Dad was at the pinnacle of his entrepreneurial career at this time. He had won a major contract to undertake the painting of all of the structural steelwork and breezeblock walling on the Milton Trading Estate. This estate had been a transit camp like the one I was born in.

Now it has become the largest inland customs port in the South of England. It was pretty big then and expanding.

I was pleasantly surprised to find that I enjoyed working for my Dad. He didn't show me any favouritism. Quite the opposite really. The other workers soon realised that I was just one of them and treated me accordingly. I was a real grafter, and that went down well too.

Dad employed a number of people according to need. There was a basic crew of about ten. I was one of them.

One major task was to spray the structural steelwork with red oxide paint. This provided a basic coat and protected the steel from rust. Spraying at the top of the steelwork was a precarious task.

I certainly could not do it. I preferred to keep my feet on the ground, so concentrated on painting the breezeblock walls that were built within the steel structures.

Spraying the steel work was left to a couple of men called Micky Welch and Charlie Burgoyne. My Dad had especially recruited them from the nearby town of Didcot.

Charlie and Micky were villains. They were proud to admit it. Both had languished at her Majesty's pleasure on a number of occasions. And not for avoiding paying their TV licences.

My Dad employed them because they were very hard workers. They were also fearless. They scampered around the steelwork at heights of 30 feet and more, spraying paint as they went. There was a certain amount of health & safety in those days. They were supposed to wear harnesses and Dad supplied them.

Of course they didn't wear them. It hampered their movement and restricted their ability to earn money. They needed to earn a certain amount to take them over the income threshold of what they could generate by stealing. Dad paid them according to the footage of steel they covered. They covered a lot.

They respected my Dad. He paid them well and did not hassle them about things like breaking all the Health & Safety rules.

The same could not be said of Mr. Nigel Pratt, who was the site agent and responsible for making sure that the site was run correctly on behalf of the main contractors. Dad was a subcontractor.

One day he came to where Micky and Charlie were working, high up in the steelwork. He noticed they were not wearing harnesses. He shouted up at them. They ignored him.

He kept shouting, asking them why they were breaking health & safety rules by not wearing their security harnesses. This carried on until eventually a couple of gallons of red oxide paint came down and landed on his head.

Nigel Pratt always wore immaculate suits, with appropriate tie and shiny shoes. To say he was shocked would be a massive understatement. Standing there he looked like a telephone box, covered in red.

Dad had to sack them of course. But he made a secret pact with them and rehired them a month later once things had died down. I don't know whether Mr. Pratt was aware they were back, but if he was he didn't say anything. Perhaps he feared the consequences if he took any further action.

Dad used to employ students in the Summer holidays. They were relatively cheap at 50p per hour and easily dispensed with if they were no good. Some were good, many weren't.

We often had students from Oxford University turn up. Dad would give anyone a fair go as the Aussies say.

One day I was painting the breeze block walls in one large unit. I was using the standard equipment of a large roller on a broom handle. The roller was constantly dipped into a large tray. It was quite hard work.

I had been given a student from Oxford University. He told me he was studying philosophy at Balliol. He was a decent guy, if a bit unfocussed at times. I assumed he was philosophising.

One of the other painters turned up to tell me my Dad wanted to see me. I had risen to some kind of unofficial supervisory role. The others didn't mind as they knew I was one of them.

There was a tray of water that was there to put the rollers in to keep them moist when you were not actually applying paint.

I told the philosopher to carry on where I had left off until I got back. I dumped my roller in the water tray. I came back about an hour later. The student had got to the end of the very long wall. I was impressed.

That was until I saw the line where I had finished painting before I had left to see my Dad. He had continued to paint using the roller I had left in the water. I could not believe he did not realise.

That was the end of his decorating career. He probably went on to become a politician. Many Oxford graduates do.

Dad made Micky Welch a foreman. The responsibility definitely went to his head. One day he had a load of students working in one of the larger units. They were painting the walls from top to bottom. The walls were high and they were using a mobile tower scaffold to get to all heights.

He called me into the unit to show me his management technique. I got on fine with Micky and Charlie. I was one of the boys.

Micky had a satchel over his shoulder full of 50p pieces. He informed me that he had a system. There were men standing on the platform at the top of the tower. They were using rollers to paint the higher walls.

There were more men in the middle of the scaffold, painting the middle part of the walls.

A few men were standing on the floor rolling the bottom part.

Then there were a number of men pushing the scaffold when it needed moving.

Micky informed me that the workers pushing the scaffold were most at risk of being given their marching orders.

However, anybody could find themselves being sent home if Micky didn't feel they were working hard enough.

Micky told me to observe his next move. He shouted OI! At the top of his voice. To a man, they all instantly looked the other way.

It was like watching a lion stalking a herd of impala. He selected his victim, called them over and gave them their hours pay, 50p. It was impressive that he knew each one that had worked an hour or less.

Micky would then adjust the hierarchical structure according to where the unfortunate person had been working. It was a brutal but effective means of motivating the workforce.

My brother is called Tim. Before I went into the Army, he had joined the RAF. He did quite a few years in the RAF.

He found out that our Dad was doing pretty well and decided to buy himself out and join the firm. I suspect he did not like the fact that I was working for Dad, assuming I might take over the business in time. I had no such plans, but I guess anything is possible.

So Tim joined the firm which was called Arron Decorations, by the way. My Dad kept that name through boom and bust. He had originally started in business with one of the many of my Mum's brothers. His name was Ron. So as my Dad's name was Arthur, put the two together and you get Arron. Obvious. But not according to my Dad. it was actually 'Our own' Yeah, right

I didn't know what happened, he must have had a big falling out with his partner, but couldn't help keeping the name on. I don't know why he did. If I became involved in the running of the business, it could be Artart as my name is the same as his. My brother would like it to be Timart. His name would have to come first before Dad's.

I have to admit that it sounds a little better than Artart. To be honest I suspected that eventually this business would eventually crash so what it was called was pretty irrelevant. Unfortunately I was right.

But before that, my brother joined. Dad made him Contracts Manager. This was odd, because my Dad had fallen out with his brothers many years before in exactly the same circumstances. He had told me about it many times.

His Father, my Grandad who we all called Poppy, had a construction business after the war. It was well established and doing well. It's still going today. Dad worked for Poppy as a painter and decorator. He worked for him for a number of years. My Dad assumed he would rise up within the family business and eventually take over.

Dad's brother Les was a lot older than Dad. He had been in the RAF during the war.

When he was de-mobbed he came home, which was and is in Reading. Poppy employed him to take over much of the running of the business. My Dad was incandescent. I don't know if he left immediately or later. But he left.

Poppy was a strong man in more ways than one. In the 1st World War his regiment was the 3rd The King's Own Hussars. He was a private. This was a cavalry regiment. This much I know to be true. Family legend has it that Poppy was involved in a battle where most of the company was wiped out and he was commissioned in the field to take control of the remaining men.

During the 2nd World War Poppy decided to get into the black market. He ran this illegal business from the family home. This was the house that he lived in until his death at the age of 96.

It is said that he had the local police force in his pay, so had no trouble throughout the War.

Nanny had a very large number of children to look after. They were always smartly turned out and very well fed, even though Poppy did not give her much housekeeping money.

Poppy used to keep a large amount of money in the middle of a chest of drawers in their bedroom. It was mostly full of white five pound notes.

What he never knew is that Nanny would open the top drawer and take out a couple of fivers now and again. Which explains why the children were so well looked after.

Poppy just thought that his wife was very good with money.

Back to Tim the Contracts Manager. The similarity was clear. Even to the particular armed force that the brother came from. The main difference is that I couldn't care less. But I have always been intrigued. Did my Dad not see that he was repeating his own history?

Tim was not appreciated by any of the men but Micky and Charlie did not like him at all. Unlike me he was not a grafter. Unlike me he did not mix with the men. He didn't seem to have any manual skills. He certainly couldn't paint. Yet he was giving them orders. Micky and Charlie were not happy about that.

I have just realised that in my current job, I have a similar situation. Being told what to do by people who wouldn't have the first idea how to do my job. I probably wouldn't do what these pair of reprobates ended up doing though.

Tim and I had gone to a pub near to a job we were working on. When I say we, I mean me and the lads, including Micky and Charlie. Tim had come over to check what we were doing and wanted to discuss it with me, hence the trip to the pub. We never drank socially.

Then Micky and Charlie walked in. 'Hi Arth' they both said. They gave my brother the evil eye then went over to the other side of the pub. They got their drinks and were talking quietly. Now and then they would glance over at our table.

After a bit they came over to us. Charlie had a pint of bitter in each hand. They knew I drank bitter. Charlie said 'would you like a beer Arth' (they all called me that) I said 'yes please' so he placed the beer in front of me.

'How about you Tim' My brother was visibly surprised but also said 'yes please'.

Charlie reached over and poured the pint all over Tim's head. I tried hard not to laugh out loud.

'Enjoy your pint Arth' said Micky

'And you Tim' said Charlie as they went out the doors, laughing uproariously.

Chapter 8

Kung Fu

It was around this time that I got into martial arts. I came up with the idea because of a series on television called Kung Fu. His beer shampoo might have motivated Tim but we started together. Kung Fu was an excellent series. There were a lot of episodes and it lasted a long time.

It was a simple plot line. David Carradine played the main character who was a Chinese man travelling around the USA being humble. Humility was important throughout the series. It is part of the Kung Fu ethos that you should be humble.

Kwai Chang Caine was the name of the character Carradine played. He kept having flashbacks to his Kung Fu training days in China where his Mentor was Master Po. Master Po called Kwai Chang Caine Grasshopper. Po himself was Chinese. He had entirely white eyes. No pupils. It was quite disconcerting. Grasshopper did not look Chinese at all. Neither did David Carradine.

In the programme he was called Caine. Master Po taught him how to meditate. He learned the importance of respect and humility. But he also learnt how to defend himself when necessary. That's the bit every boy who watched the programme wanted to see.

In every episode, Caine would walk into a new town. He wanted to be humble, but was always provoked. The Provocateurs often threatened because they were racist and didn't like strangers in their town. Caine maintained his humility until they went too far. Now and then they drew guns but they normally tried to hit him. This is the bit myself and everyone else watching was waiting for.

In fact I always felt that it took too long for the fighting to start, I was saying 'come on Caine, don't let him talk to you like that' Caine could put up with any amount of talking. It was when his antagonist got physical that he reciprocated.

He would jump into the air, spin and kick the guy in the head. The unlucky man would always try to fight back, but he was up against many centuries of Kung Fu Fighting (later to become a Carl Douglas classic) taught to his opponent by Master Po.

The best one was when he was up against a charging man on a horse. The man had a gun too. Caine ran towards him and leapt so high he could spin and kick him in the head. He dislodged the gun at the same time.

So it was this that sparked my interest. I didn't think I was up to kicking a man off a horse, but didn't feel it likely that I would need to.

We found and joined the nearest group which was in Abingdon about 3 miles from Sutton Courtenay. I enjoyed it from day one. The master was not a young man, but he was super fit. He probably could kick a man off a horse.

We soon learnt that this martial art was not all purely physical. Although there was plenty of that, after a few weeks he was like Master Po to those of us who he deemed serious enough. I had begun to get interested in the gentler side of Kung Fu. I started to enjoy the meditation and did have the odd out of body experience. That's no joke, I felt I did although who knows.

One day the Master (I never knew his name. He didn't tell us) said he was organising a trip to a very special place in Oxford. It would be for a weekend. He said we could come if we wanted but didn't have to. I know people will be sceptical about this part of my story, but I swear it is all true.

He didn't give us any further information. I completely trusted him and said I would like to go. Tim too. It was early on Saturday morning that we were taken into Oxford. I think there were four or five of us. We were led to a tall gate in a high, stone wall. There are lots of these in Oxford, normally with one of the colleges behind it.

This wasn't a college. As I recall it was a mystical place. There was a beautiful manicured lawn. Fruit trees and fragrant flowers all around. It smelled divine. The Master introduced us to this lady dressed in a nun's habit. It turned out she was a nun. She was a smiling, beatific lady who made you feel very calm in her presence.

Luckily it was not a silent order, or we wouldn't have learnt much. I learnt a lot. We were led into this ancient stone building. Having spent so much time in the Domesday book end of my village I was used to this. As a chorister in All Saints church this was all very familiar.

Incidentally, I could hold a tune but I wasn't great. I really joined the choir because we got paid five shillings to sing at weddings.

We were each allocated a room. It was more like a cell. There was a small single bed and a cabinet to the side of it. Sheets and blankets were on the bed. Once we were all settled in we were rounded up and led to a large hall. One of the nuns talked to us for a while.

She said their order believed in reincarnation. She told us that we all had seven lives to live. In each life we learned new things. You might be wealthy in one life but poor in another. At the end of each life you went to what she called the Astral Plane. There you reviewed your position in the life progression and were then re-born.

When you reached the end of your seventh life you stayed on the Astral Plane forever. She said for us to think about people we knew. Some young people were very wise. They would be far into their individual progression.

Then there are older people who seem childish and materialistic. They might have just started. I've met plenty of them.

This made a kind of sense. I've never been a particularly religious person but this sounded more plausible than the earth being created in seven days. It definitely beats the prospect of being cast down to the fires of hell.

After our talk, we were taken for lunch. There was the Master, the pupils and a few nuns including the one who greeted us and the nun that had just talked to us. The nuns were vegetarian. This was over 50 years ago and not as common as today. The meal they gave us was delicious. I can't remember what it was exactly but it was one of the best meals I have ever eaten.

Afterwards we were told that in a couple of hours we would be called to the hall for further enlightenment. Meanwhile we could go to our cells and rest. I thought when I got back to my cell that this was not unlike my sleeping area in the Army. A bed and a cupboard. Except this was not an open room and I didn't have to suffer the snoring and other noises. And the odour that came from Smelly Smith.

I laid on the bed and stared up at the ceiling. I thought over what I had heard and thought it did make a lot of sense. Certainly the bit of young wise boys and old fools.

I still believe that today. Not necessarily all of it, although I don't discount it. What happened next still takes some believing, even for me. People of my age know that looking back some things are hazy, some get distorted so you aren't fully confident that they happened or happened in the way you remember.

This however is not one of them. I remember everything with absolute clarity as if I was in that room now.

We started with a talk from a different nun. She talked about life force, Yin and Yang. Chakras. I heard about this again many years later, but at that time it was completely alien.

Then she took a chain from around her neck and held it over her palm. It started to rotate in ever widening circles. It went one way over her palm, the other way over the back of her hand. Apparently this showed the life force going through our body. The opposites of Yin and Yang.

Then we did this individually to prove it was not a trick. It worked. I wasn't sure whether it was the Yin and Yang, or my shaky hand.

Then came the main part of the event. It was early evening by now. This lady came into the room. She was not one of the Nuns. She looked mysterious to me. She sat on the floor and we sat in a circle around her.

She said she had messages for some of us in the room. Whoever she spoke to would be asked if they wanted to receive the message for them. She suggested that they accept, no matter how sceptical they might be. I thought this was definitely getting scary. She began to explain to us about reincarnation again. But she got more specific. I promise you this is true. Ask my brother if you don't believe me, he was there.

She told us that she was a conduit for those on the astral plane. She spoke in a normal voice though. I was expecting something like Darth Vador.

The woman spoke to a girl on the other side of the circle. She asked if she would accept. The girl looked absolutely terrified but said yes. She was then told some story which clearly surprised her. At the end she looked really happy.

After a few others had been spoken to, she turned to me. I looked into her eyes, and it was like looking into the abyss. It was weirdly reassuring for me, but clearly it hadn't been for the girl. She told me she had a message for me. Would I accept it? I said yes and was keen to hear it.

She said it was from Nanny. This was what we called my grandmother who had died recently. This immediately made me sad. I loved Nanny. The message was that she was fine. She had friends with her that she hadn't seen for a long time. This was all very well but could be totally made up.

But then she became more convincing. She asked me if I remembered coming to their house in the Summer. I went every Summer to stay for a week with my Nanny and Poppy. I always wished I could stay longer.

This message continued. Did I remember working with Poppy in the greenhouse, pricking out seedlings. Planting some of the plants in the garden. I thought yes, and I remember growing runner beans in the garden, tomatoes in the greenhouse. I loved it all.

Then she said my life would have ups and downs, some of which would be serious. There would come a time when it would be so bad, she would come to help me. I thought that didn't sound so good. I was on my last life, she said so when I died I would go to the Astral Plane forever. I won't be able to prove that will I?

After that we went for another fantastic meal. Once we had eaten, we went to bed. I laid in my bed once more looking up at the ceiling. I thought about that last session. I was elated that my Nan had got in touch. At that point I totally believed it. I am still quite convinced about my Nanny. There is no way a total stranger could have known all that. Unless my brother told her.

My life has indeed been a series of serious ups and downs. I have been well off and lost it to become quite poor. I haven't met my Nan yet though. Although I love her, I don't think I want to.

Chapter 9

Off to College

So, back to work. After a couple of years working on the tools, Dad thought I should use my brains. He always said I was the brightest of his two sons. He said things came easy for me whereas my brother had to work hard at what he did. I think what he meant was that I was lazy. Sometimes I was.

His idea was that I should go to the local college and study office skills so that I could work in his office. He had checked it out and found a course called the Certificate in Office Studies which seemed to fit the bill. It also had no entry requirements, which was good as I had no qualifications.

I started the course in my nineteenth year. The year my Dad and I left the family home. I had moved into a rented house in Abingdon, where the college was.

The course was incredibly easy. So I signed up for this one year course and started the first year of five O levels on top. That was easy too, especially as most of them were subjects that I was taking for the CoS such as Economics and Accounts. No Maths of course.

The course also involved things like typing and shorthand. Being a hands on, tough sort of guy I didn't like the sound of that. Until the first lesson when I realised everyone else in the class was female. The course suddenly became far more interesting.

Coming from a small council estate, my opportunities for romance were limited. I had met up with a lovely girl from over the road when I was living in Bradstock's Way. We had become engaged fairly soon after we started going out. I tended to do that. I think in the end I was engaged 6 times.

I passed the CoS easily. I got through the first year of O levels too. I realised I did not want to go back to working for my Dad yet. I was keen to carry on in college. My Dad had paid me a wage whilst I was studying and I could not carry on at college if he stopped. I wouldn't be able to pay my rent or eat which would have made it difficult.

I spoke with him and he said he would continue to pay me whilst I was at college. I was very grateful and still am. Without that supportive gesture, I could not have had the opportunities I have.

I enrolled on the Ordinary National Diploma in Business Studies. This course was worth two A levels and the entry requirements were four O levels including English and Maths. Or equivalent . Luckily CoS was equivalent. Accounts was part of the course and I was taking it at O level too. They accepted it as an equivalent to maths. Phew.

I had to complete my five O levels in the first year of the course which was two years long. I was keen to catch up on the qualifications I had failed to achieve. I knew my own potential and chose to enter into the first year of five more O levels. Again this was not as bad as it might seem because subjects were duplicated.

I decided I also wanted to do two A levels, English and Maths. Just joking, English and Economics. Both subjects I enjoyed at school. I left Art as I thought that would be too much.

The Principal of the College thought the choices I had made were already too much. I was called to his office. This was not like being called to the Head's office in school. He didn't cane me either.

Instead he said he thought taking on the first year of an OND in Business Studies with five O levels was more than enough without adding two A levels. I said I was confident I would be OK and explained my reasoning. He agreed to let me, with reluctance. He said ' You should be aware that this might make you fail some or all of your exams'.

He was wrong. I passed them all with a and b grades in the 10 O levels I took. I only passed the OND when I wanted a distinction. I got a C in Economics and a D in English. I expected to do better, so maybe the principal had a point.

Whilst on the CoS course I got to meet some attractive girls. However I was faithful to my girlfriend back on the New Estate. She was my first real girlfriend and we had been together for a while.

The first year of the OND was another matter. Some of the girls on that course were beautiful and also clever. I found that a powerful combination. Soon after starting the course I fell for a young girl called Michelle. She took my breath away.

I have always been an honourable man and I realised I had to tell my girlfriend that I had feelings for someone else. I did not know if Michelle felt the same way because at that point I hadn't spoken to her.

I knew that I had outgrown my current relationship and was certain it couldn't work out now. I had genuine feelings for my girlfriend and knew I would eventually let her down. So I thought it best that we break up now rather than delay the inevitable.

I went to see her and explained. I felt dreadful and to make matters worse, she was lovely. But then she always was. Soon after we split up she met another man and eventually married him. She has had several children which was what she wanted. I'm not sure I did so it was probably for the best. I have always wished her all the luck in the world.

Now I felt that I was free to approach Michelle. Next time she was in my class, I asked her if I could have a talk. I was a bundle of nerves and thought I must look and sound like a complete nerd.

She was a poised and elegant girl from a posh family. She must be clever too, as she had to have at least four O levels. Her dad was an architect for Pete's sake.

To my amazement she said OK. We arranged to meet up at lunchtime. I took her to a local pub in my Triumph Spitfire. That was a beautiful car. My Dad had given me a new Ford Escort to use for work. He was always generous, even if he didn't tell me he loved me.

After being in college for a while I sold the Ford and bought the Triumph Spitfire. Bit selfish, Dad was not impressed but it was a fait accompli. He still didn't punish me. He continued to pay me. He never did show me affection but this may have been his way. I have just realised I am doing the same with my sons. I must tell them I love them. They'll probably think I'm drunk.

My relationship with Michelle flourished. I was never so happy. We had a marvellous Summer, travelling around in the Spitfire, hood down, wind in our hair. I can't remember exactly what we did, but I remember that bit.

At the end of the Summer and before the Autumn term started, Michelle told me that her family was emigrating to Canada. I asked if she was going with them. She laughed, which I thought was a bit mean, as my world was falling apart. Of course she said. I asked when. In 2 weeks she replied. I was suspicious. She must have known before this. I didn't say anything.

Then she was gone. I think when you are young, you feel things far more deeply than when you are an old cynic like I am now. I was truly heartbroken. She said she would write and I said I would too, although I did not believe either of us.

But a few weeks later this thin blue envelope arrived. I had never had an airmail letter before. It was sealed and my hands shook as I opened it.

Yes, it was from her. I read it and it was about how she missed me. Some of it was hard to read because the letters had run where she had cried.

I immediately wrote back telling her I would come out as soon as I could. It might be a while because I needed to save up. I needed to do so much more. I didn't have a clue. Passports, visas, where did I start?

The details are boring, so suffice to say I got it sorted. Her family were living in Victoria on Vancouver Island which is in British Columbia. I had never been further than the Isle of Wight and had no clue about anything when it came to flying. We got the ferry to the Isle of Wight.

We continued to write. I went to the local Post Office to buy airmail envelopes and tried to use tiny writing to get as much in as possible. That's not easy with my handwriting. I told her I loved her. She said she loved me. This went on until the day was approaching for me to fly out to Canada.

I bought my flight ticket. Cost me £700. I thought it wasn't too bad, but it was still a lot. I had saved up some money and bought Canadian Dollars. I think it was about £600.

I have no idea where I got this from now. I must have saved hard. I found a belt that had a hidden zip inside for you to put money in. I stashed most of the money in the belt and kept some in my wallet.

I actually remember dates here. It was the Summer of 1975 that I flew to Vancouver. It took eight hours. I have no idea how I managed it. I get bored flying to Greece now. It wasn't as bad as when I chased another girl to Australia, but that's another story.

Chapter 10

Canada

We landed in Vancouver Airport. Once we got through passport control and into the arrivals hall, I looked for Vancouver City through the many windows. I expected to see it in front of me. It was early evening. I asked someone where the city was. I thought it would be close. He said the bus would be there in the morning. It was about 2 hours to get to Vancouver and I would have to wait till then.

In future years I would get used to being stuck in international airports for hours and days. At this time, it was all new. I was fine, I was excited to be half way across the world. I got my rucksack and settled down in a corner.

I found at that time Canadians loved the English accent. I don't know if it is the same now. Probably not. The guy I spoke to about getting to Vancouver said, 'Hey, are you from England' I confirmed that was the case. He asked if I would like to join him and his friends. I did and had a great time telling them tales about my homeland, some of which were true.

Somebody fetched out a bottle of Jack Daniels. Someone else had glasses. Another had a bottle of Coke. I was a bit disappointed that there was no ice, but you can't have everything as I have observed before. Time soon passed, and I passed out.

I woke in the morning, feeling more than slightly the worse for wear. My new found Canadian friend was still there. He was going into Vancouver so showed me to the bus. I got on the bus and pulled out one of my Canadian Dollars. We set off for Vancouver City.

After an eternity we arrived in Vancouver. I didn't really have a clue about the geography of Canada. I didn't know where Vancouver Island was. My friend was heading off to his home. He wished me well in my quest. I had told him why I had come to his country.

I can't remember how, but I knew how to get to the youth hostel in Vancouver. I am impressed by my much younger self. I am not sure that I could be so resourceful now. I found my way to the hostel and checked in. I put my stuff in the cupboard provided and settled down on the bed. I thought back to the army again.

I was exhausted and fell asleep. The next day I slept in and it was around noon when I decided to set out to explore Vancouver. I got into the centre and ended up in a place called GasTown. It wasn't until later that I found out this was the no go area of Vancouver City.

Everywhere I looked there were people who looked like Canada from the estate back home. I realised he must have been genuine. Quite a few were drunk. Some approached me and asked for money. My money was hidden, I told them I had none. It wasn't too bad. Nobody was violent. They were just desperate.

I have been to Australia as well and it is true that the indigenous people of these new lands were badly treated by the colonialists, mainly Britain. I have been told that the people of these nations had no tolerance for alcohol so it affected them badly. I saw them in Vancouver and Alice Springs, completely drunk. Aboriginals and Native Canadians with their dignity stripped from them.

I hope it's different now. I saw a sign on a building. It said ye olde English pub. I thought this looks interesting. I entered this olde English pub. Inside I attempted to approach the bar. I was told to sit at a table by a waitress. I sat down and a young lady came over. She asked me what I would like. A pint of bitter I replied. She clearly did not know what I was on about.

I questioned the veracity of their description of themselves as an olde English pub. I settled for a bottle of lager. No pint glasses. This really was no English pub.

On the table next to me was a crowd of very loud and very large gentlemen. One of them shouted over 'Hey, you from England'? This was a phrase I was going to get used to. 'Yes' I said. 'Come and join us' he said. So I did.

They turned out to be loggers down from the Yukon. Apparently they worked hard, earned their money then came to Vancouver and drank it all. They were extremely tough guys. You would not want to mess with them. They adopted me.

The drinking carried on for days. I was pretty good at drinking having grown up in a village where there was nothing to do except go to the pub.

The loggers and I travelled all over the place visiting many bars. Still no Olde English bars. They tried to find one for me but with no success. It was a good excuse for visiting a lot of bars, although they didn't need one.

At no time did they let me pay for anything which was just as well. Eventually, maybe because they had spent all of their money, they had to say goodbye. They were good enough to return me to the youth hostel. My rucksack was outside on the grass.

Apparently I had been thrown out for non payment. I tried to explain that I hadn't actually been there. They didn't want to know, I had to pay and move on.

I felt pretty good considering I had been drinking alcohol practically non stop for several days. What a bunch of guys those loggers were and despite looking like trouble they were complete gentlemen. They asked me where I was from. There was no point in saying Sutton Courtenay so I said Oxford which is quite near. They said is that in London. You get a lot of that travelling.

I decided it was time to find my love. Again the young me proved resourceful, found a ferry to Vancouver Island and took it. I ended up in Victoria, the island's capital. This was where Michelle had relocated to. There are a lot of English expats in Victoria.

I hadn't told Michelle I was coming. I wanted it to be a surprise. I had her phone number. It was the house phone, mobiles were a long way off. I called it and a man answered. I asked to speak to Michelle.

After a little while, she said 'Yes'? I announced 'It's Arthur' expecting a joyous response. There was silence. Then she said 'Where are you'? I told her that I was less than a mile away. She said she didn't want to see me. I felt my heart hit my boots.

I said that whatever her reasons, she owed me an explanation. I had come thousands of miles. I demanded that we meet and she reluctantly agreed. She named a coffee shop near her home. I said I would rather it was a bar so she named one and we met there. I needed a drink after my shock.

Michelle told me she still cared for me but this long distance affair couldn't possibly work. She had a point. I said 'but we still have today' I think I heard that on some soppy film. I suggested that as I was there, we could hang out. She said no.

She also told me that she had bought a Corvette Stingray. What a car that is. I was jealous. I had taken her all over in my Spitfire. I felt she was a bit mean not letting me even see it. I moved on again.

She left to go home. I stayed in the bar to drown my sorrows. I still hadn't touched my belt money. Which is as well because I was here for a month. It was the Summer break between my studies.

I called the waitress over. Can I have a beer please. I had learnt there was no point in asking for my preferred drink, a pint of bitter.

I heard a voice 'Hey, you from England'? I looked around and there was this guy in a check shirt. He said come and join me. So I went over. The waitress came over with my beer. She said 'that will be a dollar fifty' or whatever. The man said he would pay and ordered one for himself. I thought my belt money is going to last the whole time I'm here, the way this is going.

He told me his name was Bruce and he worked as a painter and decorator. I told him that I had been one too and was pretty good if I did say so myself. He said 'where are you from in England' I told him London.

We talked for a while about a whole range of things. He was easy to talk to and just what I needed. We had a few beers, but not too many. I stood my round although he said I didn't have to.

After a while he suggested we go to another bar where he had some friends I might like to meet. So we moved on to this other bar.

When we got there, a very pretty girl came over and said 'Hi Bruce, who's your friend?' Bruce said 'Ask him yourself' She said 'My names Laura what's yours'

'I'm Arthur' She squealed 'You're English! Oh my God. I love your accent. Say some more' I did. She wasn't only pretty, she was bright and good company too. I had a truly wonderful evening. What a turnaround!

After a while Bruce joined us. I have to say I was a little disappointed, but he had introduced me to Laura so I could not complain. He then came up with something that was going to change things. He said 'You know you said you were a painter and decorator? Can you hang wallpaper?' 'I'm reasonable at it' I said

Bruce told me that there are a lot of English expats living in Victoria (that's where I got that fact from). He said many of them liked to have wallpaper in their houses, whereas Canadians don't. Few if any local decorators could hang wallpaper.

He had a job right now where the householder wanted wallpaper. He said he could do it, but thought someone from England could probably do a better job. I said I would be happy to help as he had been so kind. And for introducing me to Laura.

He told me he could pay me $100 dollars a day. I nearly fell off my stool. 'Where is it and when can I start?' I said. He told me it was close by and I could start tomorrow if I wanted.

I suddenly thought I needed somewhere to stay. I told Bruce this, hoping he had a spare bed. Bruce said that the house he was renovating was unoccupied so I could sleep there. It was getting late by now and he suggested we go soon. I reluctantly said goodbye to Laura and we left.

The house was of wooden construction like many houses in Canada. Inside it seemed huge with several rooms, some complete, some still needing work. Bruce suggested I get some sleep, he would be back early in the morning. There were no beds in the place. There was no furniture at all. That was fine, I was 20 and could sleep anywhere. I had a sleeping bag so I put it on the floor,and climbed in.

It had been a tiring few days and I fell asleep immediately. I was still asleep when Bruce came back. He shook me awake.

I went to the bathroom and had a wash, cleaned my teeth and went back to see Bruce. He took me to where the paper needed hanging. He had brought all of the necessary tools and a paste table.

He had the wallpaper too. It was quite a big job. I reckoned about $200 worth. In the end it was $300. I was a lot better off than when I left England.

Bruce said 'We've done enough for now. Do you fancy a trip up the island'. 'Great' I said. He gave me $300 and told me I had done a good job. I could do some more when we got back if I wanted. At $100 a day I wanted.

We commenced to drive up the island. He had an old beaten up pick-up truck, as befits a painter and decorator. We were on the Trans Canada Highway. I thought this would be like the Isle of Wight. But no, it was like another country. We were heading for Long Beach, he told me.

It was too far to do in a day. When it got dark, he would park the truck, we would get in the back and have a few cans of beer that he had brought. We would then get in our sleeping bags and sleep.

The next morning after our ablutions we would be off again. It took a couple of days before we reached Long Beach. It was a beautiful place. I couldn't wait to get in the sea. I hadn't brought any swimming trunks so we both went skinny dipping.

There was no one around, just a school of dolphins offshore. Like my cows back in Sutton Courtenay, they were not really interested in our naked bodies.

It was so refreshing that when I got out I felt more alive than I ever had. I suppose it was because of my exhausting introduction to Canada. We just sat on the beach chatting and philosophising. He asked me what London was like. Caught out by my own lie. I should have said Oxford after all.

I came clean because I didn't really know much about London except Buckingham Palace and Madame Tussauds. I hadn't been to either, or indeed London. Bruce found my deception amusing and asked me to tell him about Oxford instead.

I told him about Oxford and all the things I love about the place. The Bodleian Library where I had seen the hand written letters that Kenneth Grahame had sent to his children while he was away from home. They talked about toad, mole and ratty. He later used those letters to inspire his famous series of books, The Wind in the Willows.

A few writers have been inspired this way. AA Milne wrote to his only son Christopher Robin about a bear called Winnie the Pooh. He went further than Grahame and made his son a central character of the stories.

Christopher Robin Milne became a published author himself. He died quite recently in 1996. I wonder what it was like to be the namesake of the central character in a classic English children's novel ? I don't doubt that occasionally someone would greet him with 'Where's Tigger?'

It has been said that Christopher Robin had Schizophrenia which might have led to his Father creating friends with a range of disorders. Pooh was Obsessive/Compulsive. Tigger had ADHD. These are real diagnoses by a Canadian psychiatrist. It seems a bit unlikely to me, but ideas have to come from somewhere.

I told Bruce about the Radcliffe Camera that had Winfields, I mean Gargoyles around the top. A man I interviewed once was a stonemason and had worked on ancient buildings. He told me they are not gargoyles although most people call them that. In fact the proper term used by masons is grotesques. That made sense. Winfield was certainly grotesque.

There was so much more to say about Oxford, but we ran out of day. As it began to get dark, we made a fire out of driftwood. This is all very Robinson Crusoe I thought. Bruce had brought some marshmallows. He stuck them on twigs and showed me how to toast them over the fire. That was the first time I had ever heard of this. I don't really like marshmallows. I find them too sweet. I had never seen them or tasted them this way. They were delicious, the smokiness taking the edge of the sweet taste.

Out came more beer to wash down the marshmallows. We started talking again and I realised that although we had run out of day, now we had the night. I told him a little more about Oxford, but encouraged him to talk about himself.

He spoke of hunting trips for bear and deer. But mostly about getting drunk in various places and occasionally getting into fights. I didn't like the sound of either.

Eventually we went to sleep. I slept near the fire. It was so warm and I was so drowsy I just went to sleep fully clothed and didn't get into my sleeping bag.

In the morning I woke up and saw that it was a bright, sunny day without a cloud in the sky. But it was raining.

I sat up, confused. I looked towards the sea and saw a pod of humpback whales swimming close to the shore. Every time one of them blew water out, it drifted on the inshore breeze creating the mist that had woken me. I was mesmerised and sat staring at this beautiful sight until they had gone. It was one of the most wonderful things I have experienced in my life.

I was quickly brought back down to earth when I realised I had slept with my feet too close to the dying embers of the fire. The soles of my Doc Martins were melted.

We decided to head back and get on with some work. I had a further $300 dollars when I finished everything Bruce had for me.

My time was up, my month was over. I had not had a thought for Michelle, the reason for my journey. And I had about twice as much money as when I arrived!

Bruce drove me to the airport. On the way he tried to persuade me to stay. He said he would employ me on a permanent basis. He could offer me more than $100 a day. I said I don't have a work permit or residency. He told me he could sort that out easily.

I explained that I was in the middle of my studies. My final year of OND, A levels and O levels was about to start. I said I can't stay, I wish I could. I will come back when I have finished my exams. He said you won't. He was right.

I am still unsure if I made the right choice. Canada is one of the most incredible places I have ever been to.

Chapter 11

Italy

Half way through the final year of my studies, Michelle returned. Her family couldn't settle in Canada. Somehow she was back at college too. Unfortunately she did not want to rekindle our romance. We became good friends though.

She introduced me to her friend Jess, who I went out with for some time. We got engaged. I think I had got engaged to Michelle too.

Jess came with us on a college trip which took place in the Summer of 1976 following our final exams. We had two minibuses with about 30 ex-students shared between them. There were two lecturers too, Geoff Knapp and Terry Duley. Terry was not a driver, I can't remember who the second one was.

We were all from the OND course except Jess who was not a college student at all. We drove from the college in Abingdon to Rimini in Italy. We passed through France and Germany. We went through the Brenner Pass. That goes from Germany to somewhere else.

The scenery was beautiful in some countries. We went through Austria with its chocolate box houses. And through some mountains. Probably the Alps. I said I was not too good at geography.

I had a drinking contest with Geoff Knapp at some hostelry up in the mountains. We were drinking some aniseed stuff, like Pernod or Ouzo. It was rumoured that Geoff was in the territorial SAS. He fitted the bill. Small and wiry, he loved free fall parachuting. Once he and his son parachuted out over their home in Oxfordshire. It had been the country home of Leo Tolstoy, which is irrelevant.

They landed together next to the barbecue in their huge garden. It was a garden party and everyone cheered. Nonetheless the morning after our drinking contest there he was throwing up at the roadside. I didn't and therefore won. Terry Duley had to drive that day.

We drove past Venice. There was a mighty stink and I assumed that was Venice. Others thought so too. I did not go on the day trip there.

Eventually we got to Rimini. It's just a resort town. I wasn't sure why we came here, but it was OK. Maybe I was making comparisons with Canada, against which nowhere could compete.

We found our allocated tents. They were fine. I jumped into a partitioned bit in my tent, which was effectively a separate room. I stashed my stuff in there quickly to claim ownership. I stayed there for the whole 2 weeks. It gave some privacy for Jess and me to have some cuddles too.

Once we had settled in I went for a swim. We were right by the sea. The Adriatic I think. I remembered how good it felt in Canada and how refreshing. I was tired after the long trip.

Luckily I had brought my trunks this time, which was good as there were people everywhere. I am not a good swimmer as proven by my 2 near drownings. I took it slow and didn't go too far out. Suddenly, something floating hit my nose.

At first I wondered what it was. It was a brown, solid sausage shape. I realised what it was and headed for the shore. I didn't go in again. With the smell of Venice and this floater, I wasn't sure I was keen on Italy. I haven't been back since that trip, but only because I've been there and have so many other places to go.

The holiday was very enjoyable, given my bumpy start. There were a couple of pizza parlours. There is nowhere in the world where you can get a pizza like in Italy. Except maybe in the Italian quarter of Melbourne where mostly Italians live, so it's cheating.

On the trip was my friend Gary Hunt. He spent his whole time chasing Michelle, but to his disappointment never caught her. He continued back home, with the same result. Eventually he gave up.

I don't know how, but Gary knew that Terry Duley, who taught office studies, had the OND results. They were marked internally unlike O and A levels which we had to wait till August for.

Gary kept pestering Mr. Duley, until he was told that he had failed. He was not happy. Not only had he been rejected by Michelle, he had wasted the last 2 years of his life.

He has owned his own Insurance business for many years now. He has done very well for himself financially. I have no idea how he has fared romantically. He wasn't too good at it then.

There was a time when I went to see him at his offices in a skyscraper in Oxford. He had the entire top floor and ran the business with his partner who is a Jehovah's Witness. That is also irrelevant except he was good at knocking on doors.

I needed a job. Whilst I was kept waiting in the reception area I saw a rack with his marketing brochures on it. I had a quick read of one. It said 'I studied a business course near Oxford and completed it in 1976. I then went into the Insurance Business' It was factually correct if a bit misleading. It should have said 'I studied a business course in Oxford and failed it' That would have been true but not so effective as a marketing tool.

Eventually he came out and greeted me warmly. We went into his office. He offered me a drink and we talked about the old days. I mentioned the trip, Michelle and his exam results. As I had passed everything and he hadn't passed anything, this was not the best way of securing a job with him.

Strangely enough, I didn't get a job with Gary's insurance brokerage. To be honest I didn't want one. I was desperate at the time, but whilst in with him I remembered a big favour he had done me when I was running my own business very successfully up the street from where he had a small, pokey office. It was his first attempt at working for himself.

As I said I was doing well and had a spare £10,000 laying around in a building society. I didn't need it at the time so I left it there as a contingency fund. Gary came round and told me he could invest my £10k and make me a lot of money. He showed me graphs and predictions and in the end I got so fed up I said yes. I knew how Terry Duley must have felt, worn down by his tenacity to the point that we both gave in. Terry was probably amused to tell him he had failed his course. He would not have told him if Gary had not persisted. I was not at all amused by what happened to me.

So I wrote him a cheque for £10,000. He took it and invested it. The following Friday was what they called black Friday. My £10k went to £3k in one day. When I went to his office to discuss this, he said 'Well investments can go up and down' I was tempted to make him go up and down.

He said leave it in. It will come back when the market improves. It did improve and a couple of years later it was back to £10k. He told me to still leave it in as it would probably now continue to rise. I said it might equally go down, repeating his quote to him.

I took it out and added it to some other assets to go travelling. There was a good reason for this which will become apparent later.

Chapter 12

Job Hunting

After I left college, I applied for 2 positions. I had heard of something called the open competition in the Civil Service. If taken on, you started as an executive officer and were expected to rise through the grades faster than traditional employees. It took many years to reach executive officer grade if you started as a clerical officer, which was the normal way. Many never made it at all.

It was a fast track entry for graduates mostly. The minimum requirement was two A levels and five O levels. I had the minimum, plus the OND which was worth two A levels. So I applied.

The other job I applied for was as a clerical officer at AERE Harwell. This is the Atomic Energy Research Establishment which was in Harwell, as the name suggests. They researched atomic energy, also self-explanatory.

I got a letter quite quickly for the fast track position. It was inviting me to Whitehall in London for a day of tests. As you know I love tests. As Bruce knew, London was a mystery to me. I was still resourceful and sorted out a bus trip which didn't cost too much. Dad had said he would continue to help me financially until I got a job, but he cut it down to a minimum.

I arrived in London with plenty of time for the tests. Vancouver is a big city, but it felt that there was plenty of room and it was spotlessly clean. London was a big city which was dirty, noisy, and frenetic. I did not know where I needed to go. I wandered about and time passed. I was worried that I might not make it.

I asked a policeman for directions. I said 'where's Whitehall please?'. He didn't say anything. Just pointed behind me. I turned and there was a large sign with WHITEHALL on it. 'Thanks' I said.

There was also a pretty big poster which said 'open entrance applicants this way'. There was an arrow pointing to a side door. Feeling more than a bit stupid I followed the arrow. I thought if this was a test for common sense I would be on the bus back to Oxford.

80

I came into a fairly big reception area. There were quite a few people already there. Nobody spoke. Clearly no-one had a clue what to do. A lady came out from a side room. She told everyone to go forward through some double doors. So we did.

When I got in I felt a bit intimidated. There was an absolutely enormous room. It stretched off into the distance. It was almost impossible to see the far wall. The room was also wide. There was row upon row of chairs and tables. One chair to each table. On each table was some paper and a pen.

Most of the tables had applicants on them. I was on time so I assumed they must have staggered the arrivals. Logically, there would have been a bit of a log jam if everyone had come at once. I made my way to the nearest available seat. Somehow it felt that everything was a test. Perhaps it was.

A man appeared at the other end of the hall. I went to see Bob Dylan once at a festival. He was so far away I could barely see him. There was a massive screen which carried his picture so everyone could see. This chap did not have a screen. I could barely see him, but he had a microphone so I could hear him which is what counted.

He told us that this was a timed test (I liked them) and there would be more questions than we could answer in the time available. In other words, prioritise I told myself. Hopefully others wouldn't do this.

I have a method which I employ in these situations. Quick scan through to check which questions I definitely knew the answers to. Second sweep to have a good guess at the ones I had an inkling about. Finally, go right.

Got me a C in my Economics exam which was half multiple choice. The written part I felt I hadn't done too well in and was expecting a fail, maybe an E. The multiple choice definitely saved me.

When we started, I was pleased to see a multiple choice paper. The rest was English and Maths. I employed the go right technique extensively on the Maths paper. I skipped part one, as I had no idea. Have an educated guess, then go right. If that isn't possible then leave it and concentrate on what you can do. It's all percentages.

Some people don't have a method for prioritising. They just sit scratching their heads when they reach a question they don't know the answer to. Time passes and they get far less done than they might have. It annoys me on Mastermind when people go 'ooh, mm, now then' then run out of time. I'm screaming at the telly 'Pass'

I passed a fair bit in these tests especially in Maths. I got what I knew done and some of the ones I half knew. The miniature man with the microphone thanked us and said we would be hearing from them.

I went back to my rented home in Abingdon to await the decision. The next step was a board interview at a place called Alencon Link in Basingstoke. I had made the application to Harwell at the same time as I made this one.

I had a letter from Harwell inviting me to an interview. I went along and got the job. I was pleased because I needed the money. Not so pleased as I really wanted the EO (Executive Officer) job. I soon started at Harwell. I was in the credit control department. My job was to chase outstanding debts. There were a few of us.

We had a typing pool. That sounds really antiquated now. We wrote letters to our creditors asking them to pay up, please. Later we said pay up or else. Finally it was court. These letters were all written individually, and the typists in the pool typed them up. I wondered why was it a pool? Was it something to do with having to dive in? Or keep your head above water?

After a week or two, I thought this is stupid, I will streamline the system. So I did. I called Please pay up A, Pay up now B and See you in court C. I wrote a standard letter for each. I gave them to the typing pool and explained the system. I would give them a customer account and put the appropriate letter on it. They had to type up the relevant standard letter.

The girls in the typing pool liked it as it made their jobs simpler. The other COs liked it because it cut out a lot of administration that was not necessary. The EO in charge of our section summoned me to his office.

'What do you think you are playing at', he started. I didn't know what to say. I honestly thought he was going to thank me for my innovative thinking. However I was about to get my first lesson in the way a Public Authority/Civil Service Department and any Government Department operates.

He said 'what you have done could close down this department. It might well cost me my job'. He went on 'you are not an executive officer and are operating outside of your authority. In order to remain an executive officer I need to have 6 clerical officers reporting to me. Your system will mean at least 2 will lose their jobs or be moved. Once the number of COs has been reduced I will be relocated. I might even be declared surplus to requirements.

'You don't understand the complexities of this department. We will no longer be operating this system and you must learn to stick to what you are

82

employed to do' I have worked in several such organisations and in fact still do.

Processes that have been irrelevant for years are still used, because that's how it has always been done. New ideas are frowned upon, especially from the workers. Still it won't change and you have to roll with the punches. Or you will go mad.

So I kept my head down and tried hard not to think. It was getting a bit like Mr. Orwell's 1984. I began to see where he got his ideas from. Big Brother was watching me from his office.

I had to keep telling myself that it was a job, at least I was getting paid. I find myself in a not dissimilar position now which is a shame as I, like Rowan Atkinson, am at the end of my working life. What's worse I loved my job until recently. Unfortunately the company has been taken over by accountants, IT people and yes persons.

Rowan continues to work. He is immensely talented and enjoys what he does. I also continue to work. I need the money.

I had been working at Harwell for a while when a letter plopped through my letterbox. It was from the Whitehall lot. They were pleased to inform me that I had been successful in my test and was invited to attend a board interview at the Civil Service HQ at Alencon Link in Basingstoke.

It was a bit of an anti-climax to be honest. I had given up on this and decided to grovel my way to the top at Harwell. It seemed to work for others.

I decided I might as well go so I booked a day's leave. I was going out with the blonde girl who had been chatted up by Eric Idle and Neil Innes. She said she would drive me to Basingstoke. We set out on the morning of the interview which was scheduled for early afternoon. 2 pm I think.

It's not that far from Abingdon to Basingstoke. About 40 miles. I was not in the slightest bit nervous as I had decided I could take it or leave it.

We got there and it was nothing like Whitehall. We parked easily and I found my way to the entrance. I went into the reception area and approached the desk. I gave my name and was told to sit down and wait my turn. At least I knew that I was expected. My girlfriend had opted to wait in the car.

After about an hour, I was called in. There was a high desk, a bit like in court. I know about that, which is yet another story. Behind the desk were five men, all looking sombre. I was expecting one of them to pull out a black cap and sentence me to death.

The one in the middle told me that I was going to be asked a series of questions and they wanted me to give my answers clearly and concisely. I am OK with being clear, but can struggle with being concise. I would have to stick to the point. There could be supplementary questions from any one of them. Did I understand?

No I'm stupid I thought. That was my attitude, I truly wasn't bothered. I had a job. True I wasn't entirely happy, but I could see a way forward. A bird in the hand.

So, as promised they asked me a few questions. I answered them with relative ease as they were mostly about topical issues and I liked to keep up on things. They asked me what I thought about the Icelandic Cod Wars which was big news at the time. I gave my opinion saying I thought our government was wrong in the way they were handling the situation. Eyebrows were raised, I noticed.

Then they asked me a question about my local MP who was Roy Jenkins, famous at the time. I said he seemed a decent enough bloke. He had a speech impediment and called himself Woy. They said they were interested in what I thought of the policies he supported. I hadn't got a clue. Who would?

I told them that I wasn't completely aware of all of his policies. I said MPs develop the policies but it is the Civil Service, which remains constant whilst government's change, that enact and monitor those policies.

Being concise I concluded that in my opinion the Civil Service played a more important role in the implementation of policies than the MPs. I hoped that was clear enough.

Given that I was sitting in the administrative centre of the Civil Service Commision, who prided themselves in being above politics, running an impartial and independent operation, I was taking a chance. But I did take a strong interest in politics and believed what I was saying. I might not have been quite so forthright if I was desperate for the job.

Eyebrows were more than raised. A couple of them looked ready to explode. I left, certain that I had failed the interview.

We drove home stopping on the way for a drink and a game of pool. My girlfriend was driving and had to have a Coke. I had a couple of beers. I wasn't worried, just annoyed that I had wasted a day's leave.

A few weeks later I had another letter from the Civil Service Commission. It said that I had been successful in my interview. I was astounded. I still think it was because I wasn't bothered and therefore answered the questions truthfully. Maybe they liked my forthright attitude. I knew that I had won in a huge competition against hundreds maybe thousands of others, mostly graduates. I was quite proud of myself. Take that Winfield.

In the letter sent offering me the interview I was asked which department I would prefer to work in. I said the Manpower Services Commission. This department included the newly launched Jobcentre and I was interested in joining. I wanted to work with people and try to help them to find work.

The letter telling me I was successful offered me a place in the Inland Revenue in Newbury. The collections department. I would be a tax collector. Not working with people in the way I envisaged. Apparently this was because I had a grade A O level in accounts. Nothing to do with what I had actually asked for.

I would be an Executive Officer. The same grade as my boss at Harwell. However, I didn't really want to be a tax collector.

I thought about whether to accept the offer. I would jump years up the civil service scale. I would almost double my current salary. I also knew there was a process whereby you could insist on being transferred between departments.

The letter said I had a week to decide, at which point the offer would be withdrawn and there would be no other. I wrote back immediately and said 'yes please'

I took enormous pleasure in handing Big Brother my resignation letter, informing him that I was now going to be an executive officer like him, despite being 20 years his junior.

Not in those exact words but he could read between the lines.

Chapter 13

Inland Revenue Tax Collection, Newbury

As I was driving towards Newbury for my induction into the Inland Revenue I was feeling a mixture of emotions. I don't get anxious, but I was slightly nervous. Probably because I did not have a clue what to expect. I was also excited at the start of this new chapter in my life. I was an executive officer. I would have a team of clerical officers reporting to me like my previous boss. I realised if that was the case, what would I do?

I got to the office in Newbury. It was a nondescript building in a back street of the town. I went in. There was a kind of reception area with stairs leading up. Nobody was around. I wasn't sure what to do. The letter had just told me which day and what time to arrive. This was the day and it was the right time. I expected there to be someone to meet me.

I waited a few minutes, then decided to go up the stairs. At the top was a sort of corridor with what looked like a bank counter running along it. There was a woman on the other side of it. I approached her, thinking this felt like I was going to pay in some money or take some out. I found out later that at this counter you only did the former.

I spoke to the woman, saying I was supposed to be starting work here today. She said she would get someone. She came back with a gentleman who was as equally nondescript as his building.

His name was Arthur Vickery. He reminded me vaguely of Winfield. Same build and slightly grotesque. He opened the door to let me into the main office. It was open plan with people sitting at desks all around it. It was very quiet and everyone looked miserable. It looked like a Dickensian novel. I did not feel inspired.

He told me he was Mr. Vickery. He was never Arthur. He was a pompous little fellow who was a complete non-entity. It had taken him 30 years to work his way up to his current position as department manager. He was in charge of the whole operation. He was an HEO. Higher Executive Officer.

Arthur Vickery, after a lifetime devoted to tax collecting had got to a position only one rank up from this 22 year old in front of him. He didn't like it. Not one bit.

He took me to his office, which was small and untidy, like him. There were two absolutely immense books on his desk. One was green and one was red. He said that I was going to work my way through them. He would want to see me once a week, on a Friday to check my progress.

He had one particular habit. I am not sure that I should share it, but I had to witness it every Friday and often in between. Whilst I was with him, he would sit at his desk and stick his finger in his ear, pulling out some earwax. He would roll it between his thumb and forefinger creating a nice little ball. He would then place that on the edge of the table. He ran his finger backwards and forwards over the ball until it had become part of the long brown streak that had built up over many years.

He seemed to be in some sort of trance whilst this was going on. There was no communication. When he eventually stopped he would talk to me. On this first day he explained what these huge books were about. The green one gave instructions on what you had to do in any given circumstance. It was called Collectors Notes. The size of it suggested I would have to do a lot. I don't remember what the red one was for. I spent all of my time reading the green one.

I was shown to a desk by one of the 'team'. I had my books with me and was glad to put them on the desk. They weighed a ton. Once I had been shown the desk I was left to my own devices. I found out that reading the green book was going to be my job for quite some time.

Mr. Vickery resented me because he hadn't got much further than me despite being old enough to be my father. There were two other EOs. An old chap and an equally old lady. They were OK but it became apparent that they didn't think it right that someone could have the same grade as them without doing the time. Everyone else resented me because I outranked them. I was the youngest person in the whole outfit. What had I let myself in for?

I sat at my desk. It had some filing trays. There was a phone with a brown cord running from the mouthpiece. That was old fashioned even then.

I cannot picture what else was on the desk. Today, of course, desks are full of computer monitors, keyboards, mice and so on. There was none of that then. I think it really was just a phone and paper. Lots of paper.

I opened the book. I couldn't skim read it as it was just too big. It was the size of the bible that the priest keeps on the big lectern in church and refers to when preaching his sermons. But it's contents were nothing like as interesting.

I did have a browse through before starting properly. There were two instructions that amused but also bewildered me. One was how to tie the knot required to secure the large bag that contained the confidential waste. It could only be one specific knot. There were illustrations.

The second one was about what to do if you were physically attacked by one of the tax defaulters you were trying to get money from. It said that if the attack has resulted in physical injury, you should return to your office.

It further said that when at the office you should go to the bathroom and clean yourself up, removing any blood traces. You must do this before reporting to your manager. This instruction also had illustrations. Drawings of heads being held backwards whilst the injured collector wiped off the blood.

I thought if I was attacked and left in that state, I wouldn't go to the office. Depending on the severity I would either go home or to A & E. But these are genuine instructions from the big green book I was forced to read.

This is the nonsense I had to read for the next few weeks. They wouldn't let me out until I had suffered enough. When that point was deemed to have been reached by Mr. Vickery I was let loose on the taxpaying public. Strictly speaking the non-tax paying public because we were out there to collect outstanding tax from those who had refused to pay so far.

Before we got involved just about every other means of collecting the tax had been exhausted. So we were never welcomed with open arms. Being a rural county, I was often welcomed by snarling dogs. I had been there before of course, trying to collect my wages.

We had a few ways of collecting the tax owed to the Inland Revenue as it was then. One was something called distraint. I was told that the Tax Collector was the only person who could take possessions without a court order. That was distraint, and it had its own chapter in the Big Green Book.

I never carried out a distraint in the one, long year that I worked at the Newbury Tax Collection. People did pay up when they caught you eyeing up their new car.

The area in and around Newbury has many racing stables. The people who owned them were very wealthy as were the people who stabled their race horses there. Many of them did not like paying their taxes.

Nobody likes to pay taxes, but these people just didn't pay. When I went round I frequently had dogs set on me. I seldom got payment. They would always pay up when the court summons arrived. I still had to go through the snarling dog routine. It was part of the process it would appear. It was helpful that I had a good grounding. I was far more interested in getting my pay from Old Farmer Allen than collecting taxes for the Government. When the dogs appeared I left.

As mentioned I knew that there was a rule that staff should be able to switch between departments with ease. It is now known as the OGD which is the Other Government Departments transfer list. There is a clear requirement for transfers to be completed within reasonable timescales.

The process existed in those days but was called something else. From the day I put my request in until the day I started with the MSC (Manpower Services Commission) was one year.

As previously mentioned I worked there for one year. I applied to move almost as soon as I got there. At the time I thought maybe I should give it more time. Unintentionally I did.

Apart from generally hating the job, there were a couple of specific things that made me determined to go. The first one was when I was sent to collect some tax from a sweet shop in the town centre.

I found the shop easily enough. I entered the shop and saw a little old lady behind the counter. She was on her own. Under the counter there was virtually nothing to display. She asked me what I would like. I explained that she had some outstanding tax to pay. She was confused. Her husband sorted out the tax. She didn't really understand it

She owed two years tax according to my records. Her husband had now been dead for two years. Because no tax returns had been filed, she had been given an estimated tax bill. These were based on the previous tax years when her husband was alive and business was good.

She had earned next to nothing since her husband died. If an estimated tax bill is not appealed, it becomes payable. Even if it can be proved that the bill is wrong, it has to be paid and then claimed back.

This bill was for quite a large amount. It was clear this lady had no way of paying it. I tried to do my job and ask if she had any family that might help.

I told her that she would get her money back but that it had to be paid first. She didn't understand. I didn't either to be honest. Why couldn't it just be written off. It was clearly wrong.

She was getting visibly upset. She was a tiny woman and it didn't help that she reminded me of my Mum. I told her I would do my best to get this sorted for her, I was sure that it was a mistake. How wrong I was.

I wouldn't imagine that anyone is under the delusion that the Inland Revenue, or HMRC as it now is, operates as a benevolent organisation. But I was shocked at how ruthless Mr. Vickery was.

When I got back to the office, I asked to see him. That had never happened before and he seemed annoyed at the intrusion. I waited for him to complete the ear-wax routine. When I had his attention, I outlined the situation with the sweet shop lady. I explained these estimated bills were wholly inaccurate, based on income generated before her husband had passed away. She was keeping the sweet shop open because she had nothing better to do and it kept her memory of her husband alive

She told me she collected her pension once a fortnight and bought some sweets with it. She put them on display and the local children would come in and buy them. Her stock was soon gone.

I almost had myself in tears. Not so Mr. Vickery. 'Does she own the property? ' he asked. 'I don't know, ' I replied. 'Find out. If she does we can issue a distraint on it. That will pay the tax bill' 'Isn't there some way we can cancel the bill? It is incorrect after all'. 'She should have appealed' he said. 'Now I need to get on'.

I've often encountered inflexible systems like this. Normally, they are just frustrating. In this case it was inhumane. I didn't understand why somebody could not just say this is wrong and cancel the whole thing. Obviously there are people who abuse the system. This lady was not one of them.

There were others though. The second case that helped confirm my decision to move departments was totally different. There was a very wealthy gentleman living in our area. I believe he was a Saudi Arabian prince. He was the only person in the country to pay Schedule E tax. That is a tax based on the ownership of forestry. Something like that. Anyway he was the only person in the UK who had to pay that tax. He never did.

I was passed his file. He owed thousands of pounds in tax. The interest on what he owed was far more than the sweet shop lady didn't owe. He got different treatment from Mr. Vickery. I calculated the interest on his debt, added it to his bill and issued a demand for payment, pointing out that further interest would accrue until payment was made.

Shortly after I was summoned to Mr. Vickery's room. 'What are you playing at?' He shouted

'I have had my boss on the phone. You have upset this gentleman, sending him a demand for tax that he doesn't owe'

I pointed out that the original tax bill had been generated by the Inspectorate and was still outstanding. I had merely added on the interest.

In that case the interest was removed and the original bill reinstated. I don't think it was paid.

I don't know what happened to the sweet shop lady. I hope it worked out alright. I had moved on before either case was resolved.

There were a couple of things that took place at Newbury tax collection that did make me laugh.

At the end of every day, the accounts had to be balanced. Everything taken had to balance with the overall tax bill. This was government money and if there was any discrepancy we had to stay until the balance was found.

There was one happy taxpayer who knew this. He had been disputing a tax bill for ages. It was an estimated bill which he had not incurred. But he hadn't appealed in time. The bill was for a few hundred pounds.

The office closed at 4.30pm on a Friday. He came in at 4pm one Friday and told the cashier that he had come to pay his tax bill. He pulled out a sack full of one and two pence coins and tipped them all over the counter. We were there a long time that night trying to find the balance. It's funny, but not so much at the time.

The other concerned Lord Denning, Master of the Rolls. I took Law at college, both as an O level and an option in the OND. I knew that Lord Denning was in charge of the judicial system in the UK. He was highly influential, an exceptionally clever man, and a fair one too. He encouraged judges to observe the spirit of the law rather than the letter of the law. He should have told Arthur Vickery that.

He actually could have, because he lived in Newbury at the time. For many years Lord Denning had been running rings around the Inland Revenue in

Newbury. Given his position and wealth, he must have been doing it for fun.

He contended that he should not have to pay tax. He based this on some ancient legal right which he expressed through very lengthy letters sent to the Newbury tax office on a regular basis. This had been going on for years and it was clear that the Inspectors had no idea how to deal with him.

Lord Denning will have been dead for a long time now. I doubt that the tax man ever beat him.

Chapter 14

The Manpower Services Commission (Jobcentre and PER)

I had made a successful transfer from the Inland Revenue to the Manpower Services Commision. It had taken a huge effort but turned out to be a pivotal change in my career.

I had originally wanted to join the new Jobcentre programme and that is where the Civil Service now sent me. I was based in the Oxford Jobcentre but this was a nominal base as I was sent to Manchester for training. I was one of a group of fast track EOs from all over the country. Every one of them was a graduate. I was the oldest at 23, which was the complete opposite from the tax office.

This was a golden age for me and the Jobcentres too. We stayed in Manchester for 6 months. All of us were put into a hotel on the outskirts of Manchester, close to Knotty Ash. I never met Ken Dodd in the whole six months I was there. Every day we went into the city centre spending the day in training. It was intense but enjoyable. We learnt a great deal. Unlike a lot of Civil Service and similar training, this was excellent. It seemed that no expense had been spared.

Before the Jobcentre was created, anyone claiming benefits went to the local Unemployment Benefit Office. They had their UB40 signed and waited for the money to arrive. The UBO was part of the DHSS. Occasionally the benefits clerk would point the claimant towards some local job opportunity, but it was not organised. Incidentally, yes the main benefit form was where the Birmingham group got their name

The jobcentre was created by a specially commissioned group brought in from the commercial sector by the government to tackle the unemployment problem. They came to the conclusion that a department should be created to concentrate on finding work for the unemployed. They would separate the payment of benefits from job searching.

They recommended that this department should be based in town and city centres. Whilst benefit claimants would need to 'sign on' at the Jobcentre, the claim would be processed by the local DHSS. Therefore, these Job Centres would concentrate on finding people jobs. It worked. For a while.

The training we were put through covered a wide range of subjects. We were taught how to interview by a motivational psychologist. Even now I remember the acronym they taught us. WETCHA. This stood for Work Education Training Circumstances Health, Aims and Aspirations. It was an excellent framework for an interview. Better than those used today in the Welsh careers service where I work.

We were taken around a variety of different businesses so we could understand what industry looked like and the kind of places we might be sending our customers to. I still remember the foundries we were sent to. The smell of molten metal reminded me of my days in the melting room at Burgess and Sons. That seemed a world away.

In our spare time we would go drinking in Manchester. We had a couple of Mancunians in our midst and they showed us where to go. Most nights we ended up at a curry house where the curries would blow your head off. There were contests to see who could handle the hottest curries. I competed once and then thought better of it.

There was a new film out. It was Saturday Night Fever with the incredible dancing of John Travolta. We went to disco's in town and made complete fools of ourselves. It was a great time.

At the end of the 6 months we were sent to our respective offices fully equipped to help the nation's unemployed get back to work. I returned to the Oxford office. The manager there was a lot more helpful than Mr. Vickery. Thinking back, the tax collection office in Newbury was positively Dickensian.

One thing I remember about the Oxford office has nothing to do with work or anything else. It just amused me and still does. The office was next to Oxford Jail. It was being renovated and there were wooden hoardings all the way around it. Someone had used red paint to put this message up 'Why is it that 80% of the people in this jail are working class?' It was unsigned. Some wag had painted underneath in blue paint 'Because 80% of the working class are criminals' It was signed Prince Philip, but I don't think it was really him.

On my first day working in the Oxford office, I received my first customer. I deployed the WETCHA technique. Can you tell me what your last job was? and so on. It took about 45 minutes. At the end I gave him his UB40 and directed him to the DSS.

The clerical officer next to me was saying, have a look at the jobs on the walls and come and see me if you would like to apply for anything. Then she gave the customer the form. She saw 3 to my 1.

At the end of the morning I was summoned to the manager's office. I went in and he told me to sit down. At least he wasn't rubbing ear-wax onto his desk. He said that Jane had seen 6 customers whilst I had only seen 2. It was true and to be honest who had done the most. I knew all about my customer, who went and looked at the jobs on the board after the interview. I hadn't really achieved any more than Jane and took 3 times as long.

It dawned on me that the training I had been through was not appropriate for the Jobcentre setting. However after a couple of weeks of giving out UB40s and pointing customers at the jobs board, I was called into the manager's office again. There was a man with him.

He introduced himself. He said 'My name is Derek Chadwick. I am the manager of PERs Reading office'. I had no idea what he was talking about. He went on. 'Your manager has told me that you have had some excellent training in interview techniques, but these are not really appropriate for his operation. He has suggested that I should come and meet you'

I still didn't know what he was talking about and said so. He explained. PER was the executive side of the Jobcentre. I didn't know there was one. PER stood for Professional and Executive Recruitment. They like their acronyms in the Civil Service. They only dealt with graduates and experienced management personnel who had become unemployed. Very elitist.

He told me there was one in Oxford and asked if I would like to go there. Why not, I said. We went a few doors down the street. There was a door with Professional and Executive Recruitment etched into the glass. He led me in.

There was deep pile carpet on the floor and mood music playing in the background. There was a reception area with a large table and comfortable seats. The table had a range of recent magazines on it. There was a smart gentleman sitting on one of the chairs. He turned out to be a client. Unlike the Jobcentre, PER didn't have customers. There was a smiley faced girl at the reception desk. Derek introduced himself as the manager of the Reading office. He asked if he could show me around. He took me into the first office we came to. There was a young man in there, sorting through some computer printouts.

Derek asked him to tell me what he was doing. The young man said that he had just printed off some client details from the national database. Apparently when an eligible person came into a PER office anywhere in the UK their details were taken and a brief synopsis requested. That was put on the database which anyone in the organisation could access. No-one below the grade of EO worked with clients

The EO told us that he searched for clients that matched the requirements of local employers looking for professional staff. He or she would compile a short list and call them in for an interview. This would be an in-depth interview to establish their suitability for the job they were being considered for.

A final short list of candidates would be put together and presented to the employing company. PER was a fee charging service, and the employer had to pay for the shortlist and then eventually for employing the right candidate. In the end this was to be its downfall.

The in-depth interviewing bit seemed to offer a chance to use WETCHA I thought. It would be a shame to let that training go to waste. At this point I was sold. I told Derek that I was keen. He offered me a position in the Reading office to start as soon as possible. The only problem was how to get to and from Reading when I was still living in Abingdon. I wanted this job so I thought I would worry about that later.

I had traded my Triumph Spitfire in for a Ford Capri when the Spitfire, which I was very fond of, started to develop numerous faults. No more practical than the Spitfire, it was at least more comfortable and more reliable. For a while I commuted between Abingdon and Reading, but eventually found myself a bedsit close to the office.

It was a bit small. Once in the building, which was a converted terrace house, I had to climb the stairs past other bedsits to mine which was at the top. The door to my bedsit opened outwards. It could not have opened inwards, there was not enough room. I had to edge carefully into the bedsit as the bed was close to the doorway. There was a small electric cooker at the end of the bed. I had to sit on the bed to cook on it, so I lived on takeaways.

It was on a side street but still close to the centre of town. It was very noisy. I could hear everything going on outside. Although it wasn't ideal, it was very close to the office and I didn't plan to spend a lot of time in it.

I loved working for PER. Everyone was friendly and the boss allowed me to call him Derek. It was all very informal but we did great business. Reading had some major employers even then. I did work for Digital Computers, who were a major employer in the town and always looking out for programmers. I also worked for a company called Plessey who had developed a telecoms programme called system X. I had no idea what it was about but still managed to recruit some staff for them. One company I did a lot of work for was called Racal. It was an umbrella company for several others. It had a central administration team but each company was a standalone entity.

I recruited a finance director for the admin team. One of the companies was called Racal Tacticom. They were developing mobile phones for the military. Another one was Racal Vodaphone who were developing mobile phones for use by the general public. Over the years that company has expanded and become quite successful. They left the Racal group and so stopped using their name in the company title. Their headquarters is still in the Newbury area.

Newbury is in the Thames Valley. At that time it was sometimes referred to as Silicon Valley, like the one in California. It had high technology companies everywhere you looked. It was a boom time, a period of massive growth and I had found myself in the middle of it.

I never worked with Vodaphone. I did work with Tacticom and got to know the military communications sector very well. I developed a network of contacts, which was to prove useful later in my career, which was definitely starting to take off.

Even though it was a Civil Service department and part of the Manpower Services Commision, PER was very much a commercial operation. I don't think there had been anything like it before or since. The Civil Servants that worked there did not act like Civil Servants at all. There were no books on how to tie knots and as we were helping people, clients and employers alike there was not much chance of being attacked.

Derek Chadwick ran the Reading office and he did it very well. If needed he would fight for his team and occasionally he had to. PER had its enemies. One of them was Michael Heseltine. He was a senior Tory MP in the time of Margaret Thatcher. Thatcher the Snatcher. Before becoming Prime Minister she had taken away free milk for school children. I remember the crates of milk arriving outside the Old School in Sutton Courtenay. Fatty Shepherd and I would guzzle it down. I don't know if it stopped me getting rickets, but it tasted nice.

Michael Heseltine was against PER from the start. He ran a recruitment agency in London as well as his publishing empire, Haymarket publications. I think the recruitment business was called Graduate Appointments. Michael Heseltine was nicknamed Tarzan because of his long hair. I don't think he swung around the chamber of the House of Commons with a chimpanzee on his back.

Tarzan's objection was that PER was a government organisation that charged fees for its services. Our fees were a lot lower than the commercial recruitment sector could offer. Heseltine argued this was because we did not need to make a profit. Looking back, he had a good point. He continued to try and get PER closed down and eventually succeeded. By then I was long gone.

PER featured in Hansard regularly in those days. Hansard is the official record of every day's discussions in the House of Commons. Tarzan was forever banging on about unfair competition. He was more tenacious than Gary Hunt. It's not clear whether he was more concerned about the public purse or his private pockets.

I appeared in Hansard on one occasion. I had designed a sales brochure to promote our services in the Thames Valley although it wasn't really needed. In one paragraph I actually compared our fees to a local commercial recruitment agency to show the reader that we were much better value for money.

Somehow Tarzan got a copy. He waved it around apoplectic with rage. I don't think my name was mentioned, but the entry was there and will be for evermore.

This may well have been the best time of my life. I was incredibly successful. It was probably a combination of my need to compete, decent communication skills and sheer audacity. I used to place ridiculous amounts of clients into employment. In all honesty PER was more about making money than helping anybody. I think Mr. Heseltine was right.

In the early days the Jobcentre really was about providing jobs. Employers would notify jobs because it cost nothing. Things were booming so there seemed to be plenty of work about, especially in our area. The Jobcentre did help alleviate unemployment, which was its raison d'etre.

Unfortunately, it was ultimately morphed back into the DSS, now called the Department of Work and Pensions.

The DSS was the DHSS originally. They dropped the H for some reason. Given the way the benefits system is run now it won't be long before they drop the D and reveal the true nature of their activities. I used to say, for a joke.

I have always been one to try and improve on existing systems. Hence falling foul of Big Brother in Harwell. At PER for the first time in my career this was not just allowed, it was positively encouraged.

This is how things worked: when an employer contacted us to recruit for them, Derek would decide who to allocate the job to. If it was me, I would go and visit the company at its premises, take down details of the job and define the qualities and qualifications the ideal candidate would have.

I would return to the office and put all of the details onto PERs huge client database.

There was a list of codes, each one identifying a specific job. Systems Analyst, Software Designer, Telecoms Engineer. These were some of the job codes I was always inputting because of the nature of the employers in our area.

I decided rather than input job titles each time I was given an assignment, I would create a permanent search for the most common ones that occured in our area such as the technical ones mentioned.

In order to claim benefits, it was necessary to register with us and provide details of work experience and background. I soon realised that there were people between jobs who were highly employable but just wanted some money whilst in transition.

So my search brought together a pool of relevant candidates and the market requirements in my area. In short, anyone matching my specifications that registered with us within the UK appeared on a print out that I ran every day.

Each morning I would run a search. I would go through the list of clients to seek out any likely prospect. When I found a software programmer for example, I would pull up his or her full details. I knew the requirements for each employer in my area and most were permanently looking for specialist staff. I knew that Plessey would always be interested in telecoms engineers, for example.

When I came across a likely prospect I would call my contact at the relevant company. I would describe the client's experience and was told whether they were interested or not. If yes, I would contact the client and establish their interest. Sometimes I called them in and used WETCHA on them. More often than not, I would put them in touch with the potential employer. Usually they were hired and PER got a nice fee.

Somehow I had a way of devising simple but highly effective methods to improve a system, usually to my advantage. I kept this technique to myself and started to make a lot of money for PER. I became recognised at a senior level. I was bringing in more money than anyone else in the entire company.

I was like that little boy 'bob a jobbing' but for more than a week and a lot more than a bob.

PER encouraged competition. Each month they awarded something called the Director's Cup. It went to the regional office that generated the most money in the previous month. In my most successful month I placed 10 clients into employment. There was more income from other work I had undertaken too. This amounted to a large amount of money. So large in fact, I was awarded the Director's Cup, narrowly beating Bristol.

Rod Evans was the man in charge at PER Bristol. He was a bit of a legend for getting results and I know he was not happy about his whole team being beaten by me. I was on his radar and we would meet for the first time some years from this.

I can't have been at PER for long. Over a year but less than two maybe. But in that time I achieved so much. As I get older, time becomes distorted. It seems that I was there forever.

Several of my assignments stand out in my mind. Apart from the supply of candidates from our database, we also ran one off recruitment exercises. In those days, senior recruitment was done by advertising in The Daily Telegraph on a Thursday. PER had a half page permanently reserved. Any one of us could put one of our jobs into this half page which had borders bearing the PER logo.

It was very popular with employers, as a slot with us was much cheaper than taking out their own individually. We also handled everything, providing them with a final shortlist of candidates, in my case who had all been WETCHAd and reports prepared.

I had been given a brief to recruit a Finance Director for the Institute of Marketing. They were and still are based in Moor Hall, which is in Cookham. I was about 25 at this time. I turned up at this rather grand building, set in it's own grounds. I was still driving my white Capri with its vinyl roof and 8 track stereo. I parked alongside the BMWs and Jags in the car park.

I was still being paid the same money as I earned picking up tuppeny pieces in Newbury on a Friday afternoon. I had a suit, but it wasn't Savile

Row. I did feel slightly out of my depth, but I have never felt intimidated by anyone in a business or work setting.

I walked in through a huge archway into a large vestibule. I think that's what it is called. A very elegant looking man dressed in an obviously expensive suit came towards me. He seemed to know who I was and ushered me into a plush office.

He asked me if I wanted to make myself comfortable. I later found out that this is a euphemism for using the toilet. It would be considered too vulgar to give it a more common name. I don't think this chap could bring himself to say would you like a wee.

I told him I was fine thankyou. I was very comfortable sitting here in his office. I thought I might need a wee soon though.

We had a quick chat about the recruitment exercise they wanted me to undertake. He outlined the role of the Finance Director. I had recently successfully completed recruiting for a similar role for Racal. I had done that exercise by using the Daily Telegraph. I suggested this.

He was unsure because of the cost of the advertising and our fee. I gave him a strong cost benefits analysis which I had just made up. He decided they would probably go for it, but he needed to talk with the rest of the board. It was only then that I realised I was talking to the Chairman.

I told him he would have to get a move on to meet next week's deadline, which was true, but he did not actually have to put it in at all. He didn't have to deal with me either.

He would let me know. Meanwhile would I like a spot of lunch. I had some cheese and pickle sandwiches in my car, but I thought I would see what he had to offer first.

He took me into the dining room. A large, oak panelled room with pictures of previous chairmen and other notables on the walls. A large picture of the Queen which was obligatory in all boardrooms at the time.

There was a long dining table covered in a pure white, linen table cloth. Small bunches of flowers ran along the middle. Places were set with mats and a number of different knives and forks laid out either side. I had only needed one knife and fork so far in life and wondered what the others were for.

There were several other gentlemen sitting at the table. 'Would you care to join us', he asked. 'That would be nice', I replied. I had decided that I would watch him and do what he did.

I sat down and so did he. He took a menu from in front of him. I noticed I had one too. He said 'what would you like?' I replied 'what would you recommend?' Not bad for a 25 year old from a council estate. He said he would recommend something I had never heard of. I had to go with it and say 'that would be lovely, thank you'

I don't know what it was, it tasted vaguely of chicken and was very enjoyable. He passed me the wine menu. Luckily I could say no thank you, I'm driving. It was in French and I could have ended up with anything.

Lunch was very pleasant. I talked with the chairman and the other board members. At the end of lunch the chairman told me that they had decided to go ahead with the exercise in the way I had suggested.

I said I would put things in place as soon as I got back to the office. I would write the advert and send him a copy to review. Before I left, I had to go and make myself comfortable.

The other case I remember was with a company called PHH Services. They were based in Slough and were a fleet leasing company, which was an American concept. The company supplied and maintained company car fleets, mostly for large companies, often with large sales forces. Leasing cars is common today, but wasn't in those days.

The first time I went to take an assignment from PHH, I met Mr. David Voss for the first time. David was an impressive character and I worked with him for many years. I met him in the Slough office. David was the Sales Manager. Very smart young man wearing a sharp suit with everything matching.

He had a very responsible job for a young man. He was probably a bit younger than me, so he was very young to be in his position. He was MD of the company before his 30th birthday and went on to run his own vehicle leasing company having stopped off on the way to be European Vice President for Hertz. I remember talking to him when he was negotiating his package for the Hertz job. He had been offered a nice car for himself, but they had also offered a car for his wife. She already had a very nice BMW so David was trying to get money instead. I said check out the tax implications.

The job I am thinking of was not my first with PHH. Most jobs were fairly run of the mill sales positions.

One day David phoned me up and asked me to come to Slough. Whilst I worked for PER we met at the PHH offices. Later we would more often than not meet up in different hostelries around Henley-on-Thames where he lived. I think we got on well because we were both working class boys from council estates trying to get on. He got on very well. So did I, up to a point. It was that point that changed things but that is much further off from here.

David had called me to tell me that he needed to set up a sales force in Ireland. He wanted me to fly over to Dublin and interview for the positions. We would take up a big chunk of PER's advertising space in next Thursday's Telegraph.

We sorted out the job ad between us. David had a few strange ideas. He would not employ anyone with a beard as a salesman. He said it proved they were hiding something. I told him that he could not put that in as a requirement. It was probably beardist or something.

The ad ran, we had a huge response because the package was excellent. David had made all the arrangements. I flew to Dublin airport and got a taxi to a rather swanky hotel,

I had an early start the following day and was going to be interviewing for a couple of days solid. Eight a day he wanted. I did not employ the WETCHA technique any longer, I had developed my own.

On the evening of my arrival, I decided to have an early dinner and a couple of Guinness. I had been told that the Guinness brewed in Dublin from the water's of the river Liffey was the best in the World. I decided to have a swift one before dinner.

I went to the bar. The bartender came over and asked me what I wanted. I would like a pint of Guinness please. Off he went. I stood at the bar for at least 10 minutes. Impatient, I called the bartender over. I ordered a pint of Guinness, I said, assuming he had forgotten. He beckoned me to the bar. He pointed at a long row of pints of Guinness settling on the bar trays.

I waited and when it arrived it was indeed the best pint of Guinness I ever tasted. Until I tasted a couple more.

I completed the exercise, did all the interviews and flew back to Heathrow days later. I had come a long way since the tax collection in Newbury, but still had further to go.

I thought it was time to have a chat with Derek regarding my situation in PER. I asked for a private audience. He asked what the matter was as I had never asked to see him in such a formal way before. I told him that I loved working there, but felt I should be better rewarded for the work I was doing and the money I was generating in particular. He told me to leave it with him.

A few days later he called me into his office. Despite previous experiences, that never worried me with Derek. He really was an exceptional boss, the best I have ever had.

Derek told me that he had been given approval to promote me to HEO on a temporary basis. I would do exactly the same job, but get more money. It was a ruse to keep me there. Even if it was I felt a great deal of smug satisfaction in knowing I was now at the same grade as my old mate, Arthur Vickery. And I was still young enough to be his son.

All this success was making people other than Rod Evans aware of me. A certain Gary Johnson who ran a small recruitment company called Coates-Johnson was about to come calling. Gary was ex PER and had done well in the organisation. Not as well as me, but nobody had or would. Yes I am proud of that fact. He had recently taken on Bob Thorpe, a lovely man who had been a proper HEO with us.

I don't know if it was Bob who gave him my name, but one day I was contacted by Gary. He didn't say what it was about, but it was pretty obvious.

He arranged to meet me in a local restaurant. It was clear from the start that he was out to impress me. I don't know whether that was to attract me to his company or just because he liked to show off. Probably the latter. He chose the food. I knew a bit more since the Institute of Marketing and was not impressed by his talk of food and fine wine.

He was driving his Jaguar XJS as he kept telling me. I was still in my pokey little bedsit which was only around the corner. He could not drink. I could. As he was paying, I made the most of it.

At the end of the evening he announced that he would let me know. Let me know what I asked. Whether you have got the job or not he said. I haven't applied for any job I replied. He phoned me the next day to say I had got the job that I hadn't applied for.

I wasn't all that bothered. I had just been promoted and was quite happy thank you. He offered me a 100% pay rise and a company car. I asked where I should sign.

Chapter 15

The Private Recruitment Sector

I started with Coates-Johnson in 1980. Still 25, this was a long year. They all are when you are reminiscing. It didn't take me long to realise this was a totally different job than PER. No UK wide computer database with lots of clients to place. No employers looking to use a well established service for their recruitment. In short, nothing. I was given a monthly target to achieve which would have been easy in PER. Here I had no idea how I was going to achieve it. David Voss gave me a small research based job. It was not recruitment but it was something.

I got back in touch with a few of my previous contacts. Organisations like GEC, Plessey and ICL Computers. They were all very nice, but I had to be honest there was nothing I could really offer them.

I got the odd piece of work, but never achieved my target. I did think that Johnson should have provided some sort of support, but he didn't.

It was then I came up with something I called Executive Search and Selection. I was to develop this over the ensuing years. The idea was that I would take a brief from a company looking for an executive. I would find the candidates. I would then provide a shortlist to the company. Hopefully they would take one of the candidates on. I would get my fee.

Some call this Head Hunting, which has been around forever. That's pretty much using the 'old boy network' to find potential employees and not what I was proposing to do. Others say they do this, but turn out to be agencies.

My idea was far more scientific. It involved research. Researching the company and its competitors. Researching the potential pool of candidates. At the core of this idea was the fact that most professional or executive people had specific career plans. Even in those days we had moved away from the job for life. I had observed people tended to work in job cycles of about 4 years. They then felt it was time to move on, before their motivation and skills became stale. This is about highly skilled people, often in short supply who could call the shots in their own employment.

Once I had identified a possible target, often from my client companies competitors I would make contact, usually on the phone but sometimes face to face. I would tell them that someone was interested in offering them a better and more rewarding job. That person was me because I was getting a fee. My client knew nothing about them at this stage.

The person I was talking to always thought they were being head hunted, that is the company making the approach knew of their work and admired it, which always made them feel good. This made them respond positively. Coupled with the fact that many of them were at a point in their career cycle where they were actively looking to move, I seldom got a refusal.

So my approach was more scientific and structured than others. I would expand on this approach later.

I put this idea to Gary Johnson and explained it as I just have. I had no doubt it would work and later proved it. Gary was not so sure and sacked me.

This was actually a perfect situation for me. He gave me three months salary in lieu of notice. I used this as a deposit on my first house in Abingdon. It was a small terraced house in Edward Street. This was known as the longest street in Abingdon. At one end was Knights, builders merchants. At the other end was a butcher owned by a Mr. Day. Knight at one end, Day at the other! No, not particularly funny, I agree.

What Gary Johnson didn't know was that Rod Evans had recently approached me. Somehow he had heard about my Executive Search idea and was interested in discussing it. It was probably Bob Thorpe again.

Unfortunately at the same time as all of this I was caught drink driving and given a 12 month ban. I have no excuse.

Gary demanded the company car back. It was an acrimonious parting. I had to tell him I couldn't bring it back as I had been banned from driving. He told me that he would have sacked me with no 3 months pay in lieu of notice if he had known. Too late!

He had to come and get it himself. I left the keys on the seat so I didn't have to see him. No automatic locks in those days.

I met up with Rod in Bristol. I took the train. Although forced to, I discovered that is a good way to get around. Every cloud as they say. In the past I easily found the silver lining. Now it's usually a case of pearls before swine.

I confessed to Rod up front. There was no point in trying to hide the driving ban. He saw no problem as long as I could do the job. Rod was always a very positive man. Having never used the public transport system I was not so sure. In the event it was fine.

Rod asked me about my idea. I described it to him and the science behind it. There was more detail from me, because he was interested and asked pertinent questions throughout. He was a skilled interviewer, although he didn't appear to be using the WETCHA technique.

I find that if you discuss an idea with an interested party, that idea develops further. Rod thought it would be an idea to have a specialist team doing the candidate research whilst sales oriented people like he and I went out developing business.

That is what happened. The specialist team was called Barrie.

I had met Rod in the offices of Harrison Cowley. They were an advertising agency. Some of their clients included St. Ivel and British Leyland. Big accounts in their day. Rod had convinced David Harrison to launch a recruitment company within his agency. Rod was an excellent salesman.

As with Coates Johnson where the Coates had disappeared I never met the Cowley. I only met Harrison once. I was working in their beautiful old Georgian building near Maidenhead. I had an armful of files and was going into a room that was used as my office. I gave the door a good kick to open it. He saw me and shouted something. I scuttled into the room. Luckily he didn't follow up on his obvious displeasure.

Rod told me that he was opening an office in Taplow Mill which was a mile or so outside of Maidenhead. Terry Wogan lived there, somewhere. Harrison Cowley was already established in that beautiful old Georgian mansion where the kicking incident was to take place.

He offered me a job as I had hoped and expected. It's as well that he did as my money had gone on the deposit for the house and I had no idea how I was going to make the first payment.

In order to get to Taplow Mill, I had to walk about a mile from my house to the bus stop on the other side of town. I didn't mind the walk, I went along the path by the Thames. It was very early in the morning, about 6 o'clock. The swans were just waking up. There were all types of water birds going up and down the river. Mallards, Coots the odd Great Crested Grebe. I loved all that. Still do actually.

When I got to the bus stop I had to wait until the bus arrived. It was usually on time. This bus went from Oxford to London. Same as the Thames. A boat would have been more pleasant but a bit too slow. The bus only ran every two hours, so I had to make sure I didn't miss it. I never did despite having to walk through huge snow drifts at times during the bad winter. I bought myself a pair of moon boots. They were great as they kept out the cold and snow. Unfortunately they looked stupid.

One day, My Uncle Phil appeared at the bus stop. He wasn't going to London just to Sutton Courtenay. Local buses ran from this stop too. I said hello. He must have switched off Radio Caroline, because he said hello back.

We struck up a light conversation. I don't think I had ever talked to Uncle Phil before. I wasn't going to again until the day of my Mum's funeral.

Phil said that in the war he, his elder brother Joe, Ron and Harry were in some kind of special forces outfit. He told me they would come home together on leave entering the village in one of those big army lorries with a tarpaulin across the rear. They would have this rolled up so the back was open. They would tell the driver to slow down a bit and when they reached the green, they would all jump out, perform a parachute roll then go into the Swan pub for a pint or six.

It was a great tale, but I was not sure of its veracity, especially as it was told by my Uncle Phil who thought he could tune into Radio Caroline using the metal plate in his head.

His daughter told me many years later that Uncle Phil had been in the Merchant Navy, not the armed forces. He did have a metal plate in his head, but it was caused by a motorbike accident. Another memory gone. He still might have received Radio Caroline though.

The journey took forever. The bus stopped constantly. Getting close to Maidenhead, it stopped at places like Sonning Common. This whole area was full of celebrities. George Clooney lives there now. At that time, a group that referred to themselves as the British rat pack lived there.

The rat pack included Bruce Forsyth and Kenny Lynch. Some people might not recognise the name of Kenny Lynch. I never knew what to call him. Was he a comedian or an actor? He was certainly on TV a lot in those days. He also appears on the cover of Band on the Run, by Paul McCartney's band Wings. Alongside Michael Parkinson who lived in Cookham.

One day, the bus stopped at Sonning Common. On got Kenny Lynch. I recognised him immediately. He walked up the bus and saw the seat next to me was empty. He sat down. I was struck dumb, which was rare for me in those days. I was saying to myself, speak to him. Introduce yourself. Ask him what is he a comedian or an actor.

I did none of those things. I was afraid that if I tried to speak a load of gibberish would come out and he would think I was the nutter on the bus.

He must have sensed how I was feeling. He had a copy of the Sun with him. He passed it to me and said 'Here you are son. Read this' I mumbled thanks and hid behind it. I didn't read it. I hate the Sun.

I am going to leave Kenny and I on the bus for a while. I want to return to Sutton Courtenay. I have talked about my Uncles Richard and Phil, but not about the others. The eldest son was Joe. Then there was Harry and Ron. I never met Ron. He was the second half of the Arron Decorations team. He moved to Cornwall at some point. He is probably buried there now.

Joe was an old man when I knew him. He lived at the far end of Frilsham Street. To get to his house, you had to go through a stone archway. Joe had a wife called Kit. She bore a passing resemblance to Ena Sharples or Violet Carsons who played her on Coronation Street.

Kit had a strange habit of making constant farting noises with her mouth. It was quite off putting, especially if you were trying to have a conversation with her. Which I never did. It was said that Joe was the Regimental Sergeant Major of the Intelligence Corps during the war.

Joe spoke very little, if at all. Every time I went in the Plough I saw him in the lounge with his wife Kit popping away beside him. His brothers all went into the public bar. They never seemed to talk to one another. Joe always wore a flat cap and smoked a pipe. I think he had a son called Dinger. Certainly someone had a son called Dinger, because his full name was Dinger Dodd.

I used to know Dinger quite well. He hung around with Ian Prior who was a tough guy. He was always getting into fights. One time I was at the village hall attending a disco type thing. I had a friend from Thame over. I was out in the bar when my friend came in. He had been dancing. Ian Prior had taken exception to him for some reason

Perhaps my friend had stood on his foot. Anyway Ian Prior decided to give my friend a bit of a pasting. He was bleeding profusely. He appeared to have a broken nose. A missing tooth or two. Prior had certainly done a job on him.

Ian Prior appeared in the bar. I thought he might have come for round two. Ian said to my friend 'I'm sorry mate. I didn't realise you were Arthur's friend' He said to me ' I am so sorry. You know that I wouldn't have done it if I knew he was your mate'. That was no consolation to my friend, but he still said 'that's OK' through a mouth full of blood and broken teeth. Dinger was there. He just continued with his pint. He smiled and winked at me.

Uncle Harry had a caravan at the end of his garden. He operated a barbers business from it. You got to it by walking up a back lane. He left his garden open so you could just walk straight in off the lane. There were no appointments with Harry. You turned up and waited, however long it took. He would take his lunch and pack up at 5. If you were waiting there when he went to lunch you waited longer. If you were still waiting at 5, you went home.

Uncle Harry had one of those stack shoes on one side. Presumably he had one leg shorter than the other. I never asked why, although I wanted to know.

Harry's speciality was a short back and sides. In fact that was all he did. You could ask for any style you wanted but you would get a short back and sides.

Returning to Kenny and I on the bus. I got off at Maidenhead Kenny stayed on. I assume he was going to London. Kenny got up to let me out. I said 'thanks and thank you for the paper'. 'That's alright' he said and smiled. His smile was dazzling.

To continue my journey, when I got to Maidenhead bus depot I had another mile to walk before I got to Taplow Mill. There was a long lane that I walked along to get to the site where Harrison Cowley was based.

For a while I worked from the old house, where I was given a temporary office. Later they put a portakabin in the grounds of the house. Maybe they didn't want to associate with us. Or perhaps it was David Harrison wanting to stop me damaging any more of his precious house.

When I first arrived at Taplow Mill I met Mr. Michael Grove-Dunning. He had been appointed by Rod to run the recruitment business that I had just joined. I had never met him before. He was wearing a very smart suit complete with silk handkerchief in the breast pocket. He had a tie to match. Bright shiny shoes and a bright shiny smile finished off the ensemble.

Mike and I got along most of the time. He preferred to be called Michael rather than MIke. So I called him Mike. I realised early on that he liked to claim the glory wherever possible. He lived in Weston-Super-Mare and travelled there and back every day. That made my commute pale into insignificance. He was driving though.

Rod had set up the infrastructure for the Executive Search service. There was Michael and I in Taplow and Barrie providing the research facility in Bristol. It didn't work too badly.

I was pretty good at selling our service. I should have been, I created it. I was fairly well known in the area as I had been working within it for a few years now. My first client was based in Slough. Not PHH, it was a company called Alenco. I don't remember what they manufactured but I remember my contact there very well. His name was Keith Mackney. I really liked Keith and always enjoyed going to his offices.

We were more like friends and he used to tell me some outrageous tales. It was Keith that first suggested I try Greece for my holidays. He loved the Greek islands, particularly Mykonos. I found out why when I went there.

I learned to love the islands too and had been going there for many years until I had to stop a few years ago.

Keith was one of the first people I phoned when I started looking for business. I arranged to go to his office and explain Harrison Cowley Recruitment's modus operandi. I had no trouble selling my idea, as I completely believed in it myself. I have never had to sell something I didn't believe in. It must be very difficult.

I sold the service on very simple concepts. The initial cost of retaining our services was a lot less than placing an advert in a national newspaper which had no certainty of success.

The full fee was not payable unless they employed one of the candidates we put forward.

The shortlist of candidates we provided would always be very relevant because they would come from their competitors.

The final idea was really a veiled threat, not explicitly made. If they did not retain me they became fair game should I recruit for their competitors. Unlike the other selling points this was difficult to get over. But I did.

This final 'selling point' was not used for Keith or any other of my contacts. Generally, the service was well received. The points I made were true. A service that does not deliver what is promised won't last long. It may be possible to sell once, but not twice to the same customer.

Keith gave me my first assignment for HCR. Mike was pleased and so was Rod apparently. Mike insisted on telling him. It had taken me 2 days from starting in the job to landing my first piece of business.

I felt this proved my idea worked and that Gary Johnson had made a big mistake in rejecting it. He went under within a year of me leaving. It wasn't my fault although my failure to make him any money didn't help.

I took the brief from Keith. It was for a salesman, a job I had recruited for several times when I worked for PER. So getting the information was easy. We spent most of my time there chatting about Greece and his various exploits which were always entertaining.

When I got back to the office, I typed up the job details and faxed them over to Barrie, our research team in Bristol. I was selling the research team to every company I visited. It sounded more professional than telling them once I had compiled the brief I would send it to Barrie in Bristol.

Barrie's job was to find out where the candidates for the various assignments were, then approach them with the old line 'I have a client who is very interested in talking with you because of your excellent reputation in (complete as required)'

Once he had a sufficient number of interested candidates, I would contact them and arrange to meet. It worked. I was very successful. Mike tried but did not have much success.

Things went well. In time I got my licence back. Rod brought a nice new Renault Turbo to my house in Abingdon. I had moved from the longest street in Abingdon to a quiet little cul-de-sac close to the Thames. Everything was right with my world. I was very happy, especially when the Renault arrived.

I got to Taplow in less than half the time. I did not have to walk four miles every day. On the negative side I lost the chance to meet with Kenny Lynch again. I wanted the chance to ask him what he did. Probably best that I got my licence back.

Mike had recruited a secretary for us. Her name was Sally Land. She was one of the best people I have ever met, never mind best secretary. She was extremely good at her job and organised Mike's diary as well as handling the sales and recruitment administration. I'm not sure what organising Mike's diary involved as he didn't seem to do a lot. Sally was to become pivotal in my future career.

As business was going so well, Rod decided to take on another consultant. Mike took on the task and after much research, took on his friend Guy Piercy. Guy was a laid back individual who was good looking and occasionally smoked a pipe which looked ridiculous.

In all honesty I didn't really get on with Mike. His dad was some big shot lawyer in the city and Mike thought he was a cut above. When I heard we were getting one of his pals to work with us, I expected to get something similar. A sort of Eton and Harrow wannabee. Guy was anything but. He was down to earth and easy to talk to. I liked him and we got on well.

Guy was keen to learn. I took him out with me to a few sales visits and he soon picked up the patter. Mike had always been too proud to come with me. If he had, he might have made a more positive contribution. Although Guy knew what to say, he didn't get a great deal of success. It was not clear why.

I had to fill in a sheet giving details of every assignment I had taken as they came in. At the end of every month the completed details were faxed to Rod so he could see what business was being done and by whom. Although he was a friend of Mikes, Guy was also an honest man.

One day he told me that he had to show me something. He seemed annoyed. He produced one of the end of month reports that were sent to Rod in Bristol. I have no idea where he got it from. He said look at the name next to the Alenco assignment. I looked and there were the initials MGD. Michael Grove Dunning. Guy said 'He has taken out your name and substituted it with his. It was the sort of thing he did to me in school' Guy said 'Anything to make him look good'

I did not know what to do. Guy said to leave it to him. He would sort it out. Mike Dunning would not listen to me and if I challenged him, I would suffer. Once again, I decided it was time to go. But, as always that would be a time of my choosing and to my benefit.

I had been thinking that I should set up my own business. I had been making money for others for some time. Whilst the fees I generated for PER were built on an excellent product already in place which I 'tweaked' I felt that everything I had earned for HCR was entirely down to me. The concept, the winning of business and completion of assignments. I was happy enough although I think I would have gone eventually. Mr. MGD just hastened the process.

I told Sally about Mike's duplicitous behaviour. I explained how I felt about my ideas and now business being stolen. I said I would like to have my own business but couldn't afford to take the risk as I had just bought my new house and needed to cover the costs. Sally said I'll have a talk with my Dad.

I didn't understand until Guy told me who Sally's Dad was. How he seemed to know everything was a mystery. Sally's Dad had recently resigned from his job as CEO of the National Freight Corporation. This was exactly what the name suggests. It was a massive organisation. Sally's Dad was called Peter Land. He was allegedly offered the Chairmanship of British Rail by Margaret Thatcher, but declined.

Sally told me the next day that her Dad wanted to see me at his house that evening. Sally also told me that MGD had been pestering her for months to introduce him to her Dad. She suspected that was why she was recruited in the first place. What he was after she did not know, but she did not even consider telling her Dad about him.

I felt proud, excited and nervous all at the same time. I thanked Sally constantly. She said you don't need to thank me. Just employ me as your office manager when you get started.

That was the cherry on a big fat cake. We would start up a new business, MGD would lose his main money earner and his diary organiser in one go. I was laughing as I drove over to Marlow that evening.

Marlow is in the middle of a very wealthy area and has its fair share of celebrities. There are also many people who are rich but unknown. I've always thought I would rather be rich and anonymous than rich and famous. That way you get to have a private life. I'm neither, but I'm content, having got to where I am often hanging on by my fingernails. Ups and downs like the lady said back in Oxford.

My brother has ended up rich. He has a yacht and shares in an aeroplane with properties abroad, including a villa in Florida.

I am not in the slightest bit jealous. I have a loving family and sufficient for my needs. The last time I saw him was at my Dad's funeral. He had his wife and her two daughters in tow. He has had several wives. He dumped one on the evening of their wedding. He is a deeply unhappy man.

He has told me so himself. He once said, at my youngest boys christening, that he was envious of me. I had just bought my small terraced house in Pontypool for cash. He said that I had no debt and cash in the bank. He on the other hand was asset rich and cash poor. He was living in a massive house in Cheltenham at the time. I felt really sorry for him.

I actually do feel sorry for him because on the night we got drunk on expensive whisky he said he had never loved any of his wives with the possible exception of the one he dumped on their wedding night. He ended their six hours of marriage because she got absolutely smashed at the reception and it turned out she was an alcoholic. He wished he had stayed with her.

He has paid off about five wives at the last count. He told me he wanted to do the same with his current wife and try to get back with his true love.

The problem is he doesn't realise his real love is money and the current wife says she will take the lot if he tries to divorce her.

I wouldn't wish this kind of marital stalemate on anyone. Except my brother. That might sound cruel, but I will never, ever forget the night my wife and I went to the Royal Gwent hospital to sit with my Dad. He was very close to death and we wanted to be with him.

I had just parked the car, when we saw my brother and the woman he called mother leaving the car park. They were laughing and were clearly off for a meal or something.

I haven't said much about the woman who took my Dad away. She was disgusting. The only thing that mattered to her was money. It is quite funny that she ran off with my Dad when he was doing well. She learnt in time, as I could have told her, with my Dad what goes up will come down.

They eventually ran off to Wales where she came from. Her name is, or was Audrey Jones. She might be alive. She might be dead. It's all the same to me. They ran off to Wales to escape the taxman and also to get free accommodation with her mother.

At this time my Dad owed a large amount of tax to the Inland Revenue. I know this with absolute certainty because his tax bill landed on my desk in Newbury. I was supposed to collect it. I have no idea how that happened. I put the tax demand to the bottom of my in tray and told Dad. That's when they were forced to head for the hills.

Audrey was like a cuckoo. She took over the nest and forced the old lady into one room, next to the downstairs toilet. She even made her pay half the utility bills. Not a nice lady at all.

Eventually when the old lady was nearing 100, she put her in a home. She had never been out of her own home before and within a few weeks she was dead. She had promised me a picture that I liked that hung on the wall in her room. Audrey would not give me it.

The old lady had given my youngest son Peter a small, yellow pig when he was a toddler. Audrey wanted that back. I might have not got the picture, but there was no way she was having the pig given to Pete by that lovely old lady.

As Tim and his recently acquired mother drove off laughing from the Royal Gwent hospital, Denise and I looked at each other. Neither of us could believe that anyone could behave like that.

We probably should not have been surprised. We both heard her say that if he was a dog, they would put him down as we all sat in a small room near the ICU. Death was close then.

One day when Dad was very close to dying I was sitting by his bedside with Denise next to me. He said 'sorry' very softly. I almost didn't hear it. I turned to Denise. She said 'yes, Dad said sorry'. Was he saying it to me? Or was it general, to everyone for inconveniencing them by dying. He was like that at the end.

As far as I am concerned, she made him that way. She had stripped him of his pride, knocked the stuffing out of him. I remember how proud I was of him that time in the pub in Appleford. I cried for what he had become. What she had done to him.

She did have my Dad's beloved little Yorkshire Terrier put down earlier in the year. Dad had named him Pudding when he got him as a puppy. Dad looked like Pudding. He had a little beard like him and the same sort of expression. Pudding would take any other dog on. Dad was the same with people. I guess I did love my Dad and I think he did me although he didn't show it.

One day Dad had his normal chemotherapy session. She took him to the hospital for the 8 oclock appointment. What Dad did not know was that she had made an appointment with the vet. She had planned to have Pudding put to sleep whilst my Dad was having chemo. That is what happened.

At 5 oclock she picked my Dad up and took him home. Dad always called Pudding as soon as he came into the house. The little dog would fly towards him. Not this time. Dad called but Pudding did not come.

She had to tell him then. It broke his heart. I'm sure he gave up fighting the cancer then because he did not live much longer. He had been fighting this disease for years. He told me he was 3 years past his sell by date.

On the day dad died Denise was in the hospital. He wasn't expected to die that day and I was elsewhere. That is one of my many regrets, that I wasn't with her. She loved my Dad.

No one was with him when he died. He was on a trolley being wheeled from one ward to another. After she heard he had gone Denise went to the canteen. She needed a coffee. She was in tears. She told me that when she got there she saw my brother and Audrey tucking into a meal and laughing.

My Dad was his Dad too. He was Audrey's husband. Denise was not really related to him, but it was her he confided in and she was the only one in tears. We hate both of them.

Back in Marlow on the evening that I was due to meet Peter Land, Sally had given me directions and I found his house easily. There was a private driveway shared with one other similar detached house. I parked my car and went to the front door.

Peter Land answered and invited me in. He took me into the lounge. It looked like something from those magazines that show posh people's houses. He was anything but posh. He was very smart, but for someone with his sort of background he had the common touch. That was good as I was very common.

At the back of the room were large glass doors. I could see a carefully mown lawn that gently sloped down to the Thames. The whole place was just perfect. I would love to live in a place like that. I got close but lost it, as with everything else and as my Nan predicted.

Mr. Land asked me to outline my ideas. I told him all about my ideas of search and selection. He knew about the traditional headhunting companies and that they had been around forever. He appreciated the difference in my more scientific approach.

There is a lot more to it than I can explain here. Most people would just find the small details boring but not Peter Land.

After what seemed like minutes but was actually hours, he brought things to a conclusion. He said he was sure it would work. He told me he had taken on a non-working directorship with a local insurance company called JN Dobbins and Sons. No donkey jokes please.

The original Mr. Dobbins had started the company in the distant past. He had decided to take a back seat some time ago and hand over the reins to his sons David and Jeremy. However he was worried the sons would fight over the business so asked Peter Land to take on this non-working directorship to put plans in place that would stop that happening.

As payment for his services, Peter had asked for an MG Midget. He was often to be seen driving around the area with the top down and a big smile on his face. He asked me to prepare some profit forecasts that he could show the board. He was confident he could get this set up but just needed me to show the company was viable.

Chapter 16

Roles Research Ltd.

He also suggested something that I have always repeated when talking to any budding entrepreneur. He told me to think up a name for the company first. That would make it real. A name would make it something tangible. I called it Roles Research. A play on words with quality embedded. I thought.

I had never prepared forecasts before, but my O level accounts and OND Business Studies came in handy. I worked out a sales prediction based on four possible scenarios. I called them Pessimistic, Realistic, Optimistic and finally Fantastic. These options are fairly self-explanatory. Pessimistic would mean poor sales figures. Fantastic would be off the scale.

I took these projections round to Peter Land after work one day. He laughed out loud. He said that he had seen many of these projections before. Pessimistic, Realistic and Optimistic were common categories, sometimes with different names. But he had never seen anyone use Fantastic and he was impressed, especially as the figures stacked up.

I was still working at HCR but to be honest my heart wasn't in it. My sales figures had been significantly down for the period in which I was setting up Roles Research. I was concentrating on my new business. Because of this HCR took a massive downturn. Rod was asking questions of Dunning because of course he thought it was him losing business.

MGD called me into a meeting in the boardroom of Harrison Cowley, the advertising agency based in the old house. We were not in the Portakabin.

He told me to sit at the boardroom table. There was a fire blazing in the fireplace. He placed himself in front of it. He stood there in his immaculate suit and matching accessories with his hands behind his back, rising up and down on his heels.

He told me that he was extremely disappointed at my performance in the previous quarter. He said that if things did not improve he would have to consider letting me go. I said that I would try and do better.

I would have liked to tell him to insert his job somewhere appropriate. But I bit my lip and remembered, in my time and to my advantage.

Peter Land told me that Dobbins was prepared to go ahead. I just had to go in for a meeting with the older son, David Dobbins. He was the MD.

I called to arrange the meeting. I told the girl on the phone that Peter Land had said I should arrange a meeting with Mr. Dobbins. She asked me which one, was it Mr. David or Mr. Jeremy. I found that odd, but said Mr. David. She arranged for me to see him the following Thursday at 9 o'clock.

JN Dobbins owned the building in which they were based and the land on which it stood. It was in the centre of Maidenhead and worth a fortune. There is a car park at the rear of their offices. I drove in and parked my car. I had a shirt hung in the back of the car. I can't remember why.

I found out later that David Dobbin had said that I must be well organised because I hung my shirt up in the car. He liked that.

I went into the meeting. When I first saw Mr. David, I immediately thought that he looked like Edward Fox. He told me about the history of the company and how they would set me up as part of the JN Dobbins Group.

He told me how we would work together and what my obligations would be. I was too excited to take a lot of notice of the details. I was 28 and about to launch Roles Research. That was all I could think of.

I should have paid more attention. David Dobbins told me what would be expected of Roles Research. I didn't notice that there was no mention of what I could expect from JN Dobbins (Holdings) Ltd to give them their full title. There was no discussion, he told me the terms on which the business would operate.

There were two things he told me that I should have contested. Firstly, there would be a management fee of 10% of turnover. Secondly, should we make a profit it would be shared equally between us.

Roles Research would bear all of the running costs of the business including my and Sally's salaries. JN Dobbins would have no liability for us.

It was a pretty poor deal for Roles Research and therefore me. I had never been in this situation before and I dealt with it alone. I wish Peter Land had been there with me, or even Sally, his daughter. She was more astute than me.

At the time I could not have been more happy. I drove the Renault to Taplow Mill and gave in my resignation. I was happy to put the thoughts from my last meeting with MGD into action. I was told to leave the car and vacate the premises. I did so with great pleasure.

For the last time I took the bus home. I enjoyed that trip more than any of the others. It was like all of my Christmases had come at once.

I had a long weekend and started as Manager and Sales Director of Roles Research Ltd on Monday. That was the title that Mr. David had given me. I was expecting to be MD but of course that was him. Even though he never took any part in the business.

I had suggested to David Dobbins that his well established company might make some referrals to us, his latest fledgling company. He thought that was a good idea, but nothing ever happened.

They had a large portfolio of clients. They marketed themselves as the largest private insurance company in the UK. I suppose they must have been or they would need to have included the word probably as with the Carlsberg advertisement 'Probably the best lager in the World'

Apart from the usual car and household insurance, the Dobbins group provided and maintained company pension schemes. The first company the original Mr. Dobbins sold one of his pension schemes to was Mars the chocolate bar manufacturer. They were and still are headquartered in Slough on the main trading estate. I used to drive past there often, usually on my way to see David Voss at PHH. The smell of chocolate in the air was like eating a Mars bar every time, but not as fattening.

They had other important clients. A referral to Mars would have been ideal. They would have had a very large sales team and I was always head hunting sales managers for client companies. Sales people are easy to find because they need to be seen as part of their job.

But there was no referral to Mars. Or anyone. I did ask on numerous occasions, and was always told 'Yes, we must organise something' Any salesman knows that a warm call is miles better than a cold call.

I received no help from Mr. David or his company. For that I was charged 10% of turnover.

The first week or two was taken up organising the physical setting up of the business. Dobbins had organised to rent a terraced house over the road from their offices. It had been used as an office before and so everything needed was there. Phone points and so on.

David Dobbins had a personal assistant called Julia. She organised everything. I had no say in the matter. She chose curtains, chairs, and a sofa for my office. She even picked my company car. It was a bright red Ford Escort XR3i. This car was every boy racer's dream. It even had red wheels.

I didn't feel it was appropriate for a director of a professional executive search business. I did tell DD that but was told they were not going to change it. I have to say whilst the excitement was still there, this lack of control was beginning to worry me. I wondered whether they would interfere once I was up and running.

Once we started to take assignments they lost interest. It was no longer any fun for Julia and Mr. David was more interested in playing golf and going to Sotheby's.

Sally was excellent as expected. She ran everything like clockwork and was always professional. I tried to do the same. Her Dad had told me I needed to get three good suits so I could have two on hangers. That way they didn't become creased. In the end I had five, one for every day of the working week.

I believed I looked professional and behaved accordingly. When I went out to visit a client or potential client I made sure to park the car out of sight.

Apart from her business duties, Sally sometimes used to perform the role of Barrie. She would research companies when we had a brief. She would identify individuals within those companies that could be of interest

Sally would give me a list of people to phone and I would take it from there. Even though there was only me to generate the business and Sally to help realise it, we made a small profit in the first year. That was after Dobbin had their 10% cut. They took 50% of that small profit too. Money for nothing as Dire Straits would say.

I had a letter from Peter Land congratulating me on a great start, which I have lost, of course. I am beginning to think I know where these various mementos are.

A large part of my job was to go out and sell our concept of executive recruitment. If I could get in front of a person or group of people who were looking to fill a position, I nearly always convinced them to use us.

Whilst we were generating enough income to cover our costs and pay the Dobbin fee, apparently we weren't making enough profit. I was told this by Mr. David on one of the rare occasions he spoke to me.

He had summoned me to his office across the road for a review. This was early 1985. We had been going about 18 months and had made a profit in the first year. We were paying our way so far this year. It is still my view if the 10% management fee did not exist, we would have been making a decent profit. We could have shared that profit but that was clearly not what they wanted.

I suggested we recruit another consultant with the logic that whilst he or she would cost a salary they should make a contribution to the costs of running Roles Research. Sally put the word out locally and we had quite a bit of interest. Sally and I interviewed a few people and made an offer to what seemed the best one. He certainly sold himself.

He was with us for just over a month. I can't remember anything about him other than he cost us money. I gave him his own office. We would hear him talking to people on the phone. He would say he had to go and meet with a client to discuss a possible assignment.

In those days it was quite acceptable to go to the pub at lunchtime now and then. It was referred to as a liquid lunch by some. One day I said to Sally 'We've done well, how about a pie and a pint next door?' There was a pub at the end of the street that did decent pub grub. When we walked in, there was our recent recruit propping up the bar. He was just ordering another drink. I asked him what he was doing there. 'Just having a spot of lunch' he said.

We left him to it. I went to the bar to place our order. Sally and I had been in this pub a few times since we launched Roles Research. The barman said 'Does that guy work for you' I said 'yes, why'? The barman told me that my only other staff member had been in every day for the past few weeks. He often stayed all afternoon. He had been coming in since he started with us in fact.

I asked our new recruit to pop in when he had finished his lunch. A while later he was back. Sally brought him into my office. I sacked him without compunction. Roles Research was my life then and I was trying to keep it alive. I felt like throwing him down the stairs.

We tried to recruit another two times. They were both good people and both tried as hard as they could. For some reason nobody seemed to be able to sell the service like I could. Maybe they just didn't believe in it. Whatever the reason, I decided that I would have to soldier on alone.

We were now nearing the end of 1985. I needed to come up with an idea that Sally could sell over the phone to existing clients while I was out looking for new business. It needed to provide us with some kind of ongoing income. The trouble with head hunting was that assignments were always one offs and I never knew when one would come in.

Based on the principles of the modern career cycle as I detailed earlier, I created something I called Confidential Approach and Assessment. This was a simple concept which benefited both the client and Roles Research

I came up with the idea from the work I did with one particular client. Because they were involved in developing weapon systems for the MOD I can't name them. In that sector companies nearly always work in collaboration with their competitors.

Most government contracts are huge and can cost millions to develop. By joining forces these companies can share the cost of development and personnel. That is where my simple idea comes in.

No company working in collaboration with a rival company would want to be seen poaching their staff. So I would do it for them.

I would take a very specific brief from the client. The person I was dealing with would talk to the relevant person in their workforce and ask them to find out who their counterpart was in the rival organisation.

I would then be given a list of names. These people would be doing a job at least one level down from the one I was going to talk to them about, or the benefits package on offer would have to be significantly better.

I would contact the individuals on the list one at a time. I would explain the position and tell them what was on offer. I would never reveal the client at that point. A few said they weren't interested but most said yes to a meeting.

The best thing is I didn't really have to interview them. The meeting was to assess their level of interest to make sure they weren't just there to find out who was making the approach. Then to sell them the job if I was satisfied they were serious.

A report was produced for each candidate put forward to the client company. The deal was they paid my fee, £500 for every person that they called in for an interview, irrespective of outcome. The hit rate was one in two. Therefore they got their recruit for an average £1,000. A great deal less than using an agency, advertising or any other existing recruitment method.

The benefit to them was clear. The benefit to me was extensive.

Although it sounded like a lot of time and effort for £500 that is just how it appeared. I already knew who I needed to talk to so there was no time or expense tied up in trying to find suitable candidates. I made an initial phone call to the number given to me.

Most of the time I could get the information I needed over the phone without a meeting. A virtual meeting in today's terms.

I would get enough detail from that call to compile a report. The client would see the report and if they wanted to meet the candidate, I arranged it. It wasn't until this point that I revealed the client's name to the candidate.

So nine times out of ten it was £500 for a phone call. And everyone was happy.

A final benefit was that the candidates the client did not want were now a bank of specialists that I could talk to other companies about.

As far as selling CAA is concerned I would tell any company I was outlining the service to that I could only deal with one company in any one sector. Other companies were our fishing pool. The implications were clear.

As far as I am concerned it would be a very poor salesman that could not win business with that service.

We started to present it to our existing clients initially. One of the two large software houses working on weapons software development went for it immediately. We were off to a good start. The only proviso I made with this client was that I would not approach the employees of my other client.

Although I was contacted by other companies in the sector, I would take no further business as I promised.

Chapter 17

Bipolar Begins

Then came a day which was going to have disastrous consequences for the rest of my life.

I had a sales presentation lined up with an IT company based in Marlow, where Peter Land lived. They were a small company looking to expand their salesforce. This was standard business for me and fairly easy to complete successfully.

I arrived at their offices and as usual parked the car a couple of streets away so they would not see it. When I got to the front door I was greeted by a smart young man who introduced himself as the MD. He led me up a long staircase and into a large well lit room

There were six people already in the room. I was welcomed to the boardroom by one of them who told me he was the Sales Director and as it was his team that was recruiting, he would be the one asking most of the questions. I said 'ask as many questions as you like and don't wait for me to stop talking, just jump in. That is no problem'. I smiled. He smiled. I was feeling good. Completely relaxed and in control.

There was a flip chart already set up. I started to draw a flow diagram to show how things worked, talking to the group as I drew. I had done this countless times before.

Then suddenly out of nowhere I was hit by a sledgehammer. My heart was trying to burst out of my chest and I started to sweat profusely. My hands were shaking. In fact my whole body was shaking. The people sitting in front of me started to change shape. Faces twisted, they were laughing at me. I ran.

I was out of the front door in seconds. I saw the MD shouting after me, but I kept running. It was a good job I had parked the car away from their office. When I got to it I jumped in and locked the door. I was terrified that they were after me.

I was not to know for many years that this was the start of my Manic Depression, or Bipolar disorder as it is now called. I tried constantly to find out what was wrong with me, but got no answers at all. 70% of people with Bipolar are mis-diagnosed, and it takes an age for them to discover the truth.

People like Stephen Fry make light of it. That has not been my experience. It has cost me my business, most of my possessions and my wife. On occasion it has nearly cost me my life.

Chapter 18

Jess

It was five years before this that I first went to the Greek Islands. I had taken Keith Mackney's advice and decided to see what they were like for myself. I took Jessica with me because this was our honeymoon. However we weren't married. I think I mentioned that Jess was another in a long line of fiance's.

In her case we had come close to getting married. I had been to see her Dad who was a professor of nuclear physics at Oxford University. He was a lovely man and said yes straightaway. Her mum said yes too.

Her Dad insisted that he would pay for the wedding. I had asked Jess if we could get married in Sutton Courtenay at All Saints Church. She agreed. When we spoke to the Vicar at the church, he said we would have to go to the vicarage in Tullis Close to discuss our commitment to marrying one another. When he was satisfied we were serious about getting married, he would arrange for the banns to be read.

Tullis Close turned off from Mill Lane which led to the river and our old headquarters in the split tree. I wondered then if our letter of ownership was still there. I didn't go to look as I just wanted it to be a happy memory.

All went well and the banns were duly read. The wedding day was set and invitations went out. We had letters of congratulation with some money and presents too.

I asked my best friend Peter Abbott to be best man and after going through our obligatory insults and mickey taking he said yes, he would be honoured. Peter and I were best friends for years. I think he was the only person who really understood me. We were on the same wavelength although sometimes we couldn't tune in.

As a totally irrelevant point, one day I was sitting in the lobby of a hotel in Shrewsbury, in pursuit of madness as I often was. I saw a large picture of George Orwell hanging on the wall in front of me. I realised I had never seen a picture of him before. Peter was the spitting image of him.

When we had our youngest boy we called him Peter. The older Peter was one of his Godparents. He had to travel home from Tegucigalpa, capital of Honduras where he had gone to live and work a while back.

He had a problem following some of the service as he now spoke Spanish all the time and whilst he was fluent in Spanish, his English was deteriorating by the day.

He had a big beard and with his strong Spanish accent sounded like Fidel Castro.

Peter was a truly great friend. I haven't seen him since shortly after the Christening. Our Peter is nearly thirty now, so it has been a long time since I saw my friend. He once sent me a long list of Spanish swear words and extremely rude phrases. They were translated into English and he was considerate to include the phonetic English pronunciation.

Although I haven't needed to use it yet, I still keep it in a memory box I have at home along with some letters he sent from Honduras. They are hilarious. There is a cassette too, but I can't play it as I haven't seen a cassette player for years. I would love to find one and sit listening to it with Peter, sharing a bottle of something. Peter's messages home are some of the few things I haven't lost. Or haven't been taken.

Everything was set for the wedding. All bought and paid for, it was just a case of waiting for the great day. The honeymoon was booked. It was to Greece. We were both excited about going there. Pete was working on a best man's speech. I warned him to keep it clean. He seemed disappointed.

About two weeks before the wedding Jess said she could not go through with it. She and I had been on and off for years. Since we met on the college holiday to Italy in fact. It was entirely my fault. I had got involved with another girl or two and always told Jess who was a good friend as much as a girlfriend.

After the intervening girls gave me the flick (an Australian phrase) and they always did, I would go back to Jess with my tail between my legs. She always took me back. She was an incredible and forgiving girl. It was not as though she had to forgive me. She was a truly beautiful girl, inside and out.

She told me she had done a great deal of soul searching and had come to the conclusion that she couldn't trust me to stay faithful. It was a fair comment, but I know that I would not have broken my wedding vows. I just wouldn't .

We had a dilemma. Everything was cancelled. The wedding, the invitations, the church. Everything. Except for the honeymoon. We had booked flights and a couple of nights in a hotel in Athens.

We were both looking forward to it. We had a chat about the situation and decided we would go. We were still friends. Always would be. She just couldn't marry me. I think I understood. So we flew out in July 1981.

We landed at Athens airport mid afternoon. We got a taxi to the city centre. It seemed to take a long time. I asked the driver where we were. His English was non-existent. I said to Jess I think we are being ripped off. She agreed. As he couldn't speak English we had no choice but to go with it. When we eventually got to our hotel he charged us the equivalent of £10 which was way over the £2 my guide book had said it should be.

I realised that not for the first time, I had forgotten that important rule taught to me whilst standing next to a huge pile of leaves in Sutton Courtenay.

We had a great time in the two weeks we spent in Greece. We made the most of the first two days we had in Athens. The first thing we did was walk up to the Acropolis. It's a fairly steep climb but we were both young and fit so it was not a problem. I might need to take a donkey now. There were some taking tourists up and down.

When we got to the top, we stood looking across Athens and the plains beyond. I thought about the stories of the iliad. I tried to remember the tales written by Homer. We had sat and listened to them in class two, Mr. Vales class in Big School. I still remember being transfixed by these tales of ancient Greece, the Punic wars, the Trojan horse.

We both stood taking this all in when a middle aged American couple came and stood nearby. She said 'Hey Howard, it's not as high as the Empire State Building'

We looked at each other and smiled. We walked down from the Parthenon happy, hand in hand. I never felt more in love with Jess and called myself all kinds of fool. I tried hard to woo her back whilst we were there. She was having none of it.

Halfway down the path leading to the Plaka, which is an original and ancient part of the City, I saw a sign with an arrow pointing up a track. It said Son et Lumiere. I stopped and said to Jess, 'I wonder what that says'. She pointed to the English translation which said Sound and Light Show. 'That sounds interesting', I said to her. Shall we go and see what it is?' Jess said 'Why not'. I loved her sense of adventure.

We followed the path which led to a massive amphitheatre. There was a Greek guy taking money. It was only a handful of drachma. We went down and sat on the stone steps. We had absolutely no idea what to expect as all the signs were in Greek.

The best experiences are unplanned and this turned out to be incredible. The amphitheatre was brightly lit. Far off in the distance we could see the Acropolis. All of a sudden the lights went out. It was pitch black, Although she was sitting close, I could not see Jess.

Then one bright, white laser light came from nowhere and shot across a jet black sky lighting up the Acropolis. We both gasped together. It was literally a breathtaking experience. I could see nothing but the Acropolis, set in relief against the dark sky. It was eerie but incredible..

Then a deep voice suddenly came out of the night sky. Thankfully he spoke in English. He started to tell tales of ancient Greece and the part Athens played in the many wars that happened then. I sat listening intently, I was in Mr. Vales class again.

As he spoke, more lasers of all colours appeared. It was spectacular. Then the music cut in. It was Vangelis initially. The man continued to talk of wars across the centuries. It seemed to go on forever and I loved every single second. The way the programme was weaved together will remain etched in my memory forever.

Afterwards we walked to the Plaka together. We went into a small taverna and discussed what we had seen. A waiter came to take our order. We hadn't even looked at the menu. The waiter pointed to a chalk board and told us he would recommend the Lamb Kleftico. We ordered one each and I asked what wine he would suggest. Without hesitation he said 'Retsina. It is perfect with the Kleftico'

I thought he must know what he is on about, and I said 'yes please. We'll have a litre' The Kleftico came and it was really tasty. It is still my favourite Greek meal. The Retsina came and it was disgusting. I can't describe the taste. It is apparently made from pine resin.

I have always thought even if you don't like a wine at first, if you stick with it after a while it becomes tolerable. I could not get drunk enough to tolerate Retsina. I had a beer and Jess had an Ouzo.

There are feral cats all over the Plaka, on the scrounge for food from the tourists. There was nothing warning you not to feed the cats. We had a couple of adorable little kittens playing around our feet. Jess made strange little meowing noises at them and gave them a couple of lumps of Kleftico.

The next thing, hundreds of cats appeared and surrounded our table. It did seem like hundreds, but there were definitely fifty at least. It would appear that the kittens were Trojan kittens. The waiter was not happy that we had flooded his taverna with cats. We beat a hasty retreat.

We stopped further down to have a quiet couple of drinks. I thought it best to stick with the beer. Jess was getting tipsy on Ouzo. She didn't realise its strength. She just liked the taste of aniseed. No matter how tipsy she became, she stuck with her answer of no when I asked her to marry me.

Our hotel was all marble and glass and we had a great time there, having the odd glass or two and sitting in reception eating little plates of food.

When our two days were up, I asked the receptionist to book us a taxi. She did and told us 'make sure you get a price before you get in the taxi. Some of these drivers will overcharge you' Good advice I thought.

We were heading for the port of Piraeus to get a ferry to the islands. In those days there were not many direct flights to the Greek Islands. Definitely the ones I wanted to visit. I didn't like the sound of Mykonos, but Keith also recommended the Cyclades, particularly Naxos. Not so commercialised he said. Not so many tourists.

We got to the port. There were many massive ferries anchored. We walked along looking at the destinations on their sides. We saw Crete, Santorini and many more. I wished we had gone to Santorini.

We would sit amongst the rooftops of Thira, looking down across the town at the powder blue domes of the churches with sun glinting off the golden crosses on their roofs. The sun would start to set behind anti thira the other side of the volcano that made Santorini, thousands of years ago.

The sky would turn an incredible shade of red and light up the bright white of the walls around us in a pale pink. It would be so romantic. I would turn to Jess and ask her to marry me again. She would say no, again.

We eventually found the ferry to Naxos. We went to a little ticket box on the quay and bought our tickets. Then we boarded. All Greek inter island ferries were enormous. There were several levels. We wanted to stay outside so we found our way to the upper deck. There were a lot of people, but we managed to find ourselves a space and put our rucksacks down to reserve our places. We sat down and discussed what we were going to do next. The journey was about eight hours.

Near us was a group of about ten Dutch lads. They each had a can of unopened beer. One banged his can on the deck hard, several times. He shook it hard too. Then they placed all of the cans together on the deck. They asked a nearby girl, who just happened to be very pretty, to mix up the cans. She did a very good job and none of them knew where the shaken can was.

Each of them took a can and held it against their ear. They all opened their cans together and of course one of them got an earful of cold lager. The unlucky loser in this game of lager roulette was not only ridiculed by his friends, he also had no beer.

They would then play another round. Surely he wouldn't be unlucky again? I loved the look of this game, but Jess would not let me play. Spoilsport I thought.

By the time we got to Naxos, the Dutch lads were completely drunk. They fell off the ferry onto the quay beneath. We followed. Keith had recommended that the best way to see the islands was to take the ferry and just go with one of the youngsters who was standing at the quay when you arrived. So we did.

We chose a particularly earnest looking young chap. He was probably about eight. His job was to get people coming off the ferry to go with him to the accommodation he was representing. He probably got paid. I don't know.

We went to him, he beamed, we followed. We ended up outside a local house, probably belonging to his parents. An old lady dressed in black from head to foot came out. 'Kalispera' she said. I found out later that it meant good afternoon or good evening. 'Kalispera' I replied. I could have been saying anything. She seemed happy with my response.

She beckoned us in and showed us a room. It was fine. It had a double bed and a sofa. I knew where I would be sleeping. I asked her how much, finally showing some common sense. She told me a figure in drachma which I reckoned to be the same as our taxi ride, about £10. I asked if that was for the room or per person.

After much gesticulating and pointing I understood it was for the room. 'we'll take it' I said. She clearly didn't know what I had said but when we dumped our rucksacks on the floor, she knew she had a sale. Hopefully the lad got some commission too.

As suspected I was given the sofa. I slept OK though. In the morning we woke to a bright, hot and sunny day. It was July and that was every day in Greece. We ventured out.

It was about 8 am. We went down to the quay, which was not far. Some small fishing boats were moored in the harbour. The outline of the boats were reflected in the water. It was perfectly calm and there was not a ripple on the sea.

There was a row of squid drying on the quayside. They would be cooked and served as Kalamari in tavernas around the island that night.

I asked Jess if she was hungry. She said yes. Our accommodation was not a bed and breakfast so we had to find our own breakfast. As it was the early eighties and most of the Greek Islands were still unknown to British tourists, there were no cafes selling the Full English Breakfast.

So we had to settle for a continental breakfast each. The taverna we went into sold a glass containing a mixture of yoghurt and honey mixed with fresh fruit. It was delicious. Most mornings we would have a continental breakfast followed by it. It was very healthy, but that didn't stop me.

It was July 1981. I was working for Harrison Cowley and Prince Charles was going to marry Lady Diana Spencer at the end of the month.

The yoghurt, fruit and honey came in a tall glass with massive jug handles on the side. The waiter told me that they were not just so you could get a good grip on the glass. They were also a homage to Prince Charles in the month of his forthcoming nuptials. In case it's not clear, the handles represented Charlie's ears.

They were selling cocktails in them all over the island. We tried a few.

Naxos was and possibly still is a fascinating place. There was a kind of market built into the side of a mountain that faces the harbour. Inside we would wander around looking at all sorts of trinkets. There were no kiss me quick hats here. Everything was Greek, mostly handcrafted locally. There was honey and other produce too.

One of my favourite pastimes was simply to sit in the harbour watching the world go by. Naxos has a very deep harbour. At night large boats would sail in and drop off their cargo, human or otherwise. They would then complete a 360 degree manoeuvre and exit the harbour. I enjoyed seeing the bright lights reflecting off the dark waters and the night sky.

Every Sunday the locals would dress up in their best clothes and go to church. In the evening after the service they would parade around the harbour in their finery. They dressed their children up too. That was my favourite thing, watching these proud families parading along the harbourside dressed to impress and succeeding.

We had a marvellous time but despite my best efforts I could not convince Jess to reconsider her decision.

The last time I saw her was at a petrol station in Abingdon. She had a gaggle of kids with her. She said hello and said these kids were hers. I assumed there was a man involved and my heart sank. I just said they looked lovely. I didn't tell her I still loved her. I didn't tell her I was off to Heathrow, en route to Australia via the Greek Islands. I just wished her all the best and left.

I went to the Greek Islands a lot in the 80's. I went with Pete one year. I remember him chatting up some American girls beneath the Parthenon and abandoning me to my fate whilst he disappeared with them, only to reappear many hours later with a self satisfied look on his face. Very selfish, I told him

In 1984 things had not turned out as Eric Arthur Blair had predicted. I was therefore able to fly to Corfu with a couple of my mates without worrying about the thought police. We were staying in a small village called Acharavi. It was a one donkey town then. It appears to be a major resort now. I went with Mr. Mario Granito and Mr. Paul something. There are a few Mr and Mrs Somethings in my memory, but they are not related.

Paul actually rented a room from me for a while so I should really remember his surname. But I don't. Mario never rented a room from me, but I can't forget his name.

This was a two week holiday, suggested by me to celebrate my new company Roles Research. It was a most enjoyable if confusing holiday. The confusion was mostly caused by Mr. Mario Granito.

I liked Mario a lot back in the day. Mario is an Italian as you could probably guess. He was a hairdresser and a good one by all accounts. He was always banging on about an idea he had for making a comb that could cut as you combed. It was a stupid idea so no one took much notice.

Mario was a joker. He liked to play mind games with people. He would tell one person one thing and another person something else. He loved to watch the confusion that ensued. He never did it to me though. I think.

Mario, myself and Paul had a pretty good time in Acharavi. We never actually left the village to explore Corfu. Mario, despite being married, was pursuing a young Liverpudlian girl half his age. He caught her in the end but that ended in tears.

Paul teamed up with an Australian girl. Paul was a vegetarian and liked to contemplate his navel. The Australian girl was also vegetarian and liked to contemplate her own navel. They got on well together and were often seen on the beach looking downwards.

Paul was extremely thin. I thought it was due to his vegetarianism. However his newly discovered girlfriend who was also a vegetarian was built like a brick outhouse, as her fellow Australians would nearly say.

I have a photo from this time that shows Paul lying on the beach looking wistfully out to sea. He had a haircut that was like the guy from Kajagoogoo, so his top half stood out. His torso faded into the sand. He looked like he had been run over by a tractor.

The third member of the team was me. I could say that I was still in love with Jess, which I was. The reality was that I am pretty rubbish at chatting girls up. Mario and Paul copped off straight away. I didn't.

There were two girls from London there. I fancied one of them. I tried my hardest but got nowhere. She gave me her address in London and I went there after the holiday in my nice red Escort XR3i. It was quite a way. She still wasn't interested

Mario is now a very wealthy man. Somehow his idea for the cutting comb was taken up by a client in the equine world. He is now selling it in 130 countries across the globe. Or so his marketing blurb says. Cutting the manes and tails of countless horses.

Who knew? I have to say well done Mario. Out of all the people I thought would make it, you are the last.

As I have mentioned my best friend was Pete Abbott. We got up to all sorts back then.

Everybody liked to have the odd spliff in those days. We were no different. Our routine was to go to the pub, then back to someone's house to sit down, skin up and get stoned.

In the very early days it was the house rented by Bob Osborne that we returned to. After a while passing round the joints we all started giggling, finding whatever track we were listening to hilarious. Then we would get what was called the munchies.

The frying pan would come out and we would tuck into mounds of bacon and eggs. Or if the vegetarian hippie couple Bob shared the house with joined in, mounds of brown rice and vegetables. It tasted a bit like the food

I had in the Oxford nunnery. Wonderful. Especially when we were under the influence.

I had moved on from the Beatles and the Stones to Pink Floyd and Cream. There was the occasional Black Sabbath and Led Zeppelin but mostly it was the more psychedelic music I liked.

In a group, all stoned, listening to Pink Floyd's Dark Side of the Moon was enlightening. We would have endless debates about the meaning of the music and lyrics of Pink Floyd. We would never remember what we talked about when we woke up in the morning.

When we got into the mid eighties, Pete and I liked to experiment. I had launched Roles Research by then. I had some spare cash. One evening Pete suggested we try a little bit of Cocaine. We were at my new house near the Thames in Abingdon. We walked into town along the path that I took to the bus so many times.

We were headed to the Kings Head and Bell pub, the headquarters I had moved on to from the Sutton Courtenay tree. I suppose Pete had replaced Fatty Shepherd although he was less scientific and we never went birds nesting. We certainly never murdered butterflies.

I first met Pete when he was working behind the bar at the Kings Head. We couldn't be bothered with the Bell. We got on well and he would slip me the odd pint of bitter for free. That may have been a contributory factor to his being sacked.

Anyway we arrived at the Kings Head. Several of our acquaintances were there. Andy Jones was there. He was always playing space invaders and rarely talked as he needed to concentrate. He was determined to shoot the last alien.

He had a big belly and always wore a blue t-shirt. I don't know if it was the same one but he didn't smell too bad, so I guess he had several. I called him 'Le Blob Bleu' for no particular reason. It seemed apt.

I have always given people nicknames as my colleagues at work in Wales will testify. Dicky Mint our Chief Executive would concur, if he knew. His real name was Richard Spear. Work that one out.

Pete and I went and sat in the front bar with Paddy and John. Paddy's surname was Monaghan. As was John's, because they were brothers. These two were of Irish descent although they were born and raised in Abingdon. They both worked in construction. They were always fighting with each other. Although Paddy was half the size of John, he always came out on top.

Paddy had an Uncle with the same name. He was the World bare knuckle boxing champion. He lived in a small council house in Saxton Road. It was a street full of hard men. Paddy was far and away the hardest. Some people used to say that Paddy could count Muhammed Ali amongst his friends.

We didn't believe it until a cavalcade of limousines pulled up in front of Paddys' house one day. Out stepped this huge black man. It was Muhammed Ali. Paddy was expecting him as he was standing in the doorway. Ali had to stoop to get through the entrance. You can check the local papers of the time if you don't believe me. Or you can watch the interview where Ali mentions his friend Paddy Monaghan in England after a fight. I don't remember which one.

My friend Paddy could also fight and often did. Paddy had a strict moral code, which he stuck to rigidly. He would never back down from a fight. Neither would he ever start a fight. However he did provoke a few. Quite a few.

One day Paddy was helping me move into my latest home. It was a beautiful three storey town house on Ock Street. It was grade II listed and had oak beams throughout. From the top floor at the back of the house I could see St. Helen's church with the Thames flowing past. Morlands brewery was directly behind my rear garden and I could smell the hops when the wind was in my direction.

Paddy and I were in his big white van, driving up the narrow lane that led to the rear access to my house. We hadn't reached the turn off when another big white van appeared coming towards us. Paddy put on his indicator to show we were about to turn off.

The big white van kept coming. It was being driven by a large, red faced and angry looking man. It kept coming until it blocked the entrance to the rear of my property. Paddy had stopped and was going nowhere. I knew Paddy. He never backed down or gave way. In this case I couldn't see why he should.

This angry man had plenty of time to stop and let us go. We were indicating our intention a long time before he reached the turn. He was just being awkward.

The big man got out of his van and started towards us. He was tamping as the Welsh say to signify displeasure. I deduced he was looking for a fight. He was about to get one.

Paddy undid his seatbelt. He turned to me, smiled and winked. Cool as a cucumber. The large gentleman was nearly up to the van. He was very clearly intent on inflicting damage on Paddy.

Paddy pulled back the door and flew out. He was on this man in seconds. He hit him with a right, swiftly followed by a left. He repeated this many times. His fists were a blur. The guy looked shocked. He hung in the air for a while and then dropped like a sack of King Edwards.

Paddy dropped with him. He continued to punch him with the occasional head butt as a bonus. Someone got out of the other van and started to approach the carnage. I thought I had better get out. I did not want to fight but I could not leave this man to join in the fight in support of his friend.

Well it wasn't really joining in as his friend had not had the chance to throw a single punch. Paddy asked me later why I had got out of the van. I explained that I wanted to stop the other guy from getting to him. Paddy gave me a disgusted look. 'I don't need you or anyone else fighting my battles'. He would rather go down fighting than that, he said. Another part of Paddy's code. Sometimes it was hard to understand Paddy's code.

The other man came towards me. I was a bit frightened but I stayed put. He spoke. 'Is that Paddy Monaghan' He asked. 'Yes' I replied. 'Oh dear,' he said.

Paddy finally stopped. He looked at me. I could see the red mist was clearing from his eyes. When Paddy's eyes turned red, look out!

He stood up and began to dust himself off. I noticed a speck of blood on his face. I said 'you've got some blood on your face'. He said 'it's not mine' indignantly, and wiped it off.

At this point the large man sat up. His face was a mass of blood and his eyes were already closing. He said 'you only beat me because I've had too much to drink'

Paddy had recently started his own groundworks business. He had cards printed and always had a few on him. 'You never know when some business might come up' he always said.

He took one out and threw it at the man. 'Give me a call if you ever want a rematch' Paddy said. As far as I know the bloody man never took him up on his offer.

Back in the pub, we were talking when Pete said he needed to go to the toilet. He came back a few minutes later. We carried on talking for a while. Pete said 'I have to go. Do you want to come?' I said 'yes'. We both said 'see ya' to the Monaghan brothers and left.

As I suspected Pete had scored. He showed me. It was a small amount of Cocaine. We headed back to my house. He said he had always wanted to try some cocaine with champagne.

As it happened I had a bottle of Moet in a cupboard. I put it in the freezer to chill and we unwrapped the coke. I poured us a flute of champers each. We downed it and snorted a couple of lines. The hit was instant. I felt on top of the world.

I looked at Pete and was sure he felt the same way. I said 'let's go to Oxford and pick up some girls' We jumped into the Red Devil and shot off towards Oxford in a state of high excitement.

I drove into Cornmarket Street and parked. I looked at Pete. He looked as miserable as I felt. The stuff had worn off. Pete told me he paid £50 for the cocaine. Including the champagne that was one of the most expensive and pointless twenty minutes of our lives. Pete had achieved one of his lesser ambitions. No need to do it again for either of us.

We tried a variety of drugs during our friendship although we always used marijuana as our drug of choice. Beer was the primary drug of course. Marijuana was not as strong as today's stuff. Skunk or whatever it is. It just made us feel relaxed and mildly amused.

After some time I progressed from the King's Head and Bell to the Broad Face. This pub fronted onto the main road that led to the bridge over the Thames. It's a swanky wine bar type of place now. When we were there it was very much a working class pub. Wooden floorboards, tables with fagburns around the edges and holes in the fabric seat cushions where drunken revellers had dropped their lit cigarettes.

There were beer mats to protect the tables, not that they were worth protecting. The beer mats were good for ripping a chunk out of and sticking over your nose, suggesting that someone had thrown it at you and it had embedded itself in your face.

I also enjoyed stacking them up, putting them on the edge of the table and flicking them up and over. I was only allowed to flip them once and I then had to catch them cleanly, with one hand. My record was 32. Some could do more, but they invariably had bigger hands.

In our inner circle was myself and Pete obviously. Then there was Grant. Although we were all together a long time, Grant is the only one whose surname I can't remember. The Monaghan brothers were there. John was there all the time. So was I. Pete and Paddy did not come as regularly. There were temporary members in our club. Mario would come in sometimes. Le blob bleu, but not often as there was no space invaders machine.

Grant found another use for a beermat. I had gone to the toilet. Before I went I had bought a round. My full pint was on the table. When I returned my full pint was upside down on the table. Someone had placed a beermat on top of my pint and turned it upside down. They placed it back on the table and pulled the beermat away. Initially I didn't know what to do. I hadn't seen this particular use for a beermat before.

I quickly realised there was absolutely nothing I could do. My pint was lost whatever I did. I looked around the table. Paddy was smiling, sardonically. John was chuckling. If you knew John, he had a face made for chuckling. Grant was giggling like a schoolgirl. I had my culprit. If it had been either of the brothers I would not have done what I was about to do.

I looked at them and said 'Oh well, I suppose I'll have to get another one'. In those days you always used the same glass throughout the evening. 'Does anyone else want one'. They all said no because I had just bought them one.

I put my hand on the bottom of the glass which was the top. I slid it across the table towards where Grant was sitting. When I got to just before the edge, I flicked the glass up, throwing beer all over Grant. The brothers roared with laughter. Even Paddy, who was normally coolness personified. I said 'you can have that one Grant' with echoes of Charlie Burgoyne.

Grant looked shocked. Then he looked bewildered. Then he started to laugh as well. He was a good man Grant. He didn't play that trick again though. This event became a legend. John and Paddy appeared to have a complete disregard for money. If they felt like it, they would burn five pound notes in front of you, for fun. Whether they won or lost, it didn't matter. Their reputation was what mattered and sorting out anyone who crossed them. Of course, neither of them ever started trouble.

My throwing away a pint showed a disregard for money, albeit a small one. Soaking Grant exacted my revenge on him. They had a good laugh too. After that I could do no wrong. Almost.

There was a club that ran out of the Broad Face. It was called the Winkle Club. Members of this club had a winkle (as in Cockles and Winkles) encased in a small plastic cube. For some unknown reason, one year we were all invited to become members. We accepted, apart from Paddy who was far too cool.

It was a rule of the Winkle Club that you had to have your winkle with you at all times. If another member of the Winkle Club challenged you and you did not have it on you, you had to pay a forfeit. John challenged everyone whenever he saw them, which became a bit irksome. Shopping in Tesco's John would appear and say 'where's your Winkle' It drew some funny looks from other shoppers.

Sunday was a busy night for Winklers. On this night only, a member could shout 'Winkles Up!' and every member would have to take out their winkle and hold it in the air. The last one to hold his Winkle up had to pay a forfeit. Nearly everything that happened in the Winkle club involved a forfeit. It was all for charity so nobody minded.

John was a very dedicated Winkle club member. On Sunday he would get into the Broad Face early. There was a time before which you could not shout 'Winkles Up'

I can't remember what time it was, but it was sufficiently late for most non locals to have left. One second after that time had passed John would shout 'Winkles up!' He would continue to do this frequently until the window of opportunity ended. By the end of the evening, just about every member had paid a forfeit, some more than once. Except John.

Once, the brothers decided we should have a raffle. The members of the Winkle Club were tasked with getting prizes from local businesses. Paddy was involved because although he was not a member, he knew a lot of people and none of them would refuse him.

I was tasked with getting the raffle tickets organised and printed. When holding a raffle there needs to be a designated person named on the tickets. Some sort of legal thing. When the books were prepared they were distributed amongst members to sell.

I saw the brothers the evening after the tickets were given out. I went over as usual and said hi. They both ignored me, John told me to go forth and multiply. I said 'What's up?' Paddy repeated John's instruction with an added threat of violence. I realised I was in trouble, but I didn't know why.

Later I asked Grant if he knew why. He said the brothers were not happy with me putting my name on the raffle tickets. They said I was showing off. I explained to Grant that it was a legal requirement for someone's name to be on each ticket.

I also said that I would happily scrap the tickets and have them re-printed with either John or Paddy's name on, at my expense.

Grant went over and told them. I was allowed to go over. John bought me a pint. All was forgiven. I think my offer to pay for a reprint showed my disregard for money, which impressed them.

Another time I was out for a drink with John and his girlfriend June. Everything was going fine when all of a sudden John started to shout at June. I had no idea why, but he kept on until she started to cry. I grabbed him and said what's the matter. I was trying to be a friend. I picked the wrong time to be friendly.

John turned and hit me with a massive haymaker. He knocked me out for a second. I came to, on the floor. I tried to get up, but somebody shouted for me to stay down. Apparently he was out of his mind with rage and would have taken my head off if I got up.

He calmed down slightly and realised what he had done. He left the pub and got in his car. Well it was June's but he had taken the keys. He had a lot to drink so should not have been driving. Not just because it was illegal, but also because he was not capable of driving. It is said that he drove so fast down East Saint Helen's Street that he went through the Co-op shop window.

I knew that on the following day he would be at the Fitzharris Arms which was a pub near to Paddy's house and the other side of town. It was a Sunday. There was a Ceilidh every Sunday with pipes, drums and singing. John went there before going to the Broad Face for a bit of Winkles Upping.

I walked into the pub. It was like High Noon. I looked at John. He looked at me. Paddy sat looking with interest. The pub was full of the hardest men in Abingdon. Hard men from hard families. I began to think I might have made a big mistake. John said 'You've got some balls coming in here after last night'

I don't know why, but I began to sing one of John's favourite songs, which is extremely rude and contains the word 'balls' John immediately started a jig and joined in the song.

The fiddler started to play the right tune, even though we were not singing the right words. Everyone in the pub was watching. I imagine they were thinking something like 'He's OK this English person'. Or words to that effect.

In the end I had a great afternoon and we went off to the Broad Face together. Although I enjoyed that day, I can't honestly say it was worth a punch in the face from John the Mon as we affectionately called him.

He was a great man. Somebody told me he has died, but I can't believe that. He was so full of life.

There is one final tale about the Broad Face. There was a guy called Jeff Dunbar who drank in the pub. I knew him but wouldn't call him an acquaintance, let alone a friend. I was sometimes on the periphery of his circle, but not often.

I remember on his 40th birthday a few of us had some drinks and then took a few bottles of Glenfiddich down to the Thames. We sat on the grassy bank, got drunk and together we howled at the moon. Strangely, it felt good.

Jeff is an animator and a very good one by all accounts. He did the animation for the Frog Chorus. It was a good animation but a bit of a rubbish song. Especially for Paul McCartney. Hardly comparable to Eleanor Rigby or Let it Be.

Apparently Jeff Dunbar knows Paul McCartney well. I admit I thought that he must have worked with Paul on the Frog Chorus but lots of people have worked with Sir Paul as he is involved in so many things.

I was watching Parkinson one day and Paul McCartney was on. Paul started talking about a book he was working on 'Wirral the Squirrel' He said his good friend Jeff Dunbar was going to do the illustrations. I was impressed. I don't recall seeing 'Wirral the Squirrel' anywhere. Perhaps it never happened.

I was even more impressed when Jeff came into the Broad Face one day with the Bafta he had been awarded for the Frog Chorus. He stuck it behind the bar and it stayed there for weeks.

Chapter 19

The Bipolar journey continues

I sat in the red XR3i for ages waiting for the feelings to subside. I had no idea what had just happened to me. I realised I had left my briefcase in the boardroom. There was no way I was going back. I would figure out how to get it later.

I was thinking about what had happened and trying to make some sense of it. This was just a run of the mill presentation. I had done hundreds if not thousands like it. I was not remotely worried or concerned about it. Yet that had just happened. I wanted to talk it over with Sally. I would talk to Pete later, but for now I needed to talk to someone who knew me and the business we were in.

Thinking about the situation had taken my thoughts away from the intensity of emotion I had just felt. I was ready to drive back. It wasn't far to our office, but I could not have attempted it 10 minutes earlier.

I pulled around the back of our terraced building as I always did. Somehow it all seemed different. I parked and sat for a while trying to make sense of my racing thoughts. I was afraid to go in. I told myself that was stupid and forced myself to get out of the car and walk through the back door. I carried on past the kitchen and came to the reception area where Sally was sitting, looking concerned.

'I have just had John Delyn on the phone' she said. 'He is concerned about you. He said you were talking with Alan Davies when you suddenly went very white and ran out the door. What on earth is the matter?'

I told her I had no idea. As I spoke the words did not seem to be coming from me. When Sally spoke it was though she was speaking through glass. I could see her lips moving, but her voice was distant. I was scared. What was happening to me?

I tried to describe what had happened. She didn't really understand which was not surprising because I definitely didn't.

We both agreed that we must not tell David Dobbin. I suggested we should not tell her Dad either because he might feel compromised being a director of the Dobbin Group. She wasn't happy but saw my point.

I told her I had to go home to get some rest. I was totally exhausted. Abingdon was more than 50 miles away. I didn't want to drive, but I had to. I was scared all the way home.

When I got to my house, I went straight to bed even though it must have been no later than 7 pm. I couldn't get to sleep. Eventually I must have passed out because the next thing I knew it was time to go to work.

I drove back to Maidenhead. I wasn't sure how I would be as I hadn't spoken to anyone . When I greeted Sally she responded through the glass wall. I still sounded like I was speaking from somewhere else. I realised whatever this was, I would have to live with it for now. I had some candidates to interview later. I wondered how that would go. I was no longer terrified, but I was worried. I felt that I could not let anyone else see how I was feeling.

The first interviewee came in on time. Sally showed him up to my room. She gestured good luck as she went back downstairs. She really was amazing. I said 'please sit down.' My voice came from somewhere on the ceiling. He said 'thankyou' through this glass divide that was becoming the norm. His face was blurring like through a heat haze. I felt dreadful.

Luckily I knew all the questions. At least I must have sounded plausible, I hoped. I have no idea what his answers to my questions were. I was too busy trying to not run screaming from the room.

That is how I felt in every interview I conducted. It was a dreadful time.

I don't know why, but my talks with Sally improved. The glass wall was there, but not so intimidating. Her face did not distort whilst we talked.

I had to accept that I was not likely to be able to do any presentations in the foreseeable future. It was adapt or die. At this time I felt like dying, but this was my dream and I had to keep going. I had to devise a strategy which would enable me to continue.

I thought we should push CAA. I was OK on the phone so I took care of that. We had several assignments with our regular clients. They required me to interview. It was scary, but it had to be done. Every candidate was talking through the glass wall.

Sometimes I would be talking to them and their face would change shape. It would distort terribly. I knew this was all in my mind, but it did not help knowing that.

Every day was a battle. I was determined not to give up. Somehow we managed to stay afloat with existing business, but I could not win anything new.

I read up on what was happening to me. I began to think that I might have inherited my Mum's condition. I contacted Littlemore hospital as it was the only place I knew where I thought I could discuss this.

I spoke to some young doctor who agreed to see me. I was relieved that perhaps I might find some answers and get treatment. I did not want to lose all that I had built up.

I met the young doctor at the hospital in Oxford. He asked me a load of questions about diet, lifestyle and that kind of stuff. At the end he booked me back in for the following week. This happened for the next few weeks. He seemed very thorough.

One day he thanked me for my input. He didn't need to see me again. I was confused. I asked what my diagnosis was. What was wrong with me. He couldn't tell me he said. He had been working on his dissertation.

I desperately needed help and I had been used. I felt abandoned, manipulated and above all lost. I should have realised something like this could happen. Psychiatry had done my Mum no good for all those years. Now they managed to let me down too. It was only the start of that.

I had lost the one hope I thought I had. I did see my local GP back home who referred me to a psychiatrist. When I eventually met her, she told me there was nothing seriously wrong with me. I would get through it. Be strong, she said.

Can I have some drugs to make it better please I asked. She said it would be better if I could fight it myself. Come back in a month and we'll see how it is then

When I did come back, she had gone to a better paid job.

I had now reached the conclusion that if nobody would help me, I would need to help myself. I began to talk to myself, reassuring me that I was a good bloke and very good at my job. I told myself that what I was experiencing was all nonsense. I had been successful before this and I would get there again. It was a temporary blip.

Thirty years later, I can tell the younger me that he was wrong. It's permanent. What he was doing was CBT before it had been invented. It is useful but not when you have a serious mental illness such as I found out we had. In his defence the young me did not know what the old me knows now.

Sally and I had somehow reached the end of 1985. We managed to keep the ship afloat even though it was holed beneath the waterline and slowly sinking. Without her I would have sunk without trace.

As a special Christmas present Mr. David summoned me over the road to his office. He informed me that Roles Research was not generating enough money to make a profit. I said that without the 10% management fee we would be profitable.

He disagreed saying that the fee was built into the cost structure. I found it a bit off putting that he was talking to me from a glass box and his face looked like Edvard Munch's The Scream.

He pointed at a picture on the wall. He told me that he had bought that painting from Sotheby's two years ago. It was now worth 30% more than he paid for it. I thought what's this Bargain Hunt?

He informed me that the painting had turned a better profit than Roles Research had done, year on year. I was tempted to take the painting from the wall and whack him round the face with it like the beer mats back in the Broad Face.

However I resisted. He told me that he was calling a special board meeting in a week's time. I was to be there with a business plan to show how I was going to improve our turnover and get to a profit.

I decided on what I was going to do and went over to tell Sally. She was fine. Her husband Giles ran a farm in Marlow. He would inherit it in due course, meanwhile they had a tough but good life. She wasn't desperate to keep her job with Roles Research although we'd had a good laugh over the last couple of years and done some good business.

The day of the board meeting came. I was called over the road and made to stand outside the boardroom door like my much younger self awaiting the cane.

Eventually I was called in. I looked around the room at a bunch of characters who I pictured as Butch Cassidy's Hole in the Wall gang. I was developing my own type of displacement theory, replacing a scary situation with a less threatening one. A bit like imagining the interviewer nude to take away nerves at the outset of an interview.

I definitely would not want to use that technique with this lot.

Mr. David told them about me. He called me Hutt throughout. Hutt has done this. Hutt has failed to do that. All the time the Hole in the Wall gang were snapping and snarling at me like a bunch of wolfhounds. I had already learnt to dance away from them.

Then David Dobbins introduced me to the gang. I said good morning from somewhere at the back of my head. They said nothing.

I said 'Mr. David has asked me to prepare some projections. However, I can't be arsed.' I then put my resignation letter on the table and walked out. It felt so good.

I left the XR3i in the car park of JN Dobbin. I did not leave a shirt hanging up this time. I took the bus again, even though I said the last time was the final time this really would be the last time.

Mr. David called me and asked if I would like to buy the company car. I told him I didn't want it in the first place. He tried to sell me the name of Roles Research.

I was incensed. I said I created the name and the business. You can keep it for all the good it will do you. I thought I would get the clients. They were mine in the first place.

I transferred the business to the dining room table in my lovely new home in Ock Street, Abingdon. I had just exchanged contracts on the house. In those days little phased me, despite my unknown condition. I was confident that I would meet the mortgage payments. Especially as I already had got over £4K in the bag. I was not unemployed. I was self-employed, a totally different proposition.

I also transferred an assignment I had recently negotiated with one of my defence clients. I had already been up to Oxford Street and got the brief for that one.

It hadn't yet been invoiced so I rang my contact and told him I was going into business for myself. I would bill him directly. He said that would be fine. 'Who do we make the cheque payable to?' he asked. 'Me' I replied with great relish. That was the best feeling ever.

Another client had contacted me just before Roles Research ceased to trade. They were a Swiss company that I had done business with before. I arranged to meet the MD who I knew well.Their offices were in Newbury. I was tempted to go to the tax office to see how my old mate Arthur was doing. I managed to resist the urge. The MD was called Peter Wragg.

He had no idea about the demise of RR. I told him I was setting up my own business. I did not say I was working off the table in my lounge. I had undertaken another relocation from the dining room as the lounge had the phone point in it.

Peter said wait there a minute. He disappeared and came back with two pints of lager. He handed me one and congratulated me. I took the brief while we drank the lager. I would have preferred bitter, but the lager still tasted of sweet victory.

I knew Peter so although I still felt panicky and he seemed a bit distant, the sensations were not so intense.

I had found with Sally that if I knew somebody, the feelings were somehow not so bad. It's strangers that really freaked me out.

We finished the brief. I asked Peter what the salary was going to be, I worked on a fee divided into three parts, which is standard for the industry. 18% of the first years salary in total consisting of 6% at each stage which was an up front retainer then on presentation of shortlist and finally on hiring.

He said £25k plus commission. I asked how much the commission would be. He said 'You always try that one on. Your fee will be 18% of the basic salary'. I said 'God loves a tryer' He laughed and we shook on it.

Peter said 'I'll go and get another lager'. He came back with another lager and a cheque for £1,500. I've still got a copy of it. I said thanks. I thought no 10% would come off this one.

The defence sector is very competitive and the salaries tend to be higher. My client in Oxford Street was looking for a Senior Software Designer. The successful candidate would have an in depth knowledge of working on designs for the MOD. They had to be working on Command and Control systems and Weapons Design. This person was going to need paying £45k pa. I was going to need paying £2,700.

So I had earned £4,200 in my first week of trading. I wasn't really trading as I had nothing except a telephone to trade with. I needed something to produce reports on. I needed letter headed paper and business cards. My new company was going to be named after me. I didn't need to dream that one up and I had already requested payment to myself.

I realised that I had a lot to do before I could get down to actually working on these assignments. The first thing I needed was a car. I also needed Sally to help me think about what I needed and go and get it.

Sally wasn't too keen. They were very busy on the farm. I pleaded and she relented. Only for an afternoon she said. I said that would be plenty of time. I thanked God for Sally. I knew I would struggle going out to strange places to get what I needed.

When Sally arrived I said the first thing I need is a car. We went to a couple of car sales places. In one there was a red Alfa Romeo Cloverleaf. Sally liked it and the price was right. I bought it with a card and hoped I would be able to cover it when payment became due. I would if my defence client coughed up.

I still had to bill him but had no letter headed paper to send it on. This company was part of one of the biggest groups in the world and I did not want to send a bill on a blank piece of A4. I was looking for a long term business relationship and wanted to set a high standard.

I decided this was a high priority. I wanted to send the bill. The quicker I did, the sooner I would get paid. Sally and I went to Burgess and Son printers. They said they could produce letter headed paper by the end of the week. I knew from personal experience that they could produce high quality work at a reasonable cost.

We came up with a design and I asked them to go ahead as soon as possible. I also wanted business cards but they needed to be of high quality and I didn't mind if it took time. I wanted linen backed, embossed cards.

I felt it was important that clients, old and hopefully some new, would see me in a professional light. If I had high quality cards, a decent suit and a car that wasn't bright red with bright red wheels they would hopefully take me seriously. They could not know that I was sitting in my lounge in my pyjamas talking to them on the phone. Sometimes when I am feeling paranoid or panicked, this is the best place for me.

I was coming to terms with my illness. I had been unable to find out what the problem was, but I was managing to keep going. At times it was hard. I would find myself in a cold sweat in a strange situation and had to try not to descend into a full blown panic attack.

I had decided that was what had happened to me at the presentation. I had read extensively and it made sense. I didn't want it to happen again. I was constantly on the verge of panic. It was as though my body was using this as a safety valve to avoid the big one.

Somehow I had lost the glass wall between me and others. I now had a 'bubble' that encased me. It still meant everyone outside of the bubble was somehow not connected with me, but at least I could see them without them growing two heads or turning into Jack Russells.

When I spoke it did not come from my mouth, but somewhere in the back of my head. Even that I was getting used to.

I had to accept that I would probably never be normal again. Some psychiatrists have said 'but what is normal?' trying to be clever. I have always said that I have no idea, but I do know that this sure as hell isn't.

As promised, Sally gave me the whole afternoon. We went into Oxford and traipsed around loads of stationery shops. She picked out this sort of typewriter thing. This was a long time before laptops.

This machine was state of the art. It was essentially a typewriter, but it had a memory on which a couple of pages could be stored. That is as much as I was likely to need for my reports. I like to keep them short and to the point. Instead of having to type up a report which produced one copy, I could retain it in the memory and keep it for later. Even make amendments. It was marvellous.

We had all of what I needed to get going. Anything else I could order. I was in business!

I treated Sally to a meal at Browns in the Woodstock Road. Browns is one of my favourite places to eat. We had a very pleasant meal and talked about Roles Research. I told her about my speech to the Hole in the Wall Gang. She laughed out loud. A couple next to us stared and I gave them my best Dad look. They went back to eating their food.

Sally came back to my place. She helped me set things up, ready for the new business. I was nearly ready to go. I just needed my letter headed paper so I could invoice my client. I had the typewriter ready. My typing lessons from college were finally going to be of use. If I could remember what to do.

Sally went home. Once again I thanked her profusely. After she had left, I sat down and started to think about everything. I had been so busy today and so happy over the past few days. I started to cry like a baby. It made me feel better. It was early in 1986

After sitting there for a while, I decided I didn't want to watch telly. I didn't want to be in the house. I didn't want to be alone. So I went down the Broad Face. When I got there, several of my friends were already in.

I had a word with my best friend Peter. I told him everything that had happened. Apart from the crying bit. He thought long and hard. 'What do you want to drink', he said. 'I'll have a pint of bitter mate' That's how male friends help each other in times of emotional crisis.

I had a few pints. Actually more than a few. Someone said that there was a party going on upstairs. There was a large room that was reserved for private parties. Someone from our group knew someone whose party it was.

We all went upstairs in search of wine, women and song. In my case mostly women. I failed in that quest but still had a great time. The alcohol, which I drank plenty of, took my mind away from my problems. I moved from bitter to whiskey.

Frankie goes to Hollywood were singing relax and then two tribes. I loved Frankie goes to Hollywood. I was on the dancefloor, whirling like a dervish. Then everything went blank.

I woke up in total darkness. I was the frightened little child back in Sutton Courtenay, terrified of the dark. I had no idea where I was. I shouted but nothing happened. My eyes slowly adjusted to the dark and I saw a set of curtains by the bed.

I drew them back. It was daybreak and the light was just starting to come into the room. Enough for me to realise I was in one of the bedrooms in the Kings Head and Bell. I had no idea how I got there.

I crept out of the room and headed home. My house was only a five minute walk away. I wondered why they didn't just take me home.

I got in and began to wonder what had happened. I remembered I was having a great time, but all of a sudden it stopped.

I rang Peter. I needed to know what had happened, but was too ashamed to speak to anyone except him. I begged him to come round. He seemed a bit standoffish but I knew that this illness sometimes distorted my perception of others' moods.

He did come round, which was something. I asked what had happened. He was cool with me. I hadn't imagined it.

He told me that I was making an absolute fool of myself and annoying everyone, especially the people whose party it was.

I then fell on the floor and started crying. One of the managers was called for. He came up and decided to put me to bed so I could sleep it off. They all assumed I was drunk. They were all annoyed with me because I had ruined the party. Even if they knew I had some sort of mental or emotional problem they would not have cared. No one does.

I laid low for a couple of weeks. Nobody called to see how I was, not even Peter. I began to think I had no friends. Perhaps I didn't. My paranoia grew. People will show sympathy if you have had some physical accident. But display any strange behaviour and they will stay away from you. Even your so-called friends.

I stayed at home and concentrated on my business. My letter headed paper had been completed. They looked great. I was very pleased, and immediately typed up an invoice which I sent recorded delivery to my contact. A cheque arrived by return post. I was pleased that I could pay for my Alfa.

I decided to pluck up my courage and pay a visit to the Broad Face. This was the night of the upside down beer incident. Because the Monaghan brothers were happy with me, everyone else was. I was back in favour again.

I had a strange lifestyle. Businessman by day, drunk by night. I had found that getting drunk helped to take these feelings away. They weren't gone, they were just masked. I carried on like this for a long time.

There used to be a guy called John Bowles who lived in Abingdon. He was a businessman and a really nice guy. He owned a convenience store just outside the town centre. He was very well spoken.

But he was very often drunk. When he was, he was a stumbling fool. He would blast out rock songs at the top of his voice, sometimes in the market square, full of people. He was ridiculed and laughed at. I was worried that I would turn out like that.

I was doing very well financially at the time. I was about to earn more money than I ever had or have since. I have a set of accounts which show in 1987 I earned £38,050. Not bad for a drunk. I've checked and it would be worth £114,000 today. For one years work.

I could do with that now. But I always felt it would come crashing down.

Chapter 20

Return to the Greek Islands

In the Summer of 1987 I decided to treat myself to a holiday. I had worked so hard I thought I deserved it. I still could not face looking for new business but was doing well with existing clients. I knew that putting all your eggs in one basket is risky, but I only had one basket

I flew to Athens and took a taxi to Piraeus. I walked around the harbour as Jess and I had done years before. I wasn't sure where I was going until I saw a ferry going to Paros. I knew it was part of the Cyclades group so I bought a ticket, thinking I might island hop.

The ferry set off. There were no Dutch boys playing lager roulette. It was quiet.

After several hours the ferry approached Paros. I saw a blue dome suddenly appear, standing out on the horizon on top of a dazzling white building. The capital of Paros was Parakia and it was that town I was looking at. It stood as if suspended in the turquoise sea.

A beautiful mirage in the distance, it shimmered in the heat haze. That image has always stayed with me. I felt completely at peace for a while. The madness went away. In its place was pure joy.

This was the best drug I had ever experienced. I didn't want it to end, but of course it had to. As we got closer and eventually into the port of Parakia the town became an ordinary Greek fishing village. Not that there is anything ordinary about Greece and its villages.

I have had moments of clarity there that I cannot find anywhere else. Sometimes I get close in Sutton Courtenay. I can get quite philosophical when I'm in the Greek Islands although I would never discuss this. Only with myself.

In the late 70's early 80's the islands were relatively untouched. The fishing villages were still full of fishermen bringing in their catches. Boxes of fish set out on the quayside and squid drying. Jess took a picture which I still have in a scrap album she put together. It is of me sitting next to a rack of squid. She put captions against all of her photos. This one just said 'squid drying in the sun'. I have wondered if the reference was to the squid or me.

Ladies in black dresses would come to look and buy. Always haggling over the price, it would look and sound as if the woman and the fisherman were in a heated dispute. Maybe they were. I couldn't speak the language.

I picked up a bit over the years. The Greek lads liked to teach you swear words, but I picked up some useful phrases too. It was always fun to sit in a cafe and watch, normally joined by the old men who like to sit and watch everything, smiling. They seldom say much, they just constantly flick their rosary beads. That used to annoy me. That was a clue as to the nature of my illness.

When we docked I saw a young girl, smiling sweetly at me. I decided I would choose her to find my accommodation. I followed the young girl, ending up in a small shack. An old lady appeared. This was a holiday hut, especially for tourists. It had all the essentials plus a couple of geckos for company. She gave me a price and I agreed to it.

I had a perfectly fine two days in Paros. Then I caught the ferry to Ios, a nearby island. Ios is now a party island apparently. Then, it was a quiet place with a sleepy village at the top of a very steep hill.

I didn't fancy the climb and as I had been there before when Jess and I took a day trip from Naxos, I knew there wasn't anything special to see. There were a number of hotels and tavernas around the port area. I fancied treating myself and checked into a hotel.

It was a decent hotel and made a pleasant change from the donkey shack I had just left. There were Geckos still, but they politely stayed outside on the terrace. It was on the ground floor.

I had a shower, which was bliss. I sat out on the terrace reading a book. Normally I couldn't sit still for long. I would always feel agitated and for some reason I had to get up and move. In Greece, I felt good. I could sit for hours reading a book. Or on the beach watching the sun set over the sea. Or anywhere really. The Greeks don't rush and neither do I.

That evening I went to a nearby bar. I sat on my own at a table near the door. Like Jeff Dunbar. I had a glass of Mythos, the local brew. Served in a frozen glass on a hot day, it was hard to beat. This was a warm, sticky evening. It still went down well.

I'd been there for a while, thinking about my life to date. I didn't want to go home, I felt so much better here. I thought I could buy a small bar and spend the rest of my life serving Mythos and Moussaka. It might have been possible, but never happened. Life can get in the way of your dreams.

A voice said 'Are you on your own mate?' I looked up, and there was this tall, imposing lady standing beside me. 'Yes' I said. 'D'ya mind if we join ya?' I thought 'who is we?" There was another young woman standing at the bar. I looked at her and she smiled. She had a lovely smile. I said 'No' A man of few words.

They came and sat down. The tall one seemed to do all the talking. Her friend just sat smiling. 'I am Maria Karagalonidis' the tall one said. 'People call me Mary K'. I could see why.

'This is my friend Michelle Rose. People call her Michelle' she said and laughed. 'We are from Melbun in Ostraalia' she said. Australians do not like the way we Brits pronounce the place names in their country. Even though we created them. These two from Melbourne told me it really grates with them when their home city is called Melborn, especially by us lot. Or you lot as Mary K called us.

I was surprised to realise that I felt fine in their company. Maria told me that she is a Greek Australian. She worked for her parents running a Greek cafe in Melbourne.

Michelle spoke for the first time. 'I am Jewish' she said. 'My full name is Michelle Rosenberg, but my parents shortened our surname after escaping the Russian pogrom and coming to Australia. The jews are persecuted everywhere' she said,' so it's best to stay anonymous.'

I thought, doesn't any Australian go by their proper name? So I asked Michelle who I was beginning to take a shine to. She just laughed. Michelle had now taken over as the spokesperson for the Australian duo. ' Where do you come from?' She asked. I nearly said London, but decided to be honest after the faux pas with Bruce in Canada.

'I am from Sutton Courtenay' I informed her. 'Where the hell is that?' said Maria the more forthright one. 'It's near Oxford' I replied then waited for the 'Is that near London' standard response from any foreigner.

'We are planning to go to Oxford. It looks like such a lovely city. It's older than Australia, even'

If we are talking about the white settlers, then yes by about 800 years. If it is the indigenous people then no, the dreamtime goes back to time immemorial I thought.

We had been sitting chatting for some time now. I was getting hungry. I suggested that we might go for Dinner if they would like me to join them. Not wanting to be an imposition of course.

'We would like that' they chorused. So we went in search of a decent looking taverna. As we walked along a small street with a few tavernas on it, a variety of men came out, hassling us to go into their place. We would smile and say we have just eaten. That usually gets rid of them. If any of them continued to pester us, Maria would let loose with a stream of Greek which seemed to do the trick.

We got to a clean looking taverna. Nobody came out to try and convince us to go in. The place was fairly busy and there were a few locals in, always a good sign. I said 'what about this one'

Good choice' said Maria. So in we went. The waiter showed us to a table. He gave us the menu. He was back in a flash with three glasses of ouzo which he put in front of us. 'Yes, it was a good choice' I congratulated myself.

The waiter came over again. Now what? I thought. He gave us some bread and a small bowl of brown stuff each. I dunked my bread into it and bit a piece off. I nearly spat it out. It was vile. Maria was chewing happily on hers. She laughed 'don't you like it'? 'It's horrible, what is it' 'I am not certain, I think it might be sea urchin' I drank the ouzo straight down to take the taste away.

We were in that taverna for hours. Maria showed us how to eat the Greek way. Loads of bits and pieces spread across the table, fish, salad, feta. Washed down with lots of alcohol. I had moved on from Mythos as it was too filling. We had more Ouzo. Maria ordered a bottle of retsina and I drank a glass. I must have been drunk!

There were some small fish, coated in batter. A bit like sprats they are eaten whole. I like sprats. My Dad used to bring some home wrapped in newspaper. Delicious. I ate these fish in the same way. There were some bigger fish. Maria told me you had to bite the head off then swallow the body.

I looked at the fish. It's dead eyes were looking up at me. I didn't like the look of it, but if it's the Greek way I thought I'll have to do it to avoid insulting anyone. They are a funny lot, the Greeks, easily insulted.

I plucked up courage and bit its head off. I could feel the eyes pop in my mouth. Bone crunched. I swallowed the body and grabbed a glass of Ouzo.

I looked over at Maria. She was laughing. Michelle was too. I looked around and the Greeks on the table next to us were all laughing as well. I looked at some of the other diners.

Several were eating the same type of fish that I had just bitten the head off. They were all using knives and forks. I realised I had been had. I said a commonly used Greek swear word, only mildly offensive. Maria looked surprised and then laughed.

We had moved on to port and cheese just for a change. Maria told me that throughout the evening, the waiters had been making disparaging comments about me. They spoke of my ability to keep these two women happy. Lots of insults about my physical attributes. The girls didn't escape, especially Maria. They commented about her size, her loud laugh and many other things.

When we had finished, Maria asked for the bill in fluent Greek. The waiter she asked looked surprised.

He came back with the bill. Maria hurled abuse at him. I knew a couple of the words and they were not compliments. All of the waiters stared, dumbfounded. Some of the customers looked shocked. Quite a few of the younger ones were laughing at the waiter's discomfort.

The waiter in receipt of the abuse scuttled off. A minute later the owner came out and spoke to Maria in Greek. Maria stood up and said 'Come on. We're off'

'What about the bill?' I asked. 'No charge' Maria beamed.

I suggested a nightcap at my hotel. We stopped at one of those kiosks that never seem to shut. I asked for a bottle of Metaxa. I said I would like a cigar. Maria said she would have one too. Maria was a proper Sheila.

We went out onto the terrace with the geckos. There were two chairs. I sat on the low wall. It was lucky my room was on the ground floor. I poured some Metaxa into three glasses. Maria and I smoked our cigars. Michelle coughed.

Michelle told me they were 'doing' Europe. They both said how strange it was to be visiting places that they had only seen in books back home in Australia.

They had been to Italy and seen the Leaning Tower of Pisa. They didn't go to Rimini. I said you missed a treat there, especially in the sea. Clearly that

160

meant nothing to them but it amused me. I was pretty drunk by then. I am amazed that I wasn't in a coma.

We talked about our respective homes. I told them about Sutton Courtenay and Eric Blair. Asquith too. They had heard about Asquith in school, but had never heard of Eric Blair. Until I said he is George Orwell. They had heard of him. 'What the .... hell is he doing in your churchard?' enquired Maria. I said it was because he loved the English countryside.

They told me about Melbourne. The trams that still run in the city and out to the suburbs. They told me how Cosmopolitan it is. Many different nationalities have settled in the city, Italians, Greeks, Japanese and Jews. Bit like the New Estate I thought. Many of them went to Australia to escape oppression in their home countries.

On a lighter note they told me about Aussie rules football which sounded very complicated. Probably not as bad as rugby.

When you meet somebody on holidays and hit it off, you often exchange addresses and phone numbers. You promise to keep in touch and maybe meet up in the future. But you don't. This was an exception to that rule.

The next day they took off to another Island. I was still in bed. I had an almighty hangover. I got up and had a shower. It made me feel a bit better. I decided to go out for breakfast. Luckily they don't hassle you in the morning.

I didn't go back to last night's taverna. I found another, not quite as nice but acceptable. I had some fruit and yoghurt to settle my stomach. How did I manage to drink so much without passing out? Maybe it was the continual grazing throughout the night.

I decided that I did not want to go to another island. It was time to head home. After the bottle of metaxa was consumed, I told the girls about my problem. I told them about Roles Research and its demise and I told them about my new business. Maria told me not to be so pathetic.

'Pull yourself together mate' she said. 'Or you will lose everything and it will be your own fault. There are lots of people worse off than you.' I said 'thanks a lot. That has really helped' I took the ferry back to the mainland. From Piraeus to the airport. I thought about what Maria had said. She had helped me and she was right.

When I got back to Gatwick and stepped into the arrivals hall I was hit by a wave of panic and paranoia. There were too many people, too much activity. I was back in the bubble again. I had to control my urge to disappear into the toilets and hide in a cubicle. It would not be for the first time.

Somehow I managed to retrieve my bag and clear customs. Once outside I got away from the building, sat down and tried some breathing techniques. This was all stuff I had read in books or just made up myself.

Doctors and psychiatrists can only help up to a point. It has to come from yourself. Drugs do not provide a cure it is up to the individual to want to fight mental illness. The problem is that if you cut yourself you can see the wound and dress it. With a mental illness not only can you not see it, often you think it is not there.

My Alfa was parked in the long stay car park. I retrieved it and began the long journey back to Abingdon. I had plenty of time to think about what had happened whilst I had been away. I definitely felt better for having been in the Greek sunshine and also for meeting the Australian girls. They were a breath of fresh air. Like many of their fellow countrymen they told it as it is. Especially Maria. I laughed at her little motivational speech. I would try to put it into action.

When I got back, I drove up the back lane where Paddy had his little disagreement. I parked behind the house, unlocked the gate and went in through the French Doors.

Everything was as I left it. I had also relocated the dining room table to the lounge and the typewriter thingy was on it.

I sat on the sofa. I did not put the TV on. I seldom did these days. I tried to make some sense of my condition. Nobody seemed to know what to call it. I had been given anti depressants by my GP but that didn't seem right. I did get depressed from time to time but just as often I was euphoric. I guessed I would never know, so would have to get used to it.

I was becoming increasingly convinced it would all fall apart and I would lose my house and everything else. Perhaps my nans prediction made to the 16 year old me would come true. Maybe I would end up pushing an Asda trolley around Oxford with my typewriter thingy in it.

These thoughts were constantly bubbling away. Business was drying up. I had lost my biggest defence client as they had been sold off to the opposition who dealt with another head hunter.

My Swiss company closed down their UK business.

There wasn't much left although I had some small bits of work, it would not give me a turnover like the last. I was once again keeping my head above water. My mortgage wasn't massive and I had enough to keep going for at least a year with no work. But my 'condition' I will call it that, made me negative and pessimistic

The joke goes 'I'm not paranoid, I know they are after me' Sometimes that is true. I was often paranoid. More often than not it was in my head, which is not a good place for it to be. Sometimes though people are against you, like after the night in the Kings Head and Bell.

About two weeks after I got back to the UK I had a phone call. 'G'day mate. How're they hangin? It's Mary K' the voice said.

'I would never have guessed,' I replied.'Where are you?' I asked. 'In Oxford' 'Where are you staying?' She said some hotel I can't remember. 'Why didn't you call me? You can stay here for free. I have plenty of room'

The next morning, there were two Australian girls outside my front door with large rucksacks and big smiles. I was looking forward to introducing them to the local gang. Especially Maria. I wouldn't back anyone against her in a drinking, smoking or arm wrestling contest.

In the end they stayed for just three weeks. As I suspected would happen, everybody loved them. All of the previously mentioned contests took place. Maria did indeed win them all. She slammed Le Blob Bleu's hand down after about one second in the arm wrestle.

She drank a whole table of locals under the table on one particularly memorable evening. Not so memorable for the locals. .

There was no smoking contest as such, as Maria said she only smoked cigars and only with Metaxa, in Greece.

It was generally agreed that Maria was more of a man than most of the men in Abingdon.

I took the girls all over the South of England in the Alfa. I took them to places that most tourists would not know about. White Horse hill where we went up onto the hill and walked around the horse's outline, telling tales of King Arthur and the knights of the round table.

I took them to Wayland's Smithy and told them that it was named after Wayland, the Saxon God of Metalworking. Michelle was interested in the ancient history of England. Maria looked like she wanted to find an Olde English pub.

We went to Tintagel in Cornwall and walked into Merlin's cave. It was a magical three weeks. Unfortunately it had to end as they wanted to 'do' Scotland.

In the time that they had stayed with me I had got to know Michelle a bit better than Maria. A lot better actually. I told her that I would love to visit Australia at some point in the future. She said she would like that too.

I took them to Oxford train station to begin their journey to Scotland. I told them both that I would see them some time. I didn't realise it then but that time was not too far away.

I drove home feeling quite depressed. I had enjoyed the past three weeks and hadn't thought how I would feel when they had gone. I did not feel good.

As my 'condition' took more of a hold, people were avoiding me more and more.

Business was drying up, and I was unable to do anything to generate more because of this awful condition. I had got to the point where I could see no future for myself in Abingdon.

The condition was also progressing in its severity. I felt that I was at the top of the slippery slope. I was drinking in the daytime and had given up on the business. I often went out in the day and then found myself in bed without knowing what had happened and with whom.

I decided I had to make some positive moves before it was too late. These decisions were all being made whilst I was feeling extremely vulnerable and probably not being rational.

The first thing I did was put my house on the market. I had only lived in it for just over two years. I really did not want to sell it, but I believed I was going to lose it anyway. With things going down as they were, I might well have had a point and it made sense to realise my assets before they were eaten up by normal living costs.

I put it on with a local estate agency. I thought their valuation was low. There was no interest. Not a single possible buyer. The agent said I should drop the price. The figure he suggested was less than I had paid for it.

I had seen an up market agency that sold period properties in the area. They had impressive brochures printed for each property they marketed. That's what they told me when I went into their offices in Oxford High

Street. I had decided that the high street agency was not the right place to sell my house.

The first estate agency had described my house as a mid terrace and put a photo of the front in the window. I would be the first to admit the front was not that impressive. Just a plain magnolia colour, it had no outstanding features.

Inside was a different matter. It had original oak beams on all the downstairs ceilings. There was a massive oak lintel over an equally massive brick fireplace. The front and back rooms had been knocked into one creating an open living space. There was a small galley kitchen with a double oven and hob. All very modern.

The first floor had one large bedroom with an ensuite bathroom. There was also a separate shower room on that floor. The top floor had two bedrooms. The rear one looked out towards the river, as previously mentioned. The front was high enough to see across the rooftops towards Oxford.

I was worried that the up market agency would not take my house on because compared with the rest of their properties, it was cheap. They sent an agent out to see it.

He had a good look round. He said it was a lovely property and they would be happy to promote it. He gave me a valuation which was £25,000 more than the original High Street agency. I thought that if the High Street agency couldn't get what they first priced it at, this wasn't going to work. This agent was much more professional than the other one, so I said yes, I would like them to take it on.

He went all around the house taking photos. I forgot to mention the house had a decent sized garden to the rear with a brick wall on one side, and a wooden fence on the other. It was very private which is one of the many things I loved about that house.

It had a recently built garage at the end of the garden and a gate to the rear courtyard area. There was a space to park next to the garage and behind the gate.

There was a driveway out and a lane leading to the high street.

The agent took photos of all of this.

When he left he said he would send through the brochure when it was ready for my approval. If I was happy then we could go ahead.

About two weeks later, a large brown envelope was delivered to the house. I opened it and it contained the brochure. The house looked amazing. Photos of all the rooms, with the garden and garage. A view from the courtyard to the back of the house.

The only thing which did not appear in the brochure was the front of the building.

My house looked so good that I wanted to keep it, but I was still convinced that with each mortgage payment I would be getting one step closer to bankruptcy.

Now I realise that I would almost certainly have got business from existing clients and would have easily been able to survive on the money I had in the bank.

But my mind was not working properly and by now I just wanted to get out of Abingdon. It was 1988 and I have not returned since except to pick up what was left of my belongings and once to see Paddy.

I went into Oxford hoping to see my house in the shop window of the upmarket estate agency. It was there, sandwiched between one on sale for £230,000 and one for £350,000 on the other side. Obviously on for a lot less than the other two, my place looked as good as either of them. These were 1988 prices. Both would be several million now. Mine will have reached at least £1m too.

The house went on the market in January 1988. It sold at the full asking price by February. I was on a plane to Australia via Greece by mid March.

Once the house had been sold I felt a weight had been lifted from my shoulders. Now I was no longer a businessman. I was free. I stuck on some colourful shorts, a sweat top and sandals. On with a pair of Ray Bans. I had a sweat band around my forehead. I looked crazy because I was.

I drove to Oxford. There is a sword in the flagstones outside the main gates to Christchurch meadow. I have a picture of me standing at the hilt of the sword looking off into the distance. I don't know what I was looking at and I have no idea what was going through my mind. Perhaps I was planning to take on the world. It had felt that the world was against me often enough.

There was a guy called Rob Duley who had become part of my circle of friends. His Dad was Terry Duley who had told Gary Hunt he had failed his

OND. Rob kindly offered to put me and my stuff up whilst I waited to travel. My stuff was staying once I departed.

There was a party at my house before I left. True friends like Paddy and John Monaghan turned up. Paddy brought the biggest bottle of champagne I have ever seen in my life. It was a great night. I think it was anyway because as usual I woke up in my bed and could not remember much.

I moved my stuff into Rob Duleys. There was a brand new television. A brand new three piece suite too. Most importantly to me was a box full of memorabilia. In that box was the Chinese take-away menu, the Beatles EP and many other personal items.

I had told Michelle and Maria that I was flying out and would be with them sometime in April.

I went to the travel agents to buy tickets. I was told there were several routes I could take. One stopover would be necessary with all of them, due to the length of journey which was 24 hours minimum.

There was an option to stop at Athens airport. I thought I could drop in to see Athens maybe for the last time. As I was buying the ticket anyway, it seemed obvious. Heathrow to Athens then to Bangkok and finally to Melbourne.

The night before I was due to fly, there was a party at Rob's house. Everybody was there. Perhaps they wanted to make sure I was actually going. Neil Haughey was one of them. Neil was a chef who floated in and out of our group. Sometimes he was in Scotland, his homeland and sometimes with us in Abingdon. Jimmy Lyons would have cited him as proof that as long as you had a frying pan, you could go anywhere.

Neil had a set of Sebatier knives which he carried around but expected to find the relevant pans wherever he was cooking.

Rob's house was rammed with all sorts of people. Friends and acquaintances and the odd gatecrasher.

Neil was cooking a meal for a selected few. No matter what I think of him, he was an exceptional chef. His cooking was always sublime. He could turn the most basic of ingredients into a feast fit for a King.

One of the selected few was my Mum. Neil knew her and had a soft spot for her. He went and picked her up from her flat on the other side of Abingdon. The council had moved her out of our childhood home as it was deemed too big for one person on their own. If my Dad had sorted out his credit rating, she could have stayed there.

When the council told her she had to move they asked where she wanted to move to. She said Abingdon. I was the only son that bothered to go and visit her and I lived in Abingdon. I should have gone to see her more. Her other son never came to see her at all.

Neil cooked an incredible meal. I know Mum thoroughly enjoyed it. She had settled down to a state of equanimity. I don't know if it was the drugs combination she was on but occasionally she seemed happy. That made me happy too. I asked her if she was OK with me going away. I don't know what I would have done if she had said no. She didn't. She gave me her blessing and told me to enjoy myself.

Of course I got drunk. I don't know if I behaved inappropriately but I woke up with the normal feeling of paranoia telling me I had.

I asked Neil what happened to my Mum. He had taken her home after the meal. I was already drunk apparently. I need to point out my drunkenness was never about enjoyment. It was what is termed self medication. I didn't know the term but I was trying to blunt my feelings by excessive drinking. It never works.

At the time Neil was working at a college in Boars Hill in Oxford. This was a post graduate college for students from all over the world. Some of them came from countries where their parents were high ranking politicians. I met a Nigerian student whose Father was the Finance Minister for that country. His name was Ali Chelle. Ali was completing a dissertation on Marxism. He had gained first class honours from Oxford in the subject.

I remember once I took Ali to Sutton Courtenay. I parked my car on the village green. We crossed the road and walked down to the river, passing the Wharf. I told Ali about the history of the building. He was amazed, there was nothing like it in Nigeria.

We kept walking along the towpath and across the weirs. Eventually we came out the other side into the meadow that would eventually lead to Abingdon and on to Oxford.

All the way we were talking about the idea of Communism. He knew the intellectual side of it far better than I could begin to. I came at it from a logical point of view.

I had taken a look at Das Kapital out of interest. To me it sounded like a great idea, but I could not see it working. My argument with Ali was that the theory is great, but human beings would never be able to make it work. We are too selfish, not altruistic enough.

Our discussion was lubricated by a 2 litre bottle of cider. I can still see Ali waving his arms to emphasise a point whilst holding this large bottle of cider in the other.

Chapter 21

Escape to Australia

On the morning I left Abingdon, I put my rucksack in the boot of the Alfa. I told Neil I would like to stop off and see my Mum. He said we did not have time but he promised he would pop in and see she was alright later. He also said he would take good care of my Alfa until I returned, as we had agreed.

That would have to do, I thought. I did not know that I would never see my car, or far more importantly, my Mother again.

We stopped for petrol before heading off for Heathrow. When I went to pay, there was Jess and her four kids buying sweets. I said hi, trying to be nonchalant. She said hello and introduced me to her children. My heart was breaking, so I had to go.

We got to Heathrow and I checked in. We went to a bar before I went through to departures. I said don't forget to see my Mum and say I am sorry I didn't have time to say goodbye. I also reminded him to look after my Alfa.

He then left and sold the Alfa as soon as he got back to Abingdon. Apparently he had a buyer already lined up.I didn't really care about that as long as he told my Mum goodbye for me. I hope he did.

The call for boarding came and I headed for the departure gate. I have always felt alone. Here I truly was. I was as happy as I could be.

I went through all the boring boarding procedures and got onto the plane. I found my seat and settled down. The guy next to me was fidgeting a lot and annoyed me all through the flight.

I was very uncomfortable sitting so close to a stranger. I could not look at him in case his face contorted and I would get seriously frightened. So I used the technique that Kenny Lynch taught me. Having no copy of the Sun to hand, I spent the next three hours with my nose stuck firmly into the pages of the inflight magazine. That made even the Sun seem interesting.

We arrived in Athens on time. I always stay in my seat until most people have cleared the cabin. I find all the pushing and shoving totally unnecessary. We are all going to get through as dictated by the baggage carousel and customs. I eventually headed for the exit. As I stepped from the cabin onto the top of the steps, a wave of searing heat hit me. I was in Greece.

We had to wait for the arrival of the bus to take us to the airport terminal. Everyone crowded around ready to pounce when the bus arrived. I was one of them as it could be ages before the next one came and I was standing in the blistering heat with nothing to drink. Be prepared they told us in the scouts. I hardly ever was.

I have always loved Greece, but this time I was very nervous. I didn't know then, but it was my Bipolar disorder distorting my perception. Being in crowds had become hard. If possible I would avoid those situations but sometimes there is no choice. I had to grit my teeth, keep focussed on the objective and move forward.

I was feeling a bit wobbly as I exited the plane and had to hold on as I descended the steps to the tarmac.

I was comparing this crowd pushing and jostling to get to the front with my cow herd in the early morning, back on Farmer Allen's farm. When they were heading for the milking shed they were always eager to get to their destination as were this lot.

I didn't see any of the airport crowd chewing grass, or pooing. There was a fair amount of mooing though.

When the bus finally arrived there was a large number of people waiting. The bus stopped. The doors opened and all hell broke loose. It was everyone for themselves. The elderly and infirm best get out of the way. I found myself a tiny amount of standing room. This was my worst nightmare. Thankfully it was a short trip from the plane to the terminal. Especially as I spent all of that time with my nose stuck against an extremely smelly armpit.

Athens airport is always crowded which was something I just had to put up with. It is a spacious and cool building and I was happy to be there. There was plenty of room to avoid others.

At baggage reclaim I do the same as when exiting the plane. I wait. When most people had got their bags and gone racing off to join the queues that I would shortly be joining them in, I picked mine up and strolled towards the exit.

When I got to the customs desk and the official checked my documents I was expecting to be pulled to one side and told to empty my bag. I didn't have anything on me, but I always feel that way.

Of course I was waved through with a smile and a Kalimera. I checked my watch for the time and having assured myself that it was indeed morning I said Kalimera back.The old lady at the donkey shack had taught me well.

All the way travelling to Athens airport I was trying to solve a dilemma in my head. I loved Athens, but it can be stifling. It is a huge city but I had already seen much of it. And of course the Acropolis when you stand looking out across the plains of Mycenae is still not as high as the Empire State Building.

All of these things are important. But I had walked up to the Parthenon, watched the Son et Lumiere and eaten in the Plaka with Jess. I was so happy at that time I knew I could not repeat it. In fact, quite the opposite.

I had two options. The first was to find and board a flight to Australia. The second was to spend some time in the Islands before going on. I had an open ticket which meant I could do either.

I decided to go to the islands, at least for a while. For an extremely awful reason, that turned out to be a good decision.

I had cashed in all I had and put it into a high interest account back in Abingdon. It came to quite a tidy sum. In 1988 interest rates were at a high level. This meant I had a decent income from the interest. Enough that I would not have to work whilst travelling.

I decided I did not want to take a ferry to the islands. I would fly to wherever had internal flights available.

The first one I saw on the boards was to Rhodes, leaving in an hour. I sorted out the tickets and boarded the flight on time. It was a very short flight and I was soon in Rhodes airport. Not quite like Athens it was closer to the donkey shack I had been in on Paros.

However it was not crowded which was good. I left the airport and looked around. I had no idea where to go.

With no idea what to do, I reverted to the tried and tested go right option. So I went right. There was a bus to Faliraki. I got on.

At this point it is worth putting my travels in the context of Bipolar. Symptoms include a tendency to put oneself in dangerous situations.

Talking fast with racing thoughts, a decreased need for sleep and inappropriate behaviour. Most of all for me has been forming grandiose ideas.

I arrived in Faliraki in the early afternoon. I had my rucksack with a sleeping bag tied on. And a nice big bank account with plenty of money in it. I could have gone to a hotel but for some inexplicable reason I headed for Camping Faliraki which was signposted on the side of the road close to where I got off the bus.

At this time Falaraki had not become what I would regard as a hell hole. The sort of place where hordes of young people, many from the UK would go to get drunk and get up to all sorts of inappropriate behaviour without the excuse of having Bipolar.

It was still lively enough with a few bars and a club, many of which I would sample in my time there.

With my rucksack on my back, I headed for Camping Faliraki. It was not too far. No further than my walk to big school which I did on a daily basis. I was older now and should be able to do it easily. I did.

There was a driveway that led into the camp. On the right hand side was a low building with a long reception desk. There was a smiley man behind the desk. His name turned out to be Kostas, as so many are in Greece. He owned the campsite.

I went through Faliraki a few years ago. Camping Faliraki had been replaced by a large hotel. I guess Kostas is smiling even more now.

Kostas welcomed me to Camping Faliraki. He explained the terms to me, and what was available. I could pitch a tent or sleep under the stars. Apart from the fact that sleeping under the stars sounded quite nice, I didn't have a tent. So I went for the stars option.

With this option you did not get an allocated space, you just wandered about until you found somewhere with enough room then plonked yourself down. Over the weeks that I stayed there, I became a star seeking nomad, wandering from place to place within the campsite perameters.

The campsite had its own cafe and bar area. I went in and had a few drinks. Quite a few. Enough to bring me to the attention of the camp staff. Most of the staff were Kostas' family. There were a couple of beautiful daughters and a couple of tough looking sons.

Having got somewhere that I suppose I saw as a place of safety, I began to relax. I started talking to all and sundry, whether they wanted to talk to me or not. There was a group of young Greeks who were happy to talk with me.

After confirming that I knew a few swear words, we got on well. These lads were from the mainland and about to enter into their national service. All eighteen year old Greeks had to do two years national service at that time. This was their last hurrah before going in.

They were lovely young men. They adopted me, an old man of 33 and we would sit eating, drinking and talking all day. One day I remember I had a bad eye. It happened in the bright sun in Greece. It was due to a scarring in my eyeball caused by a rather stupid attempt to explode a banger in the sandpit of the playground in Sutton Courtenay.

They were getting around on mopeds whilst in Rhodes. One of them told me to get on the back of his moped and they all roared off into Rhodes town. Perhaps roared is a bit of a strong word.

They took me to an eye doctor. She had a look and gave me some eye drops. She told me it would cost me the equivalent of about £30. Being used to the NHS I was not expecting that. I told her I did not have the money on me. I would go and get it if she would wait.

This was all being translated by the boys. They told me she said no way, you must pay now. I kindly offered one of the lads as hostage, but no.

So these incredible young men went through their combined pockets and came up with the money. Just about.

I got the lad I had travelled with to take me to a bank. I took out enough cash to pay them all back with enough left over to fund a serious eating and drinking session on me. These young men were absolutely perfect gents and would not accept my hospitality. They always paid their way and were proud young Greeks.

I pointed out to them that without their help I would have probably gone blind. I eventually convinced them and we had a fine old time. I don't think our fellow campers were too impressed at our raucous behaviour.

One German tourist sitting at the other end of the swimming pool was particularly unimpressed. We were having an impromptu game of football. Giorgios passed me the ball. It was a long pass at about waist height. The type of pass I loved as a centre back in my football days in Sutton Courtenay juniors.

I would give such a pass a massive whack upfield, so that's what I did. Unfortunately it cleared the pool and landed on this gentlemans head. The ball was more of a basketball and was not light.

In fairness to him he did signal that he was OK. I was mortified and waved back, saying sorry. This was somewhat nullified by my Greek friends who were rolling around in fits of laughter.

I had a brilliant time with this bunch of Greek lads. Probably the most enjoyable part of my whole time travelling. The time came when they had to return to the mainland to prepare for their entry into the military. I had told them about my short time in the army and how much fun it could be. They seemed to be looking forward to it. There could be worse things to do.

After they had gone things went quiet. There were some campers that I got on with. There was an English guy who had driven over in a jeep. His name was John. He used to take us out now and then, which was better than getting a bus where there was always the chance of having to share it with a goat or a few chickens.

After they had gone. I started to go out looking for entertainment. I discovered a nightclub, the name of which escapes me. I would go into Faliraki town, have a few libations then hit the club. I was always dressed like an idiot and then proceeded to dance like one too. John Travolta has a lot to answer for.

I think I might have become an international version of John Bowles.

After about a month at Camping Faliraki, the head barman, Adonis something came looking for me. Just for a change, I was in the bar. He told me there was a phone call for me. That was ridiculous. What? I said.

He confirmed what he had said and told me to follow him. We went to reception and he showed me to an office around the back. He gestured to the phone and left me to it.

I answered 'Hello?' It was my brother. He said 'You have to come home' I asked 'Why' He replied 'You must come home now' I pointed out that I was at the start of a round the world trip and I was not going back to England without a very good reason. Then it dawned on me what the reason might be. I said 'Who has died?' He told me 'Mum' 'I'm on my way'.

I could make no sense of it. She was fine when I left a few weeks previously. I immediately started to blame myself for leaving her alone. I told Adonis what had happened. He did not believe me, he knew I was a bit of a joker. Also a bit of an idiot.

I asked John to take me to the airport. I explained why. No problem, he said. I grabbed my stuff and we set out for the airport.

When we got there I knew I would get it sorted. I thanked John and offered him some money. He refused and set off back to the campsite.

The airport staff were outstanding. They got me on the next plane to Athens. I was told in Athens I could use the return part of my ticket to get back to England. That's what I did. I was soon on a plane back to Heathrow.

From Heathrow I got a train back to Oxford. I met a guy also going there. He was returning from the States. We got talking and before long, drinks were ordered.

We were laughing and joking when we arrived at Oxford Station. My brother was there with my Dad. Tim saw me with my travelling companion. He shouted 'What are you playing at? Mums just died and you are getting drunk and laughing' He was very angry.

I ignored him and asked Dad what had happened. He said he didn't really know. My brother had a phone call telling him Mum had died. He had to come down to Abingdon to sort things out.

Tim told me he had done that and I was only here for the funeral. I bit my tongue not mentioning his complete lack of support whilst Mum was alive.

He also criticised me for leaving as I did, leaving Mum on her own. He said that her flat was full of empty pill bottles and he suspected she had taken her own life. It was clear that he thought I was responsible for my Mums suicide.

I still think so too. Why did this happen just after I had left the country to go round the world? How come she died then, when there seemed to be nothing wrong with her, other than the usual stuff?

On the other hand, Mum's flat was always full of pill bottles. She often forgot to take her many tablets prescribed for her schizophrenia. Or didn't deliberately. They made her brain dead, she used to say. I know that feeling now. Tim would not have known this. He had never visited her flat.

No one will ever know, and that's the worst part of it.

On the day of the funeral some of my Mums brothers showed up. Several didn't. They were never happy with the fact that my Mum had a serious mental illness. Shame on them.

After the ceremony, standing outside All Saints Church, Sutton Courtenay by the war memorial and in front of those who had turned up, my beloved brother asked me for a cheque for £1,000. This was my share of the cost of the funeral, he said.

Everybody I tell that finds it hard to believe. I paid up as money is not that important to me. Not as much as it is to my brother, obviously.

One thing about the funeral that pleased me immensely was that Dad showed up. I know that Audrey, the wicked witch of Wales had banned him from attending his ex wife's funeral. He ignored her. I still think my Mum was his one true love. He did his best but ultimately could not cope with her illness.

I later bought a headstone for my Mum and had it inscribed. The headstone was not cheap but I paid for it without thought. I assumed my brother would pay half. I'm still waiting.

Once everything was sorted out I decided it was time to return to Camping Faliraki.

When I got there I continued as I left off, being an idiot.

One of Kostas' sons was an ex Royal Marine called Mike. Kostas had married an English girl and all of his children were as English as me. After my Mum's funeral I was even more of a drunk than I normally was.

Mike was well built and as hard as nails. When he took his shirt off, as he frequently did, he had a British Bulldog and Royal Marines tattooed on his chest and a slogan 'these colours don't run' around his navel.

We were sitting in a bar in Faliraki one night when a police car with blue flashing lights turned up. I thought, ``What's this about?" Two policemen grabbed myself and Mike and threw us into the car. They then sped off into the night.

We were taken to a police station in the middle of nowhere. Mike and I were taken into a small room with some scruffy looking man in it. The policemen who had brought us in disappeared.

We were left sitting in front of this guy who appeared to be drunk. He had a large bottle of ouzo on the desk in front of him, which he would take a swig from now and then.

He had a revolver on the desk. He would pick it up and point it at us and call us English pigs, occasionally. Mike told me this. He was fluent in Greek. Mike also told me not to worry as the bullets in the barrel of the revolver were totally rusted in. It could not possibly be used.

I still didn't like having a gun pointed at me. It was not something I was used to.

After a while Mike's dad appeared. Thank God for that I thought. He had a chat with the gunman who waved him to leave. I got up to go. Kostas said not you, with a glare. Mike and Kostas abandoned me to my fate.

Later a man appeared in a smart uniform. He accused me of being a drug dealer. 'How can you afford to be here for as long as you have, spending money as you have with no job'? I tried to explain about my investments and the high interest rate giving me a substantial yield. He clearly did not understand a word.

In the end they drove me out into the middle of nowhere. I genuinely thought my time was up. They had a gun that would work and I would be found shot to death in an olive grove.

Luckily they just threw me out of the car. I didn't have a clue where I was. It was still dark. I started walking not knowing where I was going. I walked through the night and eventually found my way back to Camping Faliraki.

I picked up my rucksack and went to the reception. Kostas was there as always. He gave me a disdainful look. I said 'it's a shame it has ended this way' He said nothing, just handed me my passport. He gave me a bill which seemed excessive, but I just wanted out of there. I paid and left. I felt no shame. I felt nothing.

Things were happening to me that seemed out of my control. That is the nature of bipolar. You find yourself in situations you had no intention of getting into. It's a miracle that I have found my way out. Frankly, it's a miracle that I'm still alive.

I did not want to stay on Rhodes. I decided to take a ferry to Kos. I had never been there but had heard it was an island worth visiting. The trip was only a couple of hours so I was soon there.

Whilst on the ferry I was approached by an old man. He asked me where I was from and what I was doing on this ferry heading for Kos. I told him I was exploring the Greek islands. I had 'done' Rhodes. Now I was about to 'do' Kos.

He spoke to me mysteriously. He told me to go to an island close to Kos. It was called Kalymnos. Once on Kalymnos I should go to a village called Vathy. It is the most beautiful place in the world, he said. I'll give it a go after I've done Kos.

Over the years I have had several psychotic episodes. Always I meet with someone who tells me outlandish things. At the time I believe them, but later realise they were a figment of my imagination. Sometimes it is impossible to tell the difference between what is real and what is not.

I sometimes wonder whether this mysterious man was made up in my head. But then if that was true, how did I know of Kalymnos and Vathy? I have thought perhaps I was being sent back to somewhere I had lived in a previous life. Maybe I was a goatherd looking after a tribe of goats on the steep slopes that surround Vathy. When I eventually got there, it felt like coming home.

The ferry sailed into the harbour of Kos town. I disembarked and looked around. It looked like a suburb of Athens. No attractive blue domed churches. Just drab buildings set around a central square. The square was more interesting. There was a statue with what looked like a mermaid cast out of metal. Someone had painted a rather inappropriate part of the mermaid's anatomy.

I decided to book into a hotel. I needed somewhere to take a shower and to try and make myself feel human again. The last few weeks had been traumatic to say the least. I had buried my Mum, been accused of drug dealing on a Greek Island and nearly shot. I needed time out.

Incidentally, my Mum wanted to be cremated. She had told me that many times. She was terrified at the prospect of being buried alive. Tim had arranged everything before I arrived back in the country. If he had asked me on the phone when I was in Greece I would have told him not to bury Mum. But my brother knows all, and certainly would not ask his younger brother for advice on anything.

I found a decent but cheap hotel just out of Kos town centre. I went to my room, had a shower then passed out on the bed. I don't know how long it was since I had a proper sleep. When I awoke, it was nighttime. I checked my watch and it was 10 pm. I had slept for hours.

I felt great. I had obviously needed that sleep. I got dressed in my best clothes. Jeans and t-shirt, but clean.

I went out in search of something to do. I wandered around the town centre. There was an open room with some lads playing pool. I thought of challenging one to a game. I was wary of talking to strangers. Not just because of the continuing problems of the bubble, but now I had additional paranoia. Also, I was rubbish at pool.

I kept walking. I found a quiet little bar and went in. I ordered a beer and sat in a corner on my own. I was happy that way. I don't know if I had realised yet that my tendency to talk too much to anyone was yet another part of my Bipolar disorder. However, recent events had made me reluctant to talk at all. Bipolar, the gift that keeps on giving.

I ended up having a few in this bar. I was left alone and enjoying my own company. I reflected back on my life and decided I had to do better. I was going to be a millionaire and live on a Caribbean island by the time I was forty. I had made a pretty good start before my illness kicked in. When your job requires you to be a strong communicator, mentally sharp and highly focussed, becoming a dribbling wreck doesn't help.

I left the bar around 12pm. I saw a club with neon signs that proclaimed to be the Playboy club. I was going to go back to the hotel, but I was wide awake and knew I would not sleep for a while yet. I entered this Playboy club. It was a bar with a bit of a dance floor. To my disappointment there were no Bunny Girls.

There was virtually no one there. I went and sat on a stool at the bar. I ordered a rum and coke. Mythos did not feel right in a club for some reason. After a while, yet another old man came and sat by me. He informed me that he was the owner of this Playboy club. He told me his life story which in many ways was like mine. He was almost certainly the result of a psychotic episode. Or I may have just been very drunk.

I left the Playboy club in the early hours of the morning. As I exited the building, I fell over. Now I really was John Bowles. I felt a pain in my right hand. I looked down. There was broken glass on the ground. I had put my hand out to break my fall and cut it just below the thumb. It would not stop bleeding. Not knowing why I lit up a cigarette and when I had smoked it down a bit, flicked the ash into the wound. It did the trick.

Over the next couple of weeks I continued to do this. Now and then I would rub the wound with any spirit I was drinking. Whiskey, ouzo, anything. I thought it would act like an antiseptic. I didn't think to go into a chemist and buy some antiseptic. Or it was a good excuse to drink more spirits.

Quite a few Greek people informed me I was crazy, which was a fair description. 'You will get a scar' they said. 'Good' said I 'I want one as a memento of my time in your beautiful country' Crazy English rude Greek word they would say. Normally I would know what the rude word meant, following my education in Greek swear words delivered by my young friends in Rhodes.

Later when the wound had healed, the scar looked a bit like the outline of Crete. I would get talking to a Greek man in a bar. I would tell him the scar looked like Crete. He would look and agree. Because it does. He would invariably ask me how I got it.

I would tell him it was from a knife fight with a Turk. I was deploying one of my Kung Fu blocking moves. I would show the man how that looks. He would be impressed. Unfortunately the Turks' knife caught my hand. Although I was being humble, I had to knock him out with a spinning head kick.

I know that the Greeks hate the Turks, and they all loved this lie. They probably knew it was a lie. But I always got a drink on the strength of it.

Apart from this Kos was pretty boring. I decided to follow the old man on the ferry's advice and go to Kalymnos.

I went to the ferry port. It took me quite a while to find the one for Kalymnos. I boarded yet another ferry. I love travelling on Greek ferries. A great way to top up your tan. Only on the upper deck though.

This was a short trip. We were soon there. We docked and I looked around. Nothing special I thought. I decided to head straight out to Vathy. There was a nearby bus with Vathy on it. The Greek spelling looked like baby to me. I saw this as significant. Perhaps it was.

I climbed on board. The bus started off. It was a normal road with the usual barren landscape except for the odd olive tree.

Then we crested a hill and things changed completely. The whole of the valley was laid out before me. There was a bright golden dome on a church off in the distance. I had only seen blue ones before. This one glistened in the bright sunshine. There were lots of bright, white buildings set in a sea of green. This was unusual for Greece, there wasn't a lot of greenery in the villages. Surrounding the village was a backdrop of tall hills. It was just possible to see tribes of goats, stepping impossibly on the steep slopes of the hills.

The bus came to a stop in the village. It was Vathy. A most magical place, it still shines bright in my memory after 33 years. I could go back but like many things it is probably best left as a memory.

I have found that when arriving in a new place it's a good idea to head for the nearest bar. This is where you can find out the best places to stay. It is also somewhere to get a drink.

I chose a taverna that was situated on the edge of the port. This became my favourite place to sit and ponder. Looking out to sea it was very calming and I could think more clearly there. I could almost forget about my condition. Almost but not quite. That is how it has and always will be. It was probably the best place that I have ever sat in. I wish I was there now.

A handsome looking chap sauntered over. He said 'G'day. What can I get you' He told me his name was Nick. He was to become a friend. I said 'Are you Australian'? He replied 'Nah mate. But I lived there for 20 years before coming back here. I lived in Sydney and worked as a chef in all the best restaurants. I was born here in Vathy'

He further told me that over half of the Greeks living on Kalymnos had gone to Australia then returned to the island having made their money. He was the same, he didn't have to work but he loved to cook. Sometimes, I would head to Nicks for some food and the place would be shut. He would be out fishing which he loved to do

After being in Greece for a while, it becomes second nature to just take things as they come. If he was shut I would either go somewhere else, or wait till he returned. Usually I waited. His cooking was the best I have ever tasted, before or since.

Before I left England a lady who I had done some business with took me to the Waterside Inn in Bray. Owned by the Roux family it has 3 Michelin stars. The food was excellent, the best of nouvelle cuisine. Nick's tasted better, and was a whole lot cheaper.

So I was chatting with Nick, having just walked into his Taverna. He asked me again what I wanted. I said I needed something to eat, but would like something to drink first. 'You look a bit stressed' he commented 'I'll get you a glass of my own wine. That will relax you'

He brought a litre carafe of this deep, ruby red wine. 'I thought you needed more than a glass, looking at how stressed you are' I didn't think I was stressed, but after a couple of glasses of Nick's home made red wine, I was so relaxed that I must have been on the verge of hysteria before.

If anything was ever good for the soul, it was that wine. The taste was divine. The texture was outstanding. It was better than any wine I had ever tasted.

I was wondering whether I was in another psychotic state and this was just a dream. Maybe it was Dionysius supplying me with this wonderful wine. If so, I might as well have some food as well.

I asked Nick what food he would recommend as he seemed to have a better understanding of my state of health than I did. He suggested his Moussaka. Home made of course. No microwave stuff from Tescos for Nick.

He disappeared for a while, returning with this impressive looking Moussaka set in a bed of Greek Salad. It was just burned enough for my taste. I tucked in. It was clearly Moussaka but definitely the best I had ever tasted in or out of Greece.

This is sounding a bit repetitive, but there was nothing that Nick cooked that wasn't the best I had ever had. It does make sense. He had been a top chef in Sydney, a place where they did not tolerate low standard cuisine in their best hotels.

Back home in his birthplace he cooked for love, not money. He could get most of the basics to create his meals locally. Lettuce, tomatoes, pepper and all the other ingredients to make a good salad were grown locally. The mince in his Moussaka came from the meat of the goats wandering around the nearby mountains. Feta cheese came from the milk those goats produced.

Then there was the sea. He would catch a lot of fish himself, swap some with locals for their produce and cook the rest. I never ate so much fish as when I was in Vathy.

I found that I loved Red Snapper. I had never heard of it before. Once I had eaten my Moussaka and finished most of my wine, I asked Nick if there was somewhere decent I could stay.

Vathy was not a tourist destination then. There were few places to stay and he inferred he would not recommend any of them. He was a friend already. He looked after me for the time I was in Vathy. Even when I went off the rails a little, as I sometimes did.

Nick told me that his friends were building a hotel in the harbour, across from his taverna. It was not fully complete, but there were rooms that could be usable, he thought. He would get in touch with them, he said.

Later this young woman came into the taverna where I was sitting sharing some wine with Nick. It was strange that his wine was strong but it never got you drunk. I found I preferred to not be drunk in Vathy.

The woman introduced herself. She was not Greek, she was from Melbourne. She had met her future husband in the Greek quarter. 'It wasn't the Saltwater cafe was it?' I asked. That was Maria's family restaurant. She looked puzzled and I explained the joke. 'You're on your way to Melbourne then' she said. 'You'll love it'

She told me that the hotel they were building was practically complete. It just needed some decoration and other bits and pieces. It was totally usable. She asked if I would like to see the rooms that were available. I said that I would love to.

We walked around the harbour to this big, brand new hotel. She took me in and showed me a couple of rooms. They were both fantastic, with large balconies facing the sea. I could see Nick's taverna from the balcony of both rooms. This was perfect. She said as they weren't ready to let rooms yet, I could have the room at a heavily discounted rate. I said yes please.

I went back to Nick's and finished off the wine. I thanked him for the food, the wine and the accommodation. He had done more for me in a couple of hours than anyone had done in years. Especially Mr. David and his 10%.

Whoever that old man on the ferry was, even if it was a previous incarnation of myself, he had done me a huge favour by sending me to this place. I ended up spending a couple of months in this small village and it helped heal me in many ways. Unfortunately not permanently.

There was a Greek family that often gathered around an Olive tree to the side of Nick's taverna. They would sit on the ground, or bring stools. They lived quite close.

They liked Nick and you could see he was fond of them. The makeup of the group would change , but there was a small group that was always there. It consisted of Grandad, Dad, Wife and daughter. The Dad was Giorgios, I remember his name. The daughter who was about five was called Poppy. I could never forget her.

Poppy and her Dad looked the same. They both had round faces with twinkling eyes. There was always a smile on their faces and they looked like they were permanently up to mischief. Poppy usually was.

Poppy used to teach me Greek. I would sit on the ground next to her and she would tell me how to say words such as flower and tree. She did teach me to say butterfly and birds. I can't remember those.

Poppy was too young to have learnt English so the teaching was conducted by her pointing at things and naming them. I had to repeat the word. When I pronounced the word incorrectly, she would look at me. I knew she was thinking you're silly. She would say the word again slowly and deliberately, staring at me all the time. I had to repeat it back and woe betide me if I got it wrong.

Preparing to write this, I looked up Vathy. Nick's taverna is now Poppy's taverna. I wonder?

At one point Nick asked me if I would like a Sunday Roast. Normally I would laugh at people who asked for a Sunday Roast when overseas. It doesn't seem right when in a foreign land that you should eat such an English meal. I knew that Nick would produce something extraordinary.

I went over to his place on Sunday. It was spectacular as expected. Roast goat meat instead of beef. Some beautiful roast potatoes, fluffy and crunchy. Many different types of vegetables in dishes around the table. Thick gravy made with his red wine.

It all looked delicious. There were several carafes of wine. I thought that's too much for me. Then in trooped Poppy and her Dad with Mum and Grandad in tow. I realised they were going to join me. This would normally annoy me, but with this delightful family I was more than happy. I looked forward to more lessons from Poppy. Roast goat, roast potatoes and more.

I had a wonderful time. Poppy taught me many words, all of which I promptly forgot. Luckily she never gave me any tests or I would have been the dunce of the class. I spoke to her Dad who had some English. I told him how proud he should be of his family. His always smiling face broke out into a huge grin. His little daughter joined in.

In the time I was there I had many lovely moments like this. One day I told Nick I had never eaten lobster. He got one of the local fishermen to go out and catch a couple for me. These guys went sponge diving regularly and could find lobsters and other crustaceans on the bottom of the harbour easily. They would dive in with no oxygen. They were under for what seemed ages then came up with something in their hands. Sponges, lobster, sea urchins whatever they could find.

You can keep the sea urchins I thought. But there were two lobsters. They were black. I said to Nick 'I thought they were red'. 'That's after they are cooked' Nick replied.

He cooked them and served them with salad and tiny potatoes, soaked in butter. I tried to get one claw open. He did not supply me with the normal implements for eating lobsters. I got a tiny piece of meat out and didn't like it. I don't like crustaceans much. I don't like crab, for example.

Although this lobster was expensive, I gave it to Giorgos and family. They got stuck in and devoured the lot in minutes. Giorgos was grateful. He didn't get to eat lobster very often, he said. I gathered they weren't a wealthy family. If you count wealth in money. In other ways they were very rich indeed.

I had great accommodation, great food and charming company. I could say here that something went wrong, but it didn't. I didn't get drunk and make a show of myself. I didn't fall foul of the law. There wasn't any there.

One day I realised that I had been several months on the islands and I should return to Athens to take the onward flight to Australia.

I said goodbye to everyone, Nick and Poppy in particular. I said I would return, but like in Canada never did.

I decided to drop into Ios on the way back. I had fond memories of being there with Michelle and Maria.

I took another ferry. I got off at Ios and quickly found my hotel from the last time I was there. I checked in. Again I took a shower and fell asleep on the bed. When I awoke it was dark. I went out onto the terrace. The geckos had moved out.

I went along the road out of the harbour. I found the bar in which I had met the girls. There was only the boss and a barman. I had a drink and then several more. I had my Sony Walkman strapped on. I looked a bit strange. They started to play music. Some people started to turn up. They clearly knew the owner and the barman. I didn't know anyone.

A couple of people moved onto the small area that was used as a dance floor. I decided to do my whirling dervish moves and was bumping into and knocking people over.

I was jumping up and down and spinning around when I felt a hand on my collar. It was the boss. He pushed me towards the door and threw me out. 'Don't come back' he shouted after me. I fell onto the floor, breaking my Sony Walkman.

I was walking back to my room when a shadowy figure approached me. He told me he was the police chief on the island. He told me that there had been a head in a bag found on the slopes beside the path leading up to the village the previous week. It was the remains of a tourist who had caused trouble on the island. Like me. If I didn't get off the island I would be next.

I went to my hotel and collected my belongings. It was about 2 am. I left and sat on the harbourside waiting for the first ferry out. I was absolutely terrified that someone would come down and cut my head off.

On reflection I am pretty certain that this was a psychotic event. Would the police chief approach a tourist who had drunkenly bumped into a couple of people in a small bar and threaten to cut his head off? It would seem a bit extreme and definitely would not help tourism on the island.

However I didn't know that at the time. The first ferry in was for Athens. I would have jumped on it if it was for the Outer Hebrides.

The ferry trip was always quite boring so I just sat on the Upper deck as I normally did, and topped up my tan. As we neared the Greek mainland we had to pass through the Isthmus of Corinth. The Corinth Canal is the only way through. I had never been this way before. The ferries I normally came on went straight to Piraeus.

The Corinth Canal is very narrow. There was less than a foot either side as we passed through. The captain must have been a superb navigator. It seemed inevitable that it would hit the sides at some point. But he got through without coming near.

As we cleared the other side a great cheer went up to praise the captain's incredible accomplishment

Chapter 22

Climbing Mount Olympus

When I eventually got to Athens, for some totally inexplicable reason I decided I wanted to climb Mount Olympus before leaving for Australia. It was something I had always wanted to do and now seemed as good a time as ever.

I took a bus to Litochoro, a village at the base of the mountain. I found a youth hostel there and checked in. I found out that there was a small group going up in the morning. I asked if I could join them. 'Sure' they said.

We left in the early morning. We took food and plenty of water. Several litres each. We set off, following the well worn path. At first it was just a path. Before too long it began to rise. After an hour or two we were about halfway up the mountain. Even there the views were spectacular.

We began to come across small troughs in the ground filled with snow. I found that strange. It was scorching hot, but there was snow. I scooped up a handful and rubbed it all over my face. The others did the same.

We came to a part of the climb where the path narrowed to about 18 inches. We had to edge along the rockface. It was like glass where many people had gone before. There was a drop of thousands of feet into the gorge below. This was not funny. I have always always had a fear of heights.

We got through it, but I realised we would have to do it again on the way down.

From thereon it got better. The views were amazing. With the clean air you could see for many miles. Small towns and villages appeared, dotted all over the landscape. It was just like the view from a plane, but without the window.

Once again I was back with Mr. Vale and his tales of the Iliad by Homer. I had spent more time there on this trip than I did in real life.

I imagined I was Zeus, casting lightning bolts down on the people below.

When we reached the top, there was a youth hostel. That seemed a bit incongruous to me. We entered and were greeted by the hostel manager. He told us the rules and showed us where we would be sleeping.

After that we gathered in the communal area with a few other climbers. Somehow alcohol appeared. I drank too much and went to bed.

The next morning I got up and had a quick wash and cleaned my teeth. I didn't hang about as the bathroom stank.

I met up with the others and we agreed to set out straightaway. We carried the water bottles we had brought with us. We had neglected to fill them up and they were only half full. Big mistake.

I had a hangover and a dry mouth so I drank a fair bit of water. We seemed to come to the small ledge quite quickly. I had been dreading it. Now it was much worse as I was dehydrated and hung over. I felt a bit wobbly.

I hung back and thought I might go back to the hostel and wait until I felt better. The rest were over and shouting at me to get moving. I stepped onto the ledge. Stupidly, I looked down. My head started to swim and I was certain I would fall. My heart was pounding. I gathered every bit of strength and courage I had and started moving again. Eventually I got through it. I was relieved and elated to have made it to solid ground.

One of the group said 'You took your time'. We carried on down. I was so happy knowing I would never have to face that again. I don't think I could.

We got a fair way down when we realised we were lost. The path we came up was nowhere in sight. Nobody had a compass. We could have used the sun to guide us. I knew it rose in the West and set in the East. Or was it the other way round? As we had no idea where we were headed there was little value in that knowledge anyway. The same would apply if we waited till night and followed the North star. We were definitely lost.

Our only option was to keep going. We wandered on getting nowhere. Our water ran out and I suddenly realised this was serious. People have died from lack of water. That will kill you a lot quicker than starvation.

We were all extremely thirsty by then. Every one of us was worried about what could very well happen. Someone called a halt so we could conserve energy. We stood looking at each other with no idea what to do. Then I thought I heard something. It sounded like faint laughter.

There was a high sand ridge to the side of the path we were on. I scrambled up it, which was not easy as I kept sliding back down, and was weak from exhaustion. I didn't think I could go on much longer.

When I reached the top and looked down, I started to howl with maniacal laughter. The others said what's up. I said 'There's a road down here. There are people walking it and a couple of tavernas'.

I rolled down the other side. Instead of going into one of the tavernas and having a beer, I found a kiosk and got some cold water. That tasted so good, better than any alcohol ever could.

We all went back to the hostel which wasn't far as we had ended up in the village in which it was situated. We all sat around and congratulated ourselves on our narrow escape. I don't know why. It was our own fault that we did not prepare properly. We didn't take enough water for the climb down. Most importantly we had not worked out our route down.

I decided it was definitely time to pack my bags and head for Oz.

I was already on the mainland so I took a bus to the airport. I arrived at Athens airport in the morning. It was now early September. I had told Michelle I would be in Australia by April. I had no excuse. I had planned to have a brief stop off in Athens before flying on. I had not phoned to say I was going to be late, which was inconsiderate of me.

I looked at flight times. There was an Olympic flight to Australia due out in about four hours. Most flights go to Perth from the UK but this one was direct to Tullamarine airport in Melbourne.

Four hours was not enough time to get to Athens and back. Not enough to have any meaningful time there anyway.

I went into a fast food place and got myself a burger and chips. Unfortunately anywhere I ate now was going to be compared with Nick's food. This was not even worth rating. The view wasn't quite as good either.

I checked in as soon as possible, to get a good seat. I always sit by the window. I like to look out, especially flying over mountains. I wondered whether we might go over Mount Olympus. I knew I wouldn't recognize it if we did. I've always thought there should be some sort of system to identify places as you fly over them. I have seen some spectacular sights when flying. Venice is pretty obvious, as is Paris. But mountains, valleys, rivers and general landscapes are practically impossible to identify.

Chapter 23

Continuing on to Oz

The next leg of the journey was from Athens to Bangkok. The first one took just over three hours. This one was going to be more than twelve hours. I was not looking forward to it. I couldn't even listen to music as my Sony Walkman had been broken when I was thrown out of the bar in Ios.

My fellow passengers began to embark. I like the Greek people, but they do like to talk. Fast and loud. Whilst I loved Poppy's family, when they were all gathered around the Olive tree it was a constant clash of voices as they all wanted to express their views at the same time. The sound was deafening. I often had to excuse myself as excessive noise is almost like physical pain to someone with Bipolar.

With a plane full of several hundred people, most of whom were Greek this was going to be a nightmare flight for me. Whilst they looked for their seats there was just constant background chatter.

But once they were settled in, the noisy talk started. It didn't help that I hardly understood a word that they said.

I suppose I should have been grateful that they didn't have chickens and goats with them as they frequently did on the Island buses.

The two people beside me were Greek. They talked at each other. They also talked at the Greeks in front and behind. I say at because there didn't seem to be much listening going on.

I don't know how I survived the flight, but I did. The first thing I planned to do in Bangkok airport was buy a Sony Walkman or something similar. I would have loved to have a set of those wireless earphones that link to your mobile phone. But yet again like the Central Heating back in Sutton Courtenay neither had been invented.

We were told within the first hour at Bangkok airport that there was a fault with our plane and we would be stuck there for eight hours, possibly more.

I was still working on Greek time, so that didn't seem too bad. I once waited a night and two days for a ferry that had been 'delayed'

I found a shop that sold lots of electrical and electronic equipment. Including the latest type of Sony Walkman. I tried it and the sound was brilliant. I had to try hard not to do my whirling dervish routine. Unfortunately the large number of cassettes I had brought with me did not fit this machine. The shop only had the one for demonstration purposes so I had to go elsewhere to find something to play on my new music machine.

I took my time looking. There was no rush after all. We had been told that we could not leave the airport. Bangkok is a very large airport with plenty to do. I enjoyed having a wander around. I found a shop selling cassettes that would fit my machine. I looked through them. There was no Pink Floyd or Cream.

What they had was current international artists like George Michael and Michael Jackson. Faith had been released the previous year. I quite liked it. I had been a fan of Michael Jackson for some time, but would not admit to it openly.

I bought those two and Holst's Planet Suite. I am partial to a bit of classical music, especially to help me wind down. I suspected I might need it for the final lap to Australia.

Having got my noise protection I went for a bite to eat. I found a cosy little restaurant serving authentic Thai cuisine. I had Thai green curry, which was delicious with noodles and several types of vegetables. I had never tasted Thai food before and enjoyed it. I had a few bottles of Chang, a Thai beer. I was quite content after this and went off to find myself a bench to grab some sleep before facing the next ordeal.

Before I knew it they were calling for us to board. I followed the queue and reached the aircraft. We climbed the steps and entered the aeroplane. I found my seat easily and as the gentlemen next to me started to talk at the people in front and behind, I stuck my George Michael cassette into my new machine, put on the headphones and was immediately carried away by George's voice.

I stayed like this, oblivious to the noise around me for a further twelve hours. This final leg of my journey was so much easier than the last one. I made a mental note to not travel back without musical accompaniment.

Everyone disembarked the plane. I stayed on. Once the crowds had cleared, chatting incessantly as they went, I found my way out of the aircraft. This time there was an air tunnel which ultimately took me to the main building.

I picked up my rucksack and headed for the arrivals hall. When I came out I saw Michelle. She did not look pleased.

'Where have you been? You were supposed to be here six months ago'. I was a bit surprised. Yes I was late, but she was only an acquaintance, not my wife. I said that I was sorry but my Mum had died unexpectedly and I had to return home.

It was a good thing that I had not been in Australia or I would have struggled to get home in time. This was true, but was in no way planned. I did admit to that.

She forgave me and we drove to her house in the suburbs. She introduced me to her family. Andrew, her older brother and Shashona her younger sister. Finally her Mother. A typical Jewish matriarch, I could tell she was not too impressed by this English Gentile.

I tried hard when I was in Melbourne but she just did not like me. Maybe it had something to do with the fact that I was going through a manic phase in my early days in her city and was acting bizarrely, even by my standards.

Michelle was an art teacher in a nearby school and was not around during the daytime for the first couple of weeks. In order to amuse myself I would don my strange garb and dance around their front room with Michael Jackson ringing in my ears.

I didn't know I was being observed, but if I did I probably would not have cared. My Bipolar had stepped up a notch. I was getting out of control. It was a good job I was in Australia, where they are more tolerant than in the Greek islands.

A couple of times I took a tram into the city and went clubbing. As usual, I made a complete show of myself. This was to become a common behaviour with me until I eventually got the help I needed. That was a long way off

Michelle was incredibly tolerant. She just ignored my outlandish behaviour. She knew the issue and just dealt with it. Nonetheless she must have wondered what she had let herself in for.

Her sister thought it was hilarious. I liked Shashona. She gave me a big fluffy Koala. A stuffed one. I still have it, although the dog has chewed its nose off.

Her brother Andrew was not sure. He worked in a bar in the city. I found out and went there to see him. The inevitable happened and I was asked to leave. He didn't seem to hold it against me.

Andrew did not embrace his faith. One day he grew a beard. I said to Michelle that it made him look like an Orthodox jew. She told him what I had said. He shaved it off the next day.

Thankfully, the Christmas break came. Michelle suggested we go on a trip. She fancied going into the middle, up to Coober Pedy through Alice Springs and eventually stopping at Ayers Rock (now Ularu)

We set off in her car, a fairly new Honda Civic. It was her pride and joy. Driving on the highways across Australia was like nothing I had ever experienced. True, I had travelled for many miles on the trans Canada highway with Bruce. But it did not have dead Kangaroos and various other animals strewn along the roadside.

One of the main methods of hauling goods around Australia is the land train. These are gargantuan lorries very long with many huge wheels with equally huge tyres. The roads are very long and very straight.

A trucker that I got talking to in Alice Springs told me that he owned his own rig, as do most of the land train drivers. He travelled at speed to get his load to wherever his destination might be. Due to the sheer size and weight of these vehicles, it was impossible to stop quickly. Like trains in this country it can take miles to stop. So they don't try.

He said if he slammed on his brakes when he saw a kangaroo or a cow wandering across the road in front of him it would be too late to avoid them and he would blow out at least one or two tyres which cost $1000 each.

This is why they have 'cow catchers' fitted to the front of their lorries. If they do hit anything, it won't damage the front of their lorry.

As a result there were dead Kangaroos all along every main road that I travelled on. Apart from in the cities of course. I didn't see any in Melbourne city centre.

Those that I did see were like statues frozen in time. Some were upright and looked like they were just taking a break. Others were on their sides or their backs. It was strange.

We left Melbourne fully loaded for the journey. Unlike my trip up Mount Olympus, Michelle had packed everything we might need. Especially lots of water. Many people have died from lack of water in the outback of Australia. It still happens. Michelle was determined we would not be joining them.

We headed out of Melbourne aiming for the centre as they call it. As soon as we were outside the city, we were into the bush. Most of the citizens of Australia live on the coast. Once clear of the towns and cities, you reach the outback pretty quickly.

We were sharing driving duties. It's difficult to imagine Australian roads living in the UK. They are very long and often completely deserted.

It is almost a surprise when you actually reach a town or city. You've been travelling through nothing for ages and then suddenly you are back in civilization.

We were heading for Alice Springs which is pretty much the centre of this huge continent. Michelle said we should stop at Coober Pedy on the way. I had never heard of the place.

Coober Pedy is the opal mining capital of the world. It was built by the opal miners who made their homes underground. Temperatures often reach 53 degrees in the Summer, so this was a way of escaping the blistering heat. They even built a church beneath the soil. There are other advantages to getting out of the open air.

Every time I stepped out of the car I would be attacked by swarms of flies. These are not ordinary house flies that are annoying but tend to leave you alone. These things are in your face, up your nose and in your mouth. Those hats with corks on that were used to portray Australians would be of no use at all. These kamikaze flies are deterred by nothing. I was constantly flailing my arms trying to keep them off. I looked like some manic human windmill.

The only way to escape them is to live underground or stay in your car. We couldn't live underground so we stayed in the car. We drove through the town. There was very little to see as the housing was mostly out of sight. There were virtually no plants as it is too hot for them to survive with little to no water either. A barren place, we decided to move on.

Passing the usual array of dead kangaroos in all kinds of poses, we were getting close to Alice. It was early evening and conditions were clear, as usual. Michelle said we should stop. I asked why. We were within a few miles of Alice Springs. She said that night falls very quickly in the centre.

When it does, the animals start to move. In the heat of the day there were few animals around. When night comes and the heat lessens, they go in search of food.

In my ignorance I decided to keep going. Suddenly it was black. Like someone had turned the lights out. It was not dark, it was black. The only lights were coming from the car. Suddenly a shape appeared in front of me. I had no time to react. There was a tremendous thump as I hit the cow that had decided to wander across the road at that particular moment.

I stopped the car and got out. The cow had disappeared. I hoped it was alright, although I doubt it. It was quite a thump. Cows are quite resilient though so maybe she had escaped. I wondered what a cow was doing there in any place. Surely there was no grass for her to munch on. Perhaps she was lost.

I also thought perhaps it had been another example of my psychosis. That is a constant possibility with this confusing 'illness'

When I saw Michelle's face I knew it wasn't. When I saw her car the next day I was certain it wasn't. Her nice new car, her pride and joy had the whole front end caved in. For some reason I said I would pay half. She accepted. I realise now I should have paid in full. It was entirely my fault. Michelle was a generous and kind person. What she saw in me I did not know. Maybe she was thinking the same thing.

We stayed in the car until day break. I had another look for the cow, but it was nowhere to be seen. I was expecting to see its dead carcase near the road. She wasn't there and I was relieved. Not because I was worried about having to recompense the farmer who should have had her penned in.

Because I genuinely cared for the welfare of the animal. I have always liked cows since I was a boy on the farm in Sutton Courtenay. Even if they did poo on my head.

We drove into Alice. The locals dispensed with the Springs, much as we left out the Head and Bell in Abingdon. Just saves time.

Alice was quite boring. Just another Australian town. We were both very tired so we booked into a hotel and stayed there until the following morning, mostly sleeping. I was having a bit of a bad time. My head was full of racing thoughts. I found it difficult to sleep. I was probably feeling guilty for wrecking Michelle's car.

I still am if I'm honest. I shouldn't have done it. I did it so I should have paid for it. I had the money. I am a bit of a skinflint I suppose.

Michelle decided that she would drive, for a while at least. Our next port of call was Ayers Rock. That is what it was called when I was there. It is now Uluru, which is the aboriginal people's name for it.

The rock was discovered in 1872 by a guy called William Gosse. He named it after Sir Henry Ayers who was Chief Secretary of Southern Australia. Why not name it after himself? Seems a bit sycophantic to me.

The rock wasn't really discovered. It had been part of Aboriginal culture for thousands upon thousands of years.

It was new to the settlers, 149 years ago. It is entirely right that it should revert to its proper name.

We were driving along when something began to appear in the distance. It was Uluru. It was ages before we got close.

It is absolutely enormous. It is also breathtakingly beautiful. It is almost red in colour and in the evening it does actually turn red for the couple of seconds before the black comes down .

There were people climbing the rock. That has recently been banned, which the aboriginal people have been demanding for years. Thousands of tourists' feet have turned the sloping sides of this monolith to glass. It makes it even more dangerous than it already is.

I considered climbing it myself. From the very bottom of the rock there is a quite easy bit to climb. It goes up about 20 feet after which there was a guide rope to hold onto. This easy bit was known as Chicken Shit rock. Excuse the language but that is what it was called. Probably not by the tour guides.

It was called that because if you got to the top but couldn't go further, you were chicken. I didn't even get halfway. I saw a lot of plaques with the names of people who had fallen from the rock and been killed. That put me off somewhat. I tell people that this was the reason for me coming down. Actually it was because I was chicken.

We decided to walk around the base of Uluru. I was expecting a nice, casual walk. It was to a point but after a few hours we realised we might not make it before the blackout blind came down. We picked up the pace and made it back just before dark. It had taken us 8 hours.

I was glad we walked around rather than climbing up Uluru. We got to see much more that way. Obviously it wasn't a conscious choice. It was based on me being a chicken. But it paid dividends.

There were caves at several points on our journey. Some had Aboriginal wall paintings. A few depictions of Kangaroos, platypus and other indigenous animals. Some were typical Aboriginal designs. Abstract pictures made up of thousands of multi coloured dots. Seeing these was far more interesting than hauling myself up a huge rock. A lot less dangerous too.

Being an art teacher Michelle was fascinated by the complexity of these designs. She had brought a set of pens and a small pad with her. She stopped at one and insisted on drawing it even though it was getting late.

I couldn't object as I had nearly written her car off. She seemed to have forgiven me, or at least put her anger on hold for later.

When you are quite close to the rock, you realise that the surface is not flat at all. There are huge indents in it. One looks like a giant head. They call that one the brain. It is head shaped but inside is a lot of loose rock which looks like a brain within the head.

There are many more that probably all have names, but I didn't know anyone to ask.

Reluctantly we had to leave Uluru. I felt sorry for those people who had got hot and sweaty dragging themselves over that huge rock. I was pleased that I was chicken.

I had noticed that when I was with Michelle, I had virtually no symptoms of Bipolar. She had a very calming manner and didn't seem to become too angry at me for the car incident. Maybe she has reached her final life and will be off to the Astral Plane as I was told I would. I was beginning to seriously doubt that the lady in the nunnery had got it right, at least as far as I was concerned.

My behaviour could be pretty stupid at times. Without Michelle and on my own, I struggled. I tried to be careful not to put myself into situations that might be a trigger. At this stage I was still 12 years away from a diagnosis and not fully aware of what those triggers could be.

On the way back to Melbourne, we stopped off at a roadside bar. There was nobody inside except for a small aboriginal man. He looked like he might be drunk, a lot of his people were often drunk. I was told it is because alcohol had never been part of their culture and they have little tolerance of it.

I went to the bar and ordered a glass of Victoria Bitter and a Coke for Michelle. I had found that VB was delicious and drank that whenever possible. I had taken the drinks back to the table where we were sitting, when the small aboriginal man came over. He mumbled something. He was drunk, but not at the falling over stage.

He had some sort of stick in his hand. It looked like a straight boomerang. I asked him what it was. He decided to give me a demonstration and stabbed it hard into my stomach. I yelped. It hurt. I saw Michelle from the corner of my eye, falling about with laughter.

I am not sure whether he was responding to my question or had just decided to stab me. I think the latter in all probability. He was looking at me belligerently. I thought he might do it again. Who knows where this time.

I asked him if he wanted to sell the stick. He started to raise it. I thought about using one of my spinning, kicking in the head moves. I realised that he hadn't got a clue what I was saying but when I spoke he saw it as a cue to attack me.

I pulled out a $20 note and waved it at him. He stared at it and tried to grab it. I pointed at the stick. He looked confused. I took hold of the end of the stick. He looked like he might kill me. Until I gave him the $20. He started to head towards the bar. He hadn't let go of the stick, but I managed to wrench it out of his hands. He stopped and turned towards me. He clearly thought I had just given him the $20. He was not aware that he had made a financial transaction.

The pull of the bar was too strong so he abandoned his stick and went to get himself a beer. $20 would buy him quite a few so we had time to drink up and go before he realised what had just happened.

As we drove off, Michelle took great delight in making yelping noises like the one I emitted after being stabbed. She told me that what I had was an aboriginal stabbing stick. There was another much bigger stick which was used to batter you round the head with. My stick was to finish you off with a stabbing motion. I was just glad he didn't have the bigger stick with him. I have the stabbing stick in the loft.

It was time for Michelle to head home. The new term was about to start. It took another couple of days to get to Melbourne. We were beginning to get a bit fed up with one another. Maybe we spent too much time together.

I think Michelle was getting tired of my bizarre behaviour. She knew the problem and that I couldn't help it. That didn't change the fact that I was and am difficult to live with. This is beginning to sound a lot like my relationship with my Mum

We arrived back at Michelle's house. It was a big place, tastefully furnished, light and airy. There was a small garden with a built-in barbecue. That wasn't used whilst I was there.

Her mother worked in marketing. She had just been given the Hugo Boss contract for Victoria and was very busy. She still managed to find time to show her contempt for me. I was not sure why she disliked me so much. Maybe it was because I am a gentile.

Perhaps she didn't think I was good enough for her daughter. Then again, she might not have appreciated me making a mess of her pristine floor coverings whilst trying to do a moonwalk, listening to Michael Jackson at full volume at 2 in the morning. Probably all three.

Roshashana got on well with me. She was a bit bonkers too. Andrew wasn't bothered either way. As Michelle and I were drifting apart, I decided to go travelling on my own.

Everyone was happy to see the back of me. I was relieved to escape the constant tension in that house. Of course it was me causing the tension, so it might come with me.

I thought about where to go. We had been up the middle to the centre of Australia. Michelle and I, despite everything, had planned to go up the East coast through Sydney and Brisbane and further on to the islands next school holidays.

Logically the place for me to go was Western Australia. I would head for Perth. I went to the central bus depot and bought a ticket.

The trip took just over two days and one night. The bus did not stop except for a brief break to look at the Great Australian Bight which is an enormous bay beneath a 200 metre drop. There are often right whales out at sea, and it is a popular spot for whale watching. Unfortunately there were none when we stopped off. It was still a spectacular landscape.

There were two drivers. One slept while the other drove. There was a cabin for the drivers to sleep. We had to sleep where we sat. There weren't that many people so I could spread out.

There were some shifty looking characters on the bus, so I was a bit worried about sleeping and someone stealing my rucksack. There wasn't anything of value in it, but I didn't want to lose my clothing. I would be a bit smelly after a few days in Perth.

I didn't get much sleep. Although it was a long trip, it didn't bother me after the days I had spent on a mini bus to Rimini. Unfortunately there was no opportunity for a pernod drinking contest with the driver.

We reached the Nullarbor desert which is a huge barren wasteland that has to be passed through to reach Perth. Going through the Nullarbor is a road called 90 mile straight. It is called this because it is 90 miles in length and does not have a single bend in all that distance. The Aussies tell it like it is.

The bus trip was boring but at least I had my music. My choice was a little bit of swaying with George or another moonwalk down the middle of the bus with Michael. I sensibly chose George.

Eventually we arrived in Perth. We were dropped off at the central bus station. When I stepped out into the bright sunlight I saw a city of tall buildings but plenty of greenery. It was best described as a pretty city. I thought I would enjoy it there.

I had checked out where the nearest backpackers hostel was. These are like youth hostels with alcohol. You don't have to do chores either. I had found them in Australia, but now they are all over the world. There is even one in Oxford. The hostel wasn't too far, so I headed off to find it. I got there quite easily which was a rare thing for me. I went in and saw a reception desk in front of me.

The man behind the desk asked me what I wanted. A bit obvious really, I thought. This is a backpackers and I have a rucksack. I didn't want to be sarcastic so early so I said I'm looking to book a room.

'How long for' he asked. 'I am not sure' I replied. 'Might be a few days, possibly longer' 'I'll put you down for a week to start with' 'That's fine' He told me my room was on the fourth floor and gave me a key.

There was no lift but getting up the stairs was not a problem. I found the room. There were two beds so I was sharing with one other person. That's fine I thought. Much better than sharing a room with seven other smelly boys.

I was tired after the bus ride from Melbourne, especially as I had hardly slept last night. I thought I would have a quick nap. It was mid-day

A sudden noise woke me up. It was my roommate. 'Hiya' this guy said. 'Hello' I said back. 'I'm George' he introduced himself. 'My name's Arthur' I reciprocated. 'Where are you from Arth?' He sounded Welsh. 'Sutton Courtenay' 'Haven't heard of that. where is it?' he enquired. 'It's near Oxford' 'I've been there. That's where they've got those gargoyles' 'They're grotesques actually' I said.

George asked what I was doing there. I explained what I had done in Australia so far. He said he meant what was I doing in Perth and in this hostel in particular. I told him about Michelle being in school so I had decided to come to Perth on my own.

He looked like he was thinking can't this bloke give me a straight answer. I'll keep it brief, I decided. Not so much detail.

'Why this hostel?' I thought 'what's with all these questions?'. A slight paranoia started. Is he after something? I told him that I had chosen this one because it was a Backpackers so there were no chores and a big bonus, they served alcohol.

'Exactly my reasons too' laughed George. The paranoia went. We're going to get on, I thought.

'So what are your plans Arth, are you going to work?' I wasn't sure I liked being called Arth by a stranger but I would give it a go. 'No, I don't have a work visa' I said. Plus I didn't have to work. I kept that to myself.

I asked him if he had a visa. He told me 'Yes, I've got a job working in a laundry in town. The money's not bad but the job is awful. I'll save up enough to buy an old Holden then I'll be off'

A Holden is a car that is commonly used by people travelling in Australia. They are cheap and reliable. People buy them, usually travel the road that encircles the whole of Australia then sell them on, often making their money back.

Time was getting on. 'What are your plans for tonight?' George asked. 'I need to get some food. Then I'll probably have a drink or two. I replied 'Is it OK if I join you?' George asked. 'That would be great,' I said. It would be good to have some company. George seemed like a decent bloke

I needed a shower. George said he did too. When we were ready, we rendezvoused back at the room. 'Any idea where to eat?' I asked him. 'The food here is not too bad. It's cheap as well' 'Sounds good to me' The dining area was spacious and clean. We went up to the counter and ordered food. I said 'I'll have steak and chips. Have you got VB?' yes they had. I like it more and more, I thought.

We ate our meals. Very nice too. A few more VBs were consumed. George was drinking Fosters, but there's no accounting for taste.

I was quite content where I was but George suggested we go into town. He said that he knew a great little bar with a pool table. He asked if I played pool. I said yes, but I was not too good. So off we went. I was feeling good. As always the bubble remained in place, but the paranoia had subsided. Shifting faces and distant voices were normal, but I did not feel panicky. I didn't feel like doing the whirling dervish thing either.

We arrived at the bar. It was just a run of the mill Australian bar. There was a pool table in the middle. Someone came over to George and said 'Hi' George said hello to him and introduced me. He said 'This is my new friend Arthur. He's from Oxford'. His friend enquired of me 'Is that near London?' I said 'Yes, quite near, what's your name, by the way?' 'Bruce' he replied.

George and I went to the bar. With our drinks, we went to join Bruce and his friends at the pool table. George put his name up for a game. He suggested I do the same. I said I would give it a miss this time.

When George's game came up, he proved to be a bit of a hustler. They were playing winner stays on. George kept winning and whilst he did, I kept drinking.

I woke up next morning with a massive hangover and several new bruises. 'What happened?' I asked George.

He said 'You were hilarious. You drank a lot of beer and moved onto spirits later. You ended up doing some strange kind of dance. It was a mixture of moonwalking, break dancing and spinning around trying to kick people in the head. That last bit was when you fell over and got those bruises'

'I am so sorry. Your friends must think I am a total waster.' 'No, He said. They're Australian. They think you are a star. They want you to go back tonight'

'I'll have to pass, I'm afraid' I didn't believe that his friends thought that. I could not face them as I was certain that in reality they thought I was a fool. I felt really guilty. That's the problem with Bipolar. You always fear the worst.

I spend a lot of time reflecting back and trying to work out whether something has actually happened and if it has, is my recollection of it correct. I have often got upset or angry about something only to find I was completely wrong in my reading of the situation. I suppose that could just be a misunderstanding. Or it could be a symptom of Bipolar.

That is the biggest problem with this condition. I am having to use my brain to work out if my brain is working properly. It's so confusing!

I didn't stay that long in Perth. One day I went to the WACA which is the cricket ground based in Perth. Many international games are played here. I went with a couple of others from the hostel to watch the West Indies play Australia.

I'm not normally a fan of cricket, but playing at this level is different to the village green version of the game. It was quite fast, which I didn't expect.

Someone told me that the huge man standing in front of us was Joel Garner, nicknamed Big Bird. He stopped everything that was headed for the boundary.

After the match we went back to the hostel. I had found that the food there was as good as anywhere. The guys from the cricket joined me. During the general conversation one of them asked me if I had been to Monkey Mia yet? I said no, what is that?

He said that it was a place further down the Western coast where you could meet and swim with wild dolphins. That is the kind of thing I love to do. He told me there was a bus that went straight there from Perth bus station. He warned that it was a 9 hour drive. Just a short trip then, I said.

Early next morning I got on the bus to Monkey Mia. We left at 7am and even I could work out that we should be there by 4pm, if we didn't stop. We actually got there at 3.30pm. There was a guide who told us that it would be the next day before we were likely to see any dolphins. There were no guarantees we would see any at all.

I am quite philosophical about these things. These are wild animals. If they turned up all the time, on time and balanced balls on their noses, you would suspect that they weren't truly wild.

I went to find a suitable place to stay the night. I checked into a small hotel and got my head down. After a couple of hours, I got up and had a shower. Putting on some clean clothes, I went out to find something to eat.

There was a little Italian place near the hotel. I went in and had a plate of spaghetti bolognese with some grated parmesan on top. It was very nice washed down with a half bottle of chianti.

There was no drunkenness that night. I was looking forward to seeing the dolphins, hopefully, and wanted all my senses to be firing as best they could.

We were told the previous day that if the dolphins did choose to put in an appearance, it would be early to mid morning. I made sure I got there early. I did not want to miss them.

Quite a crowd had gathered. I was feeling a bit anxious. I concentrated on the prospect of seeing and paddling with dolphins. I would not be swimming.

I was imagining a headline 'English man drowns whilst swimming with dolphins. His Uncle Richard is reported to have said 'I couldn't save him this time'

One of the guides said 'Here they are' I couldn't see anything. I said 'Where?' She pointed towards the horizon, and I could just make out a small dorsal fin, way off in the distance.

It got bigger and was joined by a dozen more. Then they were just a couple of hundred yards out. Jumping, spinning in mid-air and performing all sorts of aquabatics. What a glorious sight it was. I've seen reports that the dolphins in Monkey Mia are tame and perform to order. Nonsense.

These were clearly wild, free dolphins. Not a single rubber ring in sight. They were not performing for us, they were just loving life, as dolphins do. They did come in very close as the guides were offering up buckets of fish for them. This did not make them tame. It just made them sensible. Free food? Yes please.

Because they were wild you had to respect them. That's what the guide said. She told us that we could approach them, swim with them if they would let us. But in the shallows, just stroke them. They liked that.

She said that whatever you do, do not cover their blowholes. This is their only way of breathing and would cause them great distress if you did.

One particular dolphin seemed to have taken a shine to me. Perhaps because I stroked her constantly. She rolled on her back and let me tickle her belly. Not like many girls I had met before.

Suddenly there was an horrendous scream. There was a guy holding his hand in the air, blood streaming down his arm.

The guide immediately knew what had happened. She said to him 'Did you obstruct the blowhole' He said yes, he wanted to see what would happen. You could tell the guide wanted to say 'Well now you know, you idiot' Instead she took him off for treatment.

I looked at my dolphin and she looked back. I reckon she was thinking what an absolute (something rude). He deserved to get an almighty bite. Good for her friend.

If I could have high fived her I would. I just gave her a stroke. Then she was off. I'm sure she waved a flipper as she left.

Having had one of the most memorable experiences of my life, I went back to my hotel. I thought about that morning and how it made me feel so good. After my initial panic, I was fine.

My thoughts were distracted by the dolphins. Maybe this was a way to deal with my problem. I still didn't know it was bipolar of course. I tried to think how I could use the knowledge I had gained to try and lessen the impact of my condition.

Maybe I could take myself back to the feelings of joy whilst being with my dolphin. Perhaps this could become a method for the future. Sitting down with Poppy learning how to say 'butterfly' in Greek was another precious moment.

The more I thought about it, the more wonderful experiences I realised I had to draw on. Whales on Vancouver Island. Seeing the Dalai Lama and having him smile at me.

I can visualise these things when on my own and they always make me happy. It's not so easy when I am in a crowd or anywhere when I am not alone, to be honest. I have never got rid of the 'bubble' and voices will always be disjointed, particularly my own.

I can't stand groups of people chattering away inanely, especially when I can't escape them. This seems to happen a lot in my current job. I frequently have to take myself off to the loo, to sit alone and think about my dolphin. My colleagues must think I am incontinent.

Rather than head straight back to Perth, I decided to stay another night. I wandered around the town, but there was not much to see. I went back to my room and relaxed until early evening. Then I showered and changed.

I headed to a nearby bar. There were a couple of people who had been on the beach that morning. Apparently the guy who got bitten was American.

We all had a good laugh at his expense. Until he walked in, hand in bandages.

'How's your hand?' Someone asked him. 'It hurts a lot' he said. 'You won't be doing that again will you?' I said. I was annoyed at his selfish behaviour. Being American, he didn't understand my sarcasm. 'What does that mean?' he said. 'It means that you won't be blocking off a dolphin's only means of breathing in the future' He looked confused. But then he was stupid.

I caught the bus back to Perth in the morning. I had not got drunk the night before. Perhaps I was beginning to learn how to handle this thing without having to completely blot it out with alcohol.

We arrived in Perth at tea time. I went to the hostel to find that George had moved on. He must have got his Holden and set off on the next leg of his journey. Good luck to him I thought.

I didn't see any point in staying, so I left the next day, taking the bus back to Melbourne.

Michelle told me she was not ready to take our trip up the Gold Coast. The schools had not yet broken up. I thought she just didn't want to go with me. I was not sure if that was true, or whether it was paranoia.

She said she would not be ready to travel for a few weeks. I had met a guy from Sydney back in Abingdon. The girls had told him about me and he came round looking for somewhere to stay. His name was Mike and he was a thoroughly decent bloke.

I had put him up for about a month. Instead of getting on with business I took him around Oxford and other local places. He said that if I was ever in Australia I should look him up.

I decided to take him at his word. I rang him and he said sure come on up. I took the overnight train to Sydney. It was luxurious compared to British trains. I had a cabin with a proper bed and slept for much of the trip.

Mike met me at the station. He was driving a BMW special AGM or something. It looked expensive, because it was. It turned out that Mike had some big deal job in computers. He was doing all right.

We went back to his apartment. It was a big three bed affair. It was on the ground floor. There was a decked area which led into the bush. Wild animals were literally yards away. Wombats would come onto the decking at night. There was a friendly Kookaburra who would come onto the decking at any time, including during the day. This bird used to be known as the 'laughing jackass' It certainly made a very loud laughing noise.

Although we were so close to nature, we were also close to the city. From the road at the front of his apartment you could get a bus into the city centre. If you left from the back, you could easily be lost and in trouble within less than half a mile.

IT specialists were in high demand and short supply at that time. Mike was highly experienced in the field and very well paid. Apart from his BMW, He also had a Piper Comanche aeroplane and had a private pilots licence. He did have part shares in it rather than own it outright, but I was still impressed.

One day he took me out for a flight. I had never been in such a small plane. Initially it was quite scary. There was nothing much between me and a few thousand feet drop. I felt much like I did on Mount Olympus.

The view beneath me made me forget this fear. Mike flew over the Sydney suburbs. Most of the houses seemed to have large swimming pools. It was very green for such a hot country.

Then this huge metal structure appeared below us. It was the Sydney Harbour Bridge. The 'Coathanger' as the locals call it. Mike told me that he had to get special permission to fly through this particular airspace. I felt honoured

He banked left and flew straight over the Opera House. That iconic building was immediately recognisable. This whole trip was almost surreal. Very few tourists would get to see these world famous landmarks from above. Not this close up.

That was the best part of my stay by far. Mike took me to a diverse range of places in the time I was there. Quite an eclectic mix. One day he took me to a place called King's Cross. It was nothing like the train station in London. It was in fact the main red light district in Sydney. Drugs and prostitution are rife there.

I did not know this at the time. Mike did not tell me anything. He took me into a rather dingy looking building. Inside there were rows of seats set out like a theatre or cinema. I didn't know which it could be. I found out that it was closest to a theatre, but the acts were not as you would find in a Shakespearian play.

There were a small number of rather seedy looking gentlemen dotted all around the auditorium. Suddenly the stage curtains parted. A single spotlight fell on this rather unattractive woman, who proceeded to remove her clothes to the common striptease music. I don't know it's name.

I felt a bit awkward and looked at Mike who was grinning from ear to ear. It wasn't the show that was amusing him. It was my reaction. I realised I had been set up. He must have found the worst strip club in King's Cross to take me to.

I am certainly not a prude, but if beauty is in the eye of the beholder, I was not beholding much beauty here.

Things got considerably worse when several women of similar stature and countenance started to pass amongst the audience. I saw several of the seedy looking members of the audience disappear backstage.

I felt like someone at a comedy gig trying to avoid the gaze of the comedian looking for a victim.

One of these women approached me and asked if I would like to accompany her backstage. I couldn't think of anything I would like less. I mumbled 'no thank you' I noticed Mike almost doubled over in silent mirth.

I had to congratulate Mike on a well executed plan to embarrass me. It certainly succeeded. I did see the funny side. Eventually.

A totally different experience was a trip to Sydney zoo. It is much like any zoo anywhere in the world, apart from the large collection of indigenous animals many of which are marsupials. The most famous of these is the kangaroo, which everyone knows carries its' young in a pouch

Some may not realise that the Koala is a marsupial and not a bear. I only know because I was told so by one of the keepers in Sydney zoo.

When I was at university training to be a Careers Adviser I was tasked to prepare a group talk to a class of year 10 students. The subject matter was entirely up to me. I thought of the interesting fact that whilst most people talk of the Koala Bear, that is in fact incorrect.

I did a drawing of a koala looking embarrassed baring a red backside to the viewer. I may have been inspired by my experiences of being caned by Derek Hurd.

I explained this fascinating fact to a class of disinterested 15 year olds. I unveiled my excellent drawing and said this is the only Koala bare that you will see! In fact it is not a bear, it is a marsupial. Yes, it was highly tenuous. I was relying on the amazing fact that a Koala is not a bear.

It failed. Several of the class were talking to each other. One boy had his feet on the desk. Another one was chatting up the girl in front of him.

We hadn't yet completed the part of the course on effective classroom management, so I did not know what to do. I asked the class what they thought of this incredible fact. Luckily, I did not get the response that I would now expect.

Some school kids can be hard work. I should know, as I was one of the worst. At the start of every lesson, we had to take an attendance record. There was always a Micky Mouse and sometimes a Luke Skywalker from Star Wars fans. When I first saw Huw Janus it made me laugh. After a further 10 times the joke was wearing thin. Huw is Welsh for Hugh.

Mike did an excellent job of keeping me entertained and even with the odd wind up, I enjoyed it all.

I had kept in touch with Michelle and one day she told me she was ready to start our journey up towards the Gold Coast. I could have flown back, but I think I mentioned previously that I don't like to spend money unnecessarily. I took the train.

I arrived in Melbourne central station. I took the tram to St. Kilda, where Michelle lived.

Once ready, we set out along the East coast of Australia. Michelle seemed to have forgiven me for driving her car into a cow. However she chose to do all the driving herself.

We were heading along the East coast with our final destination being the Whitsunday islands. This is a group of 74 islands, most of which are uninhabited. I had never heard of them, but Michelle had always wanted to go there. She and Maria had both said whilst they were 'doing' Europe, that they had never 'done' Australia.

Our first stop on the journey was Sydney. Michelle had been there before and I had already 'done' it. So we booked into a cheap hotel near the freeway we were travelling on, ready to move on in the morning.

We grabbed a McDonalds and had a few beers in the hotel after. We talked about our future, or lack of it. We hadn't done much of that so far. I don't think either of us thought we were in love. We did talk about the idea of a 'marriage of convenience'. My visa was about to run out and marriage would enable me to stay in Australia whilst we figured out what we both wanted.

Michelle said I could get a three month extension on my visa quite easily. We would be away for about 2 weeks, so could sort it out when we got back to Melbourne. That made sense. A bit more time to decide what to do.

In the morning we resumed our journey. The first place on Michelle's itinerary was Fraser Island. Apparently it is the world's largest sand island, stretching over 120 Kilometres. We couldn't take the car onto the island as only four wheel drive vehicles were allowed, because of the sand.

That meant Michelle's plans to drive round the island were not going to be possible. Neither of us were keen on organised tours, so we took the ferry and decided we would see what we could find.

Fraser island has a diverse range of animals, including dingoes, possums and the occasional saltwater crocodile.

We were walking along the top of a beach just below the tree line when a crocodile appeared in front of us, coming out from the trees. I shouted and turned to run. The last thing you should do, as a crocodile can outrun a human.

Michelle said 'it's a Goanna you drongo' Just a lizard. This lizard was at least 5 feet long and looked a lot like a crocodile. Unless you knew it was a Goanna which looks nothing like a crocodile.

This Goanna was eating a smaller one, it's tail and back legs hanging out of the bigger lizard's mouth. Altogether it didn't appear to be a reptile I would want to spend time with, crocodile or not.

Fraser island is a truly stunning place with white sandy beaches, mangrove swamps and rainforests. The thing that I remember most about it is being frightened by this carnivorous monster lizard.

We got back on the road and continued to head for the Whitsundays. We passed Brisbane on the way but Michelle said it wasn't worth a visit. The Australian girl that my lodger Paul met in Corfu was from Brisbane. I doubted we would find her if we stopped.

I remember getting to a place called Hamilton Island. That is one of the Whitsunday Islands. It is a small place, only five kilometres square. Cars are not allowed on the island, not that one is needed. The Great Barrier Reef is nearby.

It was really hot when we got there. We got into our swimming costumes and laid on the beach. There was a small jetty which went a short way into the sea. People were standing at the end of it and pointing.

I went over to explore. When I reached the end of the jetty, I saw what everyone was so excited about. The sea was crystal clear and I could see every imaginable colour and type of fish. It was as if they were suspended in mid air, the seawater was so clear.

I noticed a couple of people snorkelling and thought that must be incredible. I had snorkelled in the Greek Islands many times, but never amongst such a myriad of colourful fish. I found a small shop just off the beach selling snorkels. I told Michelle my plan. 'Whatever' she said enthusiastically.

I went and bought my snorkel. I did not want the flippers or the speargun the proprietor tried to sell me. Why would anyone want a speargun, I thought. Shooting a clown fish would not be very nice.

I got myself set up and waded into the water. The sea was like a warm bath. It was full of salt so when I got out to my normal limit I could easily float without having to make any effort.

I went out further to a point where I could not touch the bottom. I knew I would not sink and was confident that I would not drown. I was floating looking at the fish beneath and around me. I was in my own world and had seldom felt so at peace.

Suddenly I became aware of a nearby presence. I turned slowly and saw a large shark swimming silently alongside me. Of course, I behaved in a calm fashion and started to swim slowly to the shore.

In reality I did the same as I did with the crocodile/lizard. I panicked. I started to flail my arms around in an attempt to swim. When I managed to get within my depth I tried to run towards the shore. Anyone who has tried that knows it is impossible. If the shark wanted to eat me, it would have done so and retired for a postprandial nap by now.

I got to shallow water and ran as fast as I could. I heard myself shouting 'Shark! Shark!' As I reached the beach, I must have looked terrified. I was, Jaws had nearly got me.

I saw a guy laying on the sand in front of me. He was laughing. I didn't think that was very nice as I had narrowly escaped certain death only seconds earlier.

'They're only basking sharks round here you great Galah. They won't hurt you!'

I found out later that a Galah is a pretty stupid bird, native to Australia. On reflection, I felt pretty stupid.

In my defence as a Pom I am not used to meeting sharks in the sea. I did not know what type of shark this was. I only knew of the ones that bite people in half in popular films.

Of course Michelle had witnessed all of this. As I walked towards her she tried to pretend that she did not know me. As I drew close she said 'you really are a Pommie Drongo'. What is that?

Michelle announced that it was time to return to Melbourne. Having narrowly escaped death on two separate occasions I had to agree. It had taken us a week to get here and would take almost as long to get back.

There was nothing particularly noteworthy on our return journey. We stopped off in a few places just to rest on our long trip. I did notice that there were no dead animals lining our route. It must only be the roads into the centre where that happens.

We arrived back in Melbourne. At Michelle's place nothing much had changed. Her Mum was indifferent to me, which was an improvement on contempt. Shashona continued to tell me I was mad, which I could not deny. I informed her that she was too, which amused her.

Andrew maintained his cool aloofness.

The next day, Michelle took me to some office in Melbourne to get my visa extended. I was expecting some sort of inquisition. I had to fill in a form and that was it. Another three months in Oz.

Michelle seemed to want me to stay. She arranged an interview for me with a Melbourne based recruitment company. I remember going to this high rise office block and taking the lift to one of the top floors.

I was met at the lift door by the gentleman who was my prospective employer. I had not packed a suit when I left the UK so I had to wear my best jeans and T-shirt.

We went into his office, which took up the whole floor. We were near the top of the building. The view was stupendous. The whole of Melbourne spread out before me from the Yarra River to the suburbs beyond.

He took out a bottle of wine. Australian wine was virtually unknown in Europe at that time but it was a very tasty glass of wine that he handed me. He introduced himself to me, but I can't remember his name. Not because of the wine, I just cannot remember his name. He told me that the wine we were drinking came from his own vineyard.

He told me that he owned some famous Australian rugby team too. Sydney something. I don't know if this was supposed to impress me, but it wasn't working. Eventually he got onto telling me about his recruitment business. It was a standard recruitment agency. Working for any agency is basically a sales job. Trying to get companies to employ your candidates. Or supplying contract labour.

I had no experience with that type of recruitment business. I knew I would struggle. If I couldn't sell my own business, how could I expect to sell his. I thanked him for his time, and left the building. I doubt that he would have offered me a job. I wouldn't.

I was in Australia for just over a year. For a proportion of that time I was travelling. I didn't take the traditional route going around the country, but covered more miles by travelling to and from my base in Melbourne. I got to see the centre, which many people who travelled the perimeter road did not.

I missed Darwin and some of the cities and towns at the top end of Australia. I did get to Cairns which is way up there. I cannot remember how I got there, but I know I stayed in a hostel, so I must have travelled alone.

All I can remember about Cairns was that it was extremely hot and humid. In the main street there was a huge fruit bat, hanging dead from an overhead electric cable.

I spent a lot of time hanging around Melbourne. One time I was invited to join in a Jewish religious festival. Hanukkah I think it was. One of the elder family members read from the Torah. Then we had some food which was delicious.

I used to catch the tram into the city centre now and then. Melbourne is a busy city, but retains its charm from the early days of settlement. The trams are great fun. Outside of the city centre, which is shops, businesses and bars there are old style colonial houses.

I visited Melbourne Jail which is in a park at the centre of the city. I saw the cell where Ned Kelly the famous bushranger was incarcerated. The full face iron mask he used for protection was on display. The tour of the jail ended at the spot where he was hanged. It was on a normal landing, with a trapdoor. Above there was a metal bar from which the rope would have been suspended.

I think those of us there found it all a bit gruesome. Apparently Kelly's last words were 'Such is life' Yes, indeed.

I booked my return flight. Michelle and I had a very serious talk beforehand. I told her that I could not enter into a 'sham' marriage and she agreed. I think we were both sorry for how things had turned out, but I think it would have been much worse if we had actually got married.

The day of the flight Michelle and Shona as I had taken to calling her, drove me to the airport. I was half expecting their mother to be with them to make sure I was actually going. But then she was probably at home cracking open a bottle of champagne or two.

Chapter 24

Going Home

I waved goodbye as I went through to the departures lounge. I did feel quite sad, to be leaving Australia as much as anything. I boarded the plane and we taxied off.

Another Olympic airways flight. I strapped on the headset before the whining started. I don't mean the engines.

I don't like flying. Not because it scares me. I just find it boring. Once I had got home from this flight, I promised myself I would never take another long haul trip

We stopped at Bangkok Airport again. This time there was no delay and we were re-boarded within an hour. I was walking along the corridor leading to the plane when I was confronted by an irate Thai security guard.

He really was very angry. He was shouting at me, but obviously I had no idea what was upsetting him as I don't speak Taiwanese. He kept pointing at the small rucksack that I used as hand luggage. I handed it towards him to see if that would help. He would not take it but kept on shouting and pointing.

I thought perhaps I am supposed to open it myself. I unzipped the bag and he made gestures which I took to mean that I should empty the bag. I started to do so. After a while I pulled out a small corkscrew that I always carried with me.

He went nuclear. I thought he would literally explode in front of my eyes. He took the corkscrew from me and opened out an extremely tiny blade. I didn't even know it was there.

He calmed down, kept the corkscrew and waved me on. I thought if that is how he reacts to all possible concealments, it's a miracle he hasn't died of a heart attack a long time ago.

We flew on to our penultimate destination, Athens airport. Only it turned out to be my ultimate destination.

When we left the aircraft and went to the arrivals hall, I was told that my ticket had terminated in Greece. The flight I took more than a year ago to go to my Mum's funeral had used up that part of my round the world ticket. It was obvious really. I was not going to be allowed to fly home and back for nothing.

I decided to go into Athens as I was now stuck in Greece with no onward flight. I took a bus into the city and had a wander around.

I saw a bar and decided I would like a drink, so I went in. I had a few drachma on me, enough for a quick Mythos I thought. I ordered a glass.

Whilst I was waiting this attractive young lady came over. She smiled and asked if she could sit next to me. I said of course. She asked me if I would like to buy her a drink. I said that I was only having a quick one, then I had to be off.

A large man in a dark suit appeared from nowhere. He told me that I should buy my companion a drink. I was about to say that I wasn't staying, but saw the look on his face and thought better of it. I asked her what she wanted and she ordered some sort of cocktail.

I drank my beer and asked for the bill. It was £30. I had about the equivalent of £10 on me and told the large man so. I offered him all I had. He didn't seem too impressed. He suggested I go and get the difference from a cash point. He would keep my rucksack as hostage.

I did exactly that and returned with the money. He counted it, told me to have a nice day and disappeared.

I was having a massive panic attack during this and struggled to keep things together. I headed up the street after leaving the bar, convinced I was being followed. I went faster and faster, eventually breaking into a run.

A voice said 'Shalom' I was wearing a large star of David around my neck. Was that somebody being friendly I asked myself. Or somebody after me.

Eventually I arrived at the Plaka. I knew where I was now and took a seat in a small taverna. I ordered a large carafe of red wine and downed a couple of glasses. I started to settle down.

I had a delicious Beef Stifado with a Greek salad and finished off the carafe. I ordered another. By now I was feeling very mellow and all the paranoia had gone. I realised that I could stay in Greece, maybe go back to the islands. I decided that would not be a great idea. Time to get back to reality.

I had taken more from the cashpoint than I needed to pay off the man in the clip joint, so I paid the bill and went. I left a good tip for the waiter who had helped me get through my ordeal, without realising it.

I found a travel agent and bought a one way ticket to London. I was told that there is a specific ticket designed for merchant seamen returning home having completed their contract and only needing a one way trip. This was the cheapest way to complete that type of journey. That was fine by me, as long as I didn't have to wear a sailor's suit.

I flew into Gatwick. I was well used to the airport from the trips that I had made to Greece in the past. It was good to have only been in the air for three and a half hours.

I had phoned my Dad from Athens and asked if I could stay a few days as I literally had nowhere else to go. He said he would call me back. He had to consult his wife, my step mother I suppose.

He did call me back. She had decreed that I could stay, but for no more than one week. I would have preferred for it to have been one day and for her to be out for that day. Unfortunately, I had absolutely nowhere else to go. If I had, that's where I would have been headed.

Dad was not allowed to pick me up, so I took a bus to Cardiff and then another to Pontypool, which is where Audrey's mum lived in the family home that my step mother had hi-jacked.

When I got to the house Dad was fine and showed me where my room was. His wife ignored me and did so all the time I was there, apart from the odd hostile glance. I am not sure why this was the case, but it may have been a combination of my illness and the fact that I was not rich like my brother. She liked money and anyone who had it.

I ended up staying a few months. This was certainly not by choice. I was exhausted and spent a fair amount of time in bed. I think that this was my mind recuperating after an extended period of mania. The depressive side of Manic Depression. At the time I still had no idea I was Bipolar.

The time that I spent there was primarily boring and does not warrant much attention here.

I eventually escaped when my good friend Peter Abbott offered me a place at his Mother's rental property back in England. It was in a village called Stanton Harcourt which is quite close to Oxford, so it felt like coming home. This house was new, semi-detached and made from Cotswold stone which is a sandy coloured stone which I have always found attractive . There were two bedrooms and I was going to be the sole occupant.

This was the first time in two years that I actually had a place that felt like home. I didn't have much to put in it, but luckily it came furnished.

Pete took me shopping for things like bedding and cooking utensils. I was soon fully equipped to live a normal life, or as close as possible for me.

I was coming out of my period of hibernation. This had lasted for months. The bipolar was changing in the way it presented itself. I now had lengthy periods of inactivity when I felt alright. I suspect largely because I withdrew from normal life and didn't have much to do with other people.

After a while in my new situation I began to want to do something other than lay in bed all day. I decided I needed to go and visit one of the local 'pubs' There were two in the village. There was a large impressive looking building towards the middle of the village which was called the Harcourt Arms. It was somewhere you could get a drink, but was more of a restaurant. I ate there a few times. The food was excellent but it was not really a pub as far as I was concerned.

As you entered the village from the Oxford side was the Fox. This was a proper English pub. You could eat there if you were content with a steak and kidney pie or similar. I often was.

There was a dart board and a pool table. Although pool is an American import it has become acceptable in a proper English pub. We even had one in the Plough all those years ago.

Darts has always been played in English pubs and I have enjoyed it for many years. I was a member of the Plough darts team from the age of 16. This came as a surprise to the landlord, Mr. Roy Harris when I celebrated my 18th birthday in the pub. I had become team captain by then. I noticed his headstone a while back when I visited my Mum.

Every time I go back, I see someone else I knew who has been buried in the village. Last time, there were 2 of my old classmates from big school in Sutton Courtenay.

Colin Bolton, who was a brilliant footballer. There was a small football on his grave, so he must have continued with the game he loved. I can see him clearly in my mind's eye.

The other was Kenny Vaughan. I can picture him and his brother Ronnie when they came to a party my dad had arranged one year for my birthday. Dad had made cakes and trifles. Lots of sandwiches and little party packs he had put together for the kids. An open invitation went out.

Only Kenny and Ronnie showed up. I think everyone was afraid of my mother's illness. Which was pathetic. I don't know what anyone thought a four foot and one half inch lady was going to do to them. She might well have dumped jelly on someone's head though.

I remember being disappointed, but in a way, I understood. Initially I admired the Vaughan boys, but when I witnessed them devour much of the feast dad had prepared I suspected their motives were less than altruistic. I still liked them both and was sad to see that Kenny had died.

I can still see these old school friends. But in my mind they are both eleven years old.

The Fox was a 'spit and sawdust' pub. There was a group of regulars who seemed to always be there. I suspect that is the same in many if not all pubs. It's certainly true of Wetherspoons.

Lots of people, myself included, wonder how this nucleus of drinkers can afford to stay all day in the local Wetherspoons. They can't be working as they are always in the pub. It's a mystery.

After I had challenged these Fox regulars to games of darts and usually lost them (the Plough team was exceptionally poor) I was accepted into the group. Even more so when I lost many games of pool.

The Bipolar was always there and although I had accepted it as permanent, I still did not like it. The bubble was and is my normal 'resting' state. When the extremes of depression and mania hit, they are destructive in almost equal measure.

For a while life was as good as it could be. I went to the Fox most days, but did not get drunk. I played pool and darts badly. In good weather we played Aunt Sally on a pitch by the side of the pub.

I loved Aunt Sally. It was the only pub game that I was good at. It involves throwing a lump of wood, roughly shaped like a truncheon at a 'dolly' which is placed on a metal pole some several yards away. The dolly is supposed to represent an old woman's head. I'm not sure why anyone would want to knock an old woman's head off with a wooden stick.

The player has six sticks. The aim is to knock the dolly off as many times as you can. Of course the Plough had an Aunt Sally pitch. We had inter pub matches, which we often won. Every now and then I would knock the dolly off with every stick. When six dollies were knocked off, it was recorded in the local paper. Life was quiet in the villages.

One Summer's afternoon we were playing a game of Aunt Sally at the Fox when John Patten turned up with his wife and kids. He was a well known politician at the time. His brother Chris was Governor of Hong Kong and presided over it's return to the Chinese.

I have no idea why John Patten was there, maybe he lived locally. Incidentally, Richard Branson lived locally too. He never came over for a game of Aunt Sally.

John watched for a while, clearly intrigued. He asked me about the game and I explained. He asked if he could have a go. He was a decent sort of guy for a Tory politician.

He threw one stick and nearly took the head off the man positioned to put the dolly back on when it was knocked off. He apologised, but we laughed saying that it was a common occurrence. He laughed too and left. He really was a nice guy.

I became so settled in my environment that I applied for a job. It was for a Recruitment Consultant in an agency based in Slough. The term Consultant amuses me. A bit grandiose for what it actually is.

I got an interview and to my amazement was offered the position. I started immediately. They gave me a company car and a good salary. There was a commission scheme too. It all looked pretty good.

However these are basically sales jobs and once I started to try and sell the services of the company, the usual problem returned. I did manage to make a couple of appointments, but they came to nothing as I struggled to get through the meetings. I can't have come over very well at all.

After a couple of months they 'let me go' They were a decent company but I had to admit I was no longer able to work in recruitment.

At least I had made some money for a while. I got the tax I had paid back too, which was a bonus.

One day, Pete told me that his mother wanted me to vacate the house. I didn't know why, but wondered what I was going to do. I mentioned my situation to the landlord of the Fox. His name was Jones, his first name might have been Alun. He told me that he had a spare room upstairs that I could rent off him.

I took it, gratefully. So I slept, ate and drank in the pub. Jonesy did alright out of me. I don't know whether it was the environment, but I began to drink too much. On a couple of occasions I woke up in the morning thinking I had done something wrong the night before. Usually I hadn't. Sometimes I had.

Eventually Mr. Jones had enough. He asked me to leave. For some time I had been thinking of moving to Wales. Whilst staying with my dad, I had noticed how cheap the houses were. I still had hardly touched my money and easily had enough to buy a reasonable terraced house in Pontypool.

I asked Jonesy for time to sort something out. In the meanwhile I would not enter his bar area. He agreed. I contacted a couple of estate agencies in Pontypool. I received details of lots of properties.

I chose a few to see, hired a car and went up to Pontypool to view them. Most of them were of no interest to me, for a variety of reasons. There was one I really liked. It was in an area called Wainfelin. A mid terrace, it was advertised as having 4 bedrooms. It was a 3 bed really, the large front room had a stud wall put in to create a very small office space.

It had a downstairs bathroom which I did not like, but I planned to move it upstairs in time. There was plenty of room to do this.

They say that once you start to make plans like that, you are sold. I was, and made an offer of the full asking price. I was told I could have got it for less, but I was happy enough as I was comparing it with prices in the South of England.

Also the man selling it was moving out because he had recently lost his wife and couldn't stand to stay in the house that they had made their home. I felt sorry for him.

I returned to Stanton Harcourt and told Jonesy that I was buying a house in Pontypool and would move out as soon as the transaction was complete. The house was vacant because the vendor, Les Jones, did not want to stay there so the sale should go through quickly.

Jonesy, the landlord of the Fox, was from the Welsh valleys himself and was OK about my staying until I could move there. It seemed to me that everyone from Wales was called Jones. Even my dad's new wife used to be Audrey Jones.

One of the pub regulars sold old bangers on the side. I told him I was interested in buying a cheap but reliable car to move to Wales in. I bought a beaten up old Ford Estate. It turned out to be an excellent purchase which gave me no problems for the time that I owned it.

I had to go to Pontypool a couple of times to sort out the documentation for buying the house. The solicitor who was acting for me was a very attractive young woman. She told me her boyfriend was a bricklayer. I wondered what such an attractive and intelligent woman was doing with a builder. I convinced myself I was a better bet. Unfortunately she did not agree.

When everything went through and I was ready to move into my new home, I decided to go to see Rob Duley and get my property back. I would have to hire a van for the new TV and three piece suite. The various boxes of possessions I had left could go in the back of the estate. I had nothing much else to put in there.

I had no contact details so drove over to Abingdon and went to his house. It was odd approaching the front door and remembering the last time I was there. It seemed like a lifetime ago.

I rang the doorbell and he appeared. Initially he looked surprised. I said hi, and asked him how he was. He muttered something and ushered me in.

Once inside, he was joined by a woman I had not seen before. He did not have a girlfriend before I left, but he told me this was his partner. She looked at me stony faced, saying nothing. He was just wearing a pair of jeans and was sucking in his stomach and puffing out his chest. I had no idea why.

I had not seen him for years, but he did not offer me a cup of tea or anything. I did not like this atmosphere at all. I told him I had come for my stuff. He went off and returned with one cardboard box. It was one of the ones I had used to store my worldly possessions.

I said I had left more than one box. He said that this was all I had left with him, and puffed his chest out further. His partner looked like a Greek Gorgon. I expected to be turned to stone when I looked at her.

I asked where my TV and three piece suite were. The TV had broken. They did not have room for the suite so had sold it. The money they got for the suite paid for the storage. Of one small cardboard box.

I could see I was going to get nowhere and thoroughly disgusted with this thieving pair, I left.

I didn't check the contents of the box, there was no point. When I did, my most treasured things had gone.

I really was upset, not at the duplicity of my ex friend, but by the loss of my Chinese menu and my Beatles ep.

I went back to Stanton Harcourt and packed up my few possessions. I set off to Wales for the next part of my adventure.

Chapter 25

Moving to Wales

When I got to my new home, I could not have been happier. This house really was mine. I had no mortgage and the fear that I might end up homeless had gone. It was a big old place and the few things I owned were lost in it.

I had bedding, but did not have a bed. No three piece suite thanks to Rob Duley. I had seen a place in the town where they sold second hand furniture. I went down and bought some chairs and a bed. It was delivered the next day. The first night I slept on the floor in my sleeping bag. I had been in worse positions.

When I had been lodging with my Dad, I had been into the covered market in Pontypool town centre. For some totally inexplicable reason, I thought it would be a good idea to rent a unit and start up some sort of business.

I had seen a guy in Cwmbran town centre selling hot jacket potatoes, cooked in an old Victorian oven. He did a roaring trade.

I thought I could do the same, selling out of the market. It wasn't a bad idea apart from location. Cwmbran has a very busy town centre and there was a lot of passing trade.

Pontypool market had quite a few visitors, but nothing like as many as Cwmbran. Also my bipolar was going to change dramatically whilst the planning and implementation of my new business took place.

I talked to my Dad about my plans. He was very interested and supportive. I found a company that fabricated and sold the ovens. When I visited them, they also sold me aluminium display units which could be used to keep fillings hot. I bought a large glass fronted fridge for cold fillings and drinks.

Dad came and fitted a gas supply into my rental unit in the market. He got a carpenter friend to build cabinets to hold the display units and a stand for the fridge, so it could be seen from the other side of the counter. Water was connected, sinks and basins fitted.

Everything was moving along nicely. Except for me. I can only recognise with hindsight what happened. At the time everything seemed fine. That is the nature of my illness and probably most other mental illnesses.

I think I moved into a state of permanent mania. My actions became irrational. Although I had a perfectly usable car, I went out and bought a Renault 5 Turbo. It cost a big chunk of my remaining capital. I spent a lot of time speeding around the Welsh countryside when I should have been concentrating on my new business. I employed a couple of scoundrels who took pay and did nothing for it.

The business was actually operating, everything was in place and supplies were there. It probably would have worked but I was useless and there was no-one to help. After his initial interest my Dad had withdrawn from any involvement. I don't know how much his wife influenced him.

Chapter 26

Denise and the Boys

There was one good thing that came out of my madness. One evening I was sitting at home, feeling sorry for myself. Although I had a bottle of whisky to keep me company, I felt very alone.

I did something I had never done before in my life. I picked up a copy of a local free paper that had been posted through the door. I turned to the personal ads. I am not sure what I was looking for. I saw a 'lonely hearts' ad.

I read one that caught my eye. I thought 'why not' and dialled the number. A quiet voice answered 'hello'. I said hello and said I had seen this ad. The little voice said she hadn't placed it, her friend had. Her husband had left her for another woman and the friend thought it would be a good idea for her to look for a man. She wasn't particularly interested. She was happy on her own for the time being.

We kept talking. For hours. Her name was Denise. She had 4 sons, 2 in the army 2 at home. That did not put me off. We got on really well. She told me about her husband, who did not sound like a pleasant person. I decided I wanted to meet her and said so.

She said she lived in Crewe. I had no idea where that was. I told her I was phoning from Pontypool. 'Where's that?' she enquired. We were both clueless, but she said she would like to meet too.

I said where would she suggest we meet in Crewe. She said in the car park of her local squash club. I had not drunk much of the whisky and it had been several hours since then. I figured I was OK to drive.

When I stepped outside, it was early morning. I got into my Renault 5 Turbo and set off.

I stopped at the garage on the edge of Pontypool, filled up with petrol and bought a map. I looked at where Crewe was and realised it was going to take a long time to get there.

I headed in what I thought was the general direction of Crewe. A sat nav would have been really useful. Unfortunately like the central heating and double glazing in my first house in Sutton Courtenay, it had not been invented.

I drove around in circles for several hours. I stopped at one point and bought a load of Easter eggs for Denise and her boys. I also bought some flowers for her.

I eventually got there. I was about 5 hours late and expected her to have gone. I could not phone her because mobiles had not been invented either. I could have used a public phone but I had cleverly forgotten to bring her number.

She was there! Standing in the corner of the squash court car park, soaking wet because it had been raining. I got out and apologised non stop for about 5 minutes. She forgave me and climbed into the car. She directed me to her house. I didn't tell her about my bipolar for a long time because I didn't have a name for it then. It definitely played a big part in my lack of direction.

At her house I met her two youngest sons, Colin who was 16 and David who was 12. I was expecting some resentment from the boys, but there was none. There never has been. David called me Dad from the off and would not hear anything else. He still gets annoyed if anyone suggests that he has a different father.

When he started school in Pontypool he was told he had to accept that he would be called Piggott which was his biological father's name. Colin was at the same school. They both refused to accept this. Colin told the Headteacher that he had every right to call himself whatever he wanted. He was also in the process of legally changing his name by deed poll.

They both left the school and came home refusing to go back until they could be called by my surname. I have learnt over the past 30 years that there is no point in arguing with either Colin or David. Even less point in taking on their Mum.

The school backed down and everyone was happy. I did not have to intervene at all. They sorted it out for themselves.

As previously mentioned my bipolar was changing. I was frequently exhibiting strange behaviour although of course it all seemed completely normal to me. In Crewe I bought some outlandish clothes and insisted on going to a local disco with Denise. Here I tried to impress her with my usual mix of moonwalking and Kung Fu. It did not have the desired effect. She took me round to meet her mum.

Denise told me later that her mum thought I was a bit puddled. She was not far wrong.

I stayed the weekend. I left on Monday morning. Most people would have waved me goodbye and locked the door after me. Not Denise though. Perhaps she took pity on me.

I had been getting on well with the boys. Colin said he wanted to come back to Wales with me. This might all seem a bit rushed, but I was happy with the arrangement. We went together and this time went in the right direction. Mostly because Colin was navigating.

Colin was always a practical, outdoors sort of person. He liked nothing better than being out all night Carp fishing or running around the hills surrounding Pontypool with a rucksack full of two litre bottles of water on his back. He was extremely fit.

On our way back from Crewe we stopped at a village called Knighton. There was a lad about Colin's age kicking a ball around in the park where we stopped. I shouted to him asking if we could have a kickabout. He came over and we all booted the ball around for a bit. We had a chat and he told us his Dad was an officer in the army. He told us some improbable tales of his fathers exploits.

I told him some equally tall stories from my six months in the army. Sometimes when I tell someone that I was a soldier, I leave out the six months bit. After a while we said goodbye and continued on to Pontypool.

Shortly after we got home, I had a call from Denise. She was extremely upset. Apparently this Piggott character had found out that she had met someone who had taken Colin off to Wales. David had gone to school Monday morning as usual.

Piggott turned up and tried to take David away. The school called the police and he was thrown off the school premises. Denise was terrified he would come to the house and attack David and herself. I told her to come to Wales and she could stay with me. There was plenty of room for her and the boys. She said she had no money. I asked if she could get some. She said her Mum might be able to lend her some but she would need it straight back.

I said for her to go and see her Mum and I would make sure she would get the money back as soon as possible. I told Denise to just pack a few things and get out. We would go back and pick up the rest of her stuff in a day or two, when I would repay her Mum.

A few hours later I picked Denise and my son David up from Pontypool station. We drove back to my house in Wainfelin. They have stayed in Wales ever since, making it their home.

Colin has his own engineering business and David is a GSM (General Store Manager) with Asda. They both earn a lot more money than me, which I regard as a success for them, not a failure for me.

A few days after we had settled down together, I hired a large removal van and we went back to Crewe. We emptied the house into the van, including their cat. I was warned it could be a bit vicious and to be careful. I left it to the boys to load the cat, I concentrated on the furniture.

I forgot to mention the family dog, Sandy. He had been taken to Wales with Colin on the first trip. He was a lovely dog who looked and howled like a wolf, much to the neighbour's annoyance.

Colin went up into the loft to see if there was anything there worth taking. He put his foot through the ceiling and decided to come down. David still complains that he missed his Millenium Falcon.

We returned to Wales, this time to stay. I realised that I had fallen for Denise. God knows what she thought of me. I was still behaving in strange ways. I would go out drinking in Pontypool on my own.

One time I was seen rolling a cigarette in the toilets of a town centre pub. The next thing I was being accused of smoking Cannabis in the loos. Back in Abingdon that might have been true. But not here. Nonetheless I was banned for life.

Shortly after Denise and David came to live with me, I had a visit from Pontypool police. This was the first of several. They had been contacted by the father of the boy in Knighton. He accused me of acting inappropriately with his son.

Because of my erratic behaviour, the police had started to show an interest in me. I am not sure if they are any better now in their treatment of people with mental health problems. It was suggested to Denise that I might be a paedophile.

I had returned to drinking heavily to mask the effects of bipolar.

So I was flat out upstairs when the police arrived. Denise dealt with them initially. The police officer suggested that her boys could be in danger. What did she know about me? She told them that she knew I was not a threat to her sons and asked them to leave.

They continued to grill her. Colin had been listening in. He came downstairs and asked the policemen to go. He was only 16, but was more of a man than many older men that I know. Was this further proof of the theory of life progression suggested to me back in Oxford when I was a similar age to Colin?

Eventually the police realised they were going to get nowhere and left. A couple of weeks later they came around again after someone had reported that there was a lot of shouting going on in the house. They knocked on the door and again Denise answered. They asked if there was a problem. She said no.

I came to talk to them. They suggested that I step outside for a second. Completely unaware of the tricks the police use, I complied. As soon as I was out of the door I was grabbed and a pair of handcuffs were slapped on me.

I was shocked. Why did this happen? I had done absolutely nothing wrong. Yes we had been shouting at one another. Is that an offence? They took me down to Pontypool police station and locked me in a cell. I had never been in this sort of situation. Why were they doing this to me?

Denise came down to the station to tell them to let me go. She said nothing had happened and she was shouting as loud as me. They refused to listen to her and also would not let her see me.

The next day I was sent to the magistrates court where I was found guilty of a breach of the peace. I believe this is the sort of thing people with mental health problems are still suffering today.

Whilst all this was going on, my market takeaway continued to decline. I suppose it had never risen. I had called it Arfur's Daily a play on words based on a popular TV character on a show called Minder. He was Arthur Daly, a rogue and the main character. Of course this had nothing at all to do with the business. I just liked the name.

The boys decided they wanted to help out with my doomed catering business. Whilst I was running around in the Renault 5 Turbo with their Mum, Colin and David had a go at running the business. David sold a display pizza that I had on top of the oven. It was rock solid and completely inedible. The purchaser worked in the market and was not impressed, apparently.

With one thing and another, I ran out of money. Luckily I still owned the house so we had somewhere to live. Denise still accuses me of conning her as I said I had money. I did for a short time, but lost it soon after our meeting.

This was not a great time. We had a lot of disagreements, looking back sparked by my mental illness. Of course I was not aware at the time and thought everything was everybody else's fault.

Throughout this period, I was experiencing the worst episode of mania that I had up until that date. It was constant with no respite. I thought all was fine. One night Denise had enough and left me in the house alone. She had taken the boys to my Dad's nearby. Apparently he was constantly telling her to leave me. I never knew at the time.

When I realised everyone was gone I went into a complete panic. I went looking for Denise all over the area. I went down to the town and around the park. I must have walked miles. Eventually I gave up and began to walk up the hill towards home. There was a church half way up between the town and my house.

Outside the church stood an old man. I asked him if he had seen a lady dressed in black. He turned to me and said 'She's no lady' I didn't know what he meant.

I am fairly certain that this was another psychosis like the police chief on Ios. It's impossible to know for certain as they appear so real.

I can only use logic to tell me that this old man would know nothing about Denise and she certainly is a lady. A lady so strong she stuck by me during this time, which must have been awful for her. Our sons were equally strong. God knows what would have happened had she not been there for me.

Although I am not a religious person by any means, I entered into the church. I had vague memories of how to behave from my time at All Saints church in Sutton Courtenay. It was very late, but there were a few people sitting in complete silence.

I went to an empty pew at the back of the church, knelt down and began to pray. I prayed that I would see Denise again. She meant the world to me and still does although I know she has her doubts. I prayed for myself although I did not know why. Perhaps I had a moment of clarity and realised my behaviour was bizarre, to say the least. I can look back at these moments of mania and remember with almost total recall. At the time I have absolutely no clue. That is my reality and I am often in a happy place in my head, despite everything.

I left the church and walked the short distance to my house. When I got home, Denise was there with the boys. Apparently she had walked out the house, waited for me to go looking for her and went back in.

Denise thinks she is 'thick'. I believe because she was told so by her school and later constantly by her heroic husband. He also kept telling her she was fat, which drove her into an eating disorder.

She is dyslexic, not thick. She is also one of the brightest people I have ever known. She certainly runs rings around me. Perhaps I am thick.

Eventually the mania subsided. I went into another period of hibernation. Depression I suppose, although I wasn't particularly unhappy. My son Peter arrived on 31st March 1992 which was a very happy event.

Peter was born at the Royal Gwent hospital in Newport. I wanted to go and see him. I had given my old Ford Estate to my Dad after I got the Renault 5 Turbo. I had wrecked the Renault when I was taking a corner at speed near Abergavenny and left the road, embedding the car in a large oak tree.

I asked Dad whether I could borrow my old car to go and see my new son. Despite the fact it stood on his drive unused, he said no. The witch again. So I took a bus. The bus terminated at Newport bus station and I began the fairly long walk to the hospital.

On the way I saw a scruffy looking bear in a shop window. He looked very endearing and I had to have him despite the fact that he was not cheap. At this time I was on benefits and every penny counted. He is named Raggy Ted and sits in Peter's bedroom to this day. Peter turns thirty on his next birthday.

I named my new son Peter after my friend Pete Abbott. I asked Pete to be Godfather. This time he actually got to fulfil the role, unlike when I asked him to be my best man . He came to Wales and we had a great time. I was definitely happy then.

Mostly though, I was in a state of suspended animation. I was signing on for almost 3 years. This was due to a lack of suitable opportunities in the area and the state of my mind. Denise must have frequently wondered why she had come to Wales with this madman. She says not and has absolutely no regrets about relocating her family. I have to admit they have done well here.

The Jobcentre was on the edge of Pontypool town, near to the park. Pontypool park is a lovely place to go for a walk, and I used to go there when I signed on. That was a particularly demeaning experience I recall.

One time I had a particularly rude woman deal with me. She was completely dismissive and talked to me like I was something she had found on her shoe. I got annoyed and said 'do you realise that I used to work for the Jobcentre and was at the same level as your Jobcentre's Manager'. She looked at me and said ' Well, I have never been out of work' I was lost for words.

I was forced to attend something laughingly called a Job Club. Going there was a condition to get benefits. The members of this not so exclusive club had to prove they were actively seeking work.

It was required that you sent out a minimum number of letters begging for a job each time you attended. The HR departments of Asda and Tescos must have resented that particular target. Some claimants had devised standard letters which they fired off to these local stores every time they came in. Completely pointless for all concerned, but it met the targets.

I was to find out that this was a common approach when dealing with and working for public authorities in Wales.

I think it's time they renamed the Jobcentres. When I was there in the early days this novel concept was to locate the new Jobcentre in the centre of town and display jobs on it's walls. It worked well.

Now they have no jobs on display and are often out of town. They are back to the old role of policing the benefits system. In fact they are much worse, imposing a range of sanctions which can stop the claimant receiving the meagre amount of money they struggle to exist on.

I interviewed a client who had been made redundant from her job as a Manager in a local Jobcentre. She told me that she had targets to achieve a certain amount of sanctions each month. 'What if no-one is doing anything to warrant a sanction?' I asked. She told me that it was a requirement to achieve those targets and if you didn't it was a disciplinary offence.

She refused to comply. She believed that was the reason she had been offered voluntary redundancy. She was more than happy to take it.

From the start of my benefit claiming period I used to periodically go to the careers office which was also by the park and near to the Jobcentre. I thought it might be somewhere I could discuss my career prospects.

The first time I went there I was invited in by a very polite man. He was Irish. I could tell by his accent. I wanted to know why he had come to Wales but never got round to asking.

He took me upstairs to his office which had a large window looking out onto the hills above the town. He pointed at those hills. He told me that although they looked very picturesque, they were in fact slag heaps made from the spoils of years of mining in the area.

I said that was very interesting, but could I talk to someone about getting my career restarted. He told me that the careers service only dealt with young people, there was no provision for adults. I got the same answer when I returned to check things out from time to time.

I remember I contacted the Newport Inland Revenue offices to see if I could get back into the Civil Service. I knew they were normally desperate for staff. After a while I got a letter back telling me that they had accessed my service record and in my last appraisal report, my Manager had said that I was not a team player. For that reason alone, I was rejected.

This was PER where I had generated a fortune through my individual efforts. I suppose it's how you look at things. I do remember my Manager telling me at the time that my success was due to the whole team, not just me. I couldn't see how that was, but didn't argue. Because I was a team player.

This would have been around 1993. Two interesting things happened that year. At the beginning of the year David who was then 14 had a rather unfortunate accident. Before that point, he would not be impressed to know that I had thought David was the weaker of the two brothers. Colin was 17 so it was unfair to make comparisons, but my opinion changed totally after this event.

David was mucking about with some friends at the front of the terrace. Suddenly he came in and told us he had accidentally fallen on one of the spikes on the railings in front of his friend's house. He wasn't crying. In fact he seemed completely calm.

Denise got him to lay on his front on the sofa. On inspection, he had a massive wound in his backside. It turned out that he had fallen onto the spike which embedded into his rear. Somehow he had hauled himself off and come home.

Perhaps he was in shock, but at no point did he show any fear or pain. I have to admit I was impressed and still am. I would have been howling like a banshee.

We took him to hospital. He was taken through to a side room for treatment. Denise would not go in as she can't stand the sight of blood. Which is strange as she ended up working in hospitals.

I went with him. The wound was so deep the doctors had to stitch inside it before closing the outer skin with further stitches. I would imagine he still has a scar, but he has never shown me.

I can't imagine what sort of a lie he could make up to get a drink out of a Greek in a bar. Or even more how he would demonstrate it.

On the 18th of October in that year, we got married. The wedding ceremony was a low key affair at Pontypool registry office. Although late in the year it was a beautiful sunny day. We crossed the road to stand in the park for photos.

Peter was 19 months old and dressed in a little suit with a bow tie. He looked adorable. His mother was wearing an off the peg number from Tescos, that well known fashion house. My suit was from Asda. Just call me George.

Initially Peter was being looked after by Sue, my brother's wife. David soon wrested him away from her. David always looked after his little brother. When Peter came home from hospital, David looked at him and said 'I am NOT changing his nappies' Within a month he was.

We spent very little on the wedding. I had been saving up for many months to get the money to put on a great reception. I think we achieved that. We hired a room at the Three Salmons, a well known hotel and restaurant in Usk.

The room was prepared immaculately, with crisp linen tablecloths on tables laid out in a square. A lovely floral centrepiece, silver cutlery, it really looked impressive.

There were a large number of guests including my Dad, his wife and her Mother. Denise's oldest son Darren was there, unfortunately. She thought she had to invite him, but now thinks it was a mistake. I knew it was. He sat with his usual surly expression and did not say anything to anyone throughout the meal or after. There are tales I could tell about this 'man's' behaviour but it's not worth the effort.

At least he didn't cause trouble as he had many times before. We had a great time and everyone seemed to enjoy themselves. The food was good and the wine was excellent.

At the end as everyone was saying their goodbyes, my brother came over to us and congratulated us on our marriage. He then said he had booked the bridal suite in the hotel for us. He had even paid for it. I was absolutely speechless. In all our years he had never done anything like it. It was the one and only selfless gesture he had ever made towards me. I looked for the ulterior motive, but there was none.

We sat with Tim and Sue and had a truly pleasant evening. It had never happened before and hasn't since. But for that one night hostilities were ceased.

They were heading home after our drinks with them. Sue had been drinking soft drinks all day and drove. Tim, like me, was decidedly merry. I really was. Not drunk but very happy.

I thanked Tim, again not something that happened often. They left and we headed for the bridal suite which was over the road from the main hotel. The room was amazing. Denise had always said she wanted to sleep in a four poster bed. There was a huge one right in front of her, draped with curtains.

To the side of the bed was an ice bucket on a stand. In it was a bottle of champagne. Bollinger. I was impressed.

I said to Denise, 'Shall we open it?' She told me that she was hungry. I realised I was too. 'Let's go to the chippy' she said. 'Great idea' said I. So we headed off to the fish and chip shop that was just up the road.

We came back with a large bag of cod and chips. There was no crockery in the place but that didn't matter. Fish suppers are always best eaten out of the wrapper.

Fish and chips washed down with a bottle of Bollinger. The perfect end to a perfect day.

One day I went to sign on. As I stood in line feeling the same sense of shame that I always did, I saw a notice on the wall. It said that Adult Directions (I think) were operating out of the local careers office and how to contact them. They had finally realised that there was a demand for careers advice amongst adults.

I didn't contact them as advised. I went straight around to the offices that I had been to many times before and went in. The Irish man was nowhere to be seen. Perhaps I had imagined him.

A young lady came to meet me. She took my name and booked me in for a careers interview.

Chapter 27

A Fresh Start

I went to the interview as agreed. My Adviser was a smart woman in every sense of that word. Her name was Judith Evans and in the following hour, she was to turn my life around. I don't think she realises what a profound impact she had on my life, on that day.

She asked me a couple of questions but basically I babbled on telling her about my career as an interviewer in the Jobcentre. I probably mentioned WETCHA. I told her about PER and then my time in the private sector. I had packed in a lot over those few short years.

She told me that with my sort of experience I would make a good Careers Adviser. I was aware of the job and had thought about it in my early days as an Executive Officer in the Jobcentre. I found out it required a degree and not having one, I dismissed the idea.

Judith told me that I didn't necessarily need a degree. My previous experience could count as Accredited Prior Learning (APL). There was no guarantee, but it was worth an application, she said.

She wrote down a list of things for me to do. First on the list was to contact Glamorgan University and enquire about the Diploma in Careers Guidance. She even gave me the phone number. Another was to contact Margaret Noakes who was a manager in the Cwmbran office. I was to arrange to go and see her. A further one to contact the local council to find out about grants.

She covered everything needed for me to get going. I was elated. I went home to put these plans into action. The course leader at Glamorgan, Andy Fosterjohn offered me an interview. Margaret Noakes was charming and agreed to meet. The council made positive noises about a grant.

I met Margaret Noakes first. She turned out to be English as well. She told me all about Gwent Careers which was the careers company she and Judith worked for. Their various offices and locations. She also gave me a lot of insight into the work of a Careers Adviser which was to prove invaluable in the upcoming interview. I thanked her very much, and meant it.

Next was the interview at Glamorgan University. There were two people interviewing me. Andy and a lady named Theresa something. She was the lecturer in psychology on the course. They asked me lots of questions. I cannot remember any of them.

Interviewers make the worst interviewees. I went home convinced I had made a mess of the interview. Later that day I had a phone call from Andy offering me a place on the next course which was commencing September 1994. To say I was pleased would be the understatement of that century.

I was going to find my way back to a normal life at last. To build some respect for myself. To offer something more to my family and in particular Denise. All of these things had been made possible through the intervention of one excellent Adviser. I know that there are plenty that would not have been capable of doing what Judith did that day, so I thank God she was my Adviser.

I got a letter from the University confirming my place. I had applied to the council for a maintenance grant. I had been told that these were being phased out. Nonetheless I was given a full grant. It came to more than I was getting in benefits. Quite a lot more in fact.

I found out that I was one of the last people to be awarded a full grant. It made life a lot easier and I was going to be doing more than sitting in front of the TV playing Sonic the Hedgehog all day.

I told my Dad that he would have to give me my car back as I needed it to get to and from University. Glamorgan University is in Pontypridd and a long way from Pontypool. He said that he had promised it to his step daughter. I suggested that he unpromise it as his son needed it more. No was his answer.

Luckily Colin had bought himself a car that was even more of an old banger than mine. He was 19 and had a job in an engineering works in Cwmbran. He had already proven to be highly skilful in all matters mechanical.

After buying the car for next to nothing which was close to its true value, Colin got it into our garage, rigged up a rope and pulley system from the roof beam and with his friend, lifted out the engine. He worked on that engine for weeks. He got an old Haynes manual and basically taught himself to be a mechanic.

Once the engine was back in the car, it went well. I asked Colin if I could borrow his car for the year that I would be at Uni. He said yes without hesitation although he had no idea how he was going to get to and from work. In the end he took the bus until I finished the course. That's how families help each other out.

So I started at University in the Autumn of 1994. I was so happy to be taking this step in the right direction. I had to put the past behind me and concentrate on making the most of this opportunity. I never thought for one minute that I would make it to University. I was on a post graduate course without having ever graduated! It was almost surreal.

Most of the others on the course were more mature, like me. One lady had actually given up her job and paid her way through a history degree to enable her to get on this course.

When she found out I had got on without a degree, she was a bit put out. When she also found out I was getting a full maintenance grant, which she wasn't, she was even more annoyed.

At last, things were going my way! I have to say, I thoroughly enjoyed my time at Glamorgan University. It was good to be using my brains again. There was a student bar which I couldn't use as I had to drive in and back every day. With the discounted beer, that was probably a good thing. The canteen was good, but I seldom ate there. I preferred to spend my grant on the family. I brought sandwiches.

I will always remember my very first day on the course. It was called the Dip CG. (Diploma in Careers Guidance) The year at University was the first part of the qualification. The second part was completed in the workplace through a series of assessments.

One of the first things we did on that first day was to undertake mock interviews with each other. I was paired up with a young business graduate named Mark Hoban. I had been interviewing for years so I had no problem with Mark.

I treated it like a real interview and found out that he had a decent degree in Business Studies and had graduated that year. No previous work experience so we talked about his school and hobbies.

When I finished my interview, it was Mark's turn. He started as I had by asking my name. I told him my name was Arthur. He asked me why I had applied for the course, which I thought was an excellent opening question. I told him why. He said 'Well Dave, what do you think you will do after the course?' A good question I thought, except my name is not Dave. I pointed that out to him. He apologised and said 'So, can you tell me what your plans are for the future, Dave?' I realised he was just nervous, which was understandable as he had never done this before. His questions were excellent though. It still makes me smile when I think back.

Mark went on to work for Gwent Careers after the course. He is still in the Careers service after all these years. He runs the company's website, and other marketing functions. His is a senior position.

I saw him a while back in our Caerphilly office. He recognised me and said hello. I reminded him of that first day and our interviews. He did not remember it. I suppose that is not surprising as he could not remember my name for the space of a few seconds.

We were taught all sorts of things on the course. It really was very good. In many ways it was like the course I did in preparation for working in the Jobcentre. Except it was meant to be used and actually was.

I have always been given the time to interview properly. Noone has ever called me into their office and told me to concentrate on giving out forms.

There was a guy called Alun Connick who taught us presentation techniques. He had all sorts of little tricks for improving the delivery of group sessions. One was when wanting to emphasise a point by using a drawing on a flipchart, he suggested drawing that picture in outline, using a pencil which could not be seen by the group.

It sounds simple, but is not something I would ever have thought of. I've never used it though. I didn't realise it then, but Alun was a senior member of the management team of Mid Glamorgan Careers. They were to be my future employers.

Alun had a couple of eccentricities. One was when he was doing presentations himself. If he was talking to a sizable audience from a variety of backgrounds, he would adopt a Mid-Atlantic accent, almost American.

Alun is originally from Merthyr Tydfil. Inhabitants of that town have a distinctive accent. When Alun is on home turf, he delivers with that specific accent. I am not sure why, probably the Merthyr accent is his natural one and the Mid Atlantic one is an affectation. It doesn't really matter, he was good at his job.

The DipCG was a challenging course. There was a lot of theory about models of guidance, much of which I thought was nonsense. I still do. I relate it to the study of Economics. A complicated way of stating the obvious.

I had no problems with the interviewing on the course. Groupworks was another matter. They would bus in a local school's year group for us to practice on. Before and in between sessions, these pupils would get together in the main hall and plot ways to cause mayhem in my groups. Or so it felt.

I have already mentioned the hugely successful Koala Bare session. Most were like that. Often I would start to feel a bipolar panic start to develop in the middle of one of these group sessions.

It was natural to feel a sense of panic I am sure. But this was on another scale. Sometimes I had to muster all of my strength to finish a session. These group works were recorded and knowing that didn't help.

There was a period when the rest of the group would be watching live via a camera placed in the room. That was really intimidating. I always got through these sessions, but I don't know how. I suppose if I told the course leaders about my bipolar I might have been given some extra support.

Nobody ever said anything, so it probably was not as bad as I thought. Anyway, I could not tell them I was Bipolar as I didn't know myself and wouldn't for a further five years.

In early 1995, Denise announced that she was pregnant. We were both over the moon. Perhaps her sixth child would be the daughter she had always wanted. She called her tuppence. At the sixteenth week scan, everything was fine.

I was in a lecture when I was called out by Andy Fosterjohn. I needed to phone Denise. She told me that she thought she was losing tuppence. I immediately left for home.

When I got home, Denise was in a terrible state. I took her to the Royal Gwent straightaway and went to A&E. We sat for an hour. Denise was in tears. I went to the reception and demanded to be seen. Of course, that got us nowhere.

Eventually we were seen, after having been triaged. Some tests were taken. We were sent through to see a consultant. He told Denise that she wasn't pregnant and never had been.

We knew that was rubbish, but he was having none of it. He said that the tests showed that she was not pregnant. He explained, but his accent was so strong that we could not make out what he was saying.

I said to Denise, we are getting nowhere here. Let's go home. On the way back I had an idea. Why don't we go to Nevill Hall hospital I said. I knew that to be a better hospital. We had always found it to be so. I don't know why I had gone to the Royal Gwent. I guess it was because Peter had been born there.

I can't remember the time but I know it was late. We arrived at Nevill Hall and I explained what had happened to a nurse I found at the entrance. She said for us to wait. A couple of minutes later she came back with a doctor who took us to a room further into the hospital. It had an ultrasound machine.

The doctor asked Denise some questions. He asked us to stay in the room and went off. He came back with a nurse who turned on the ultrascan. She completed a scan and said she had to see the doctor. She promised they would return as soon as possible.

We sat there, fearing the worst. The doctor came back with the nurse. They had clearly been discussing the scan. The doctor said that he was so sorry, but that our baby had died. Tuppence was gone. The nurse comforted Denise as she cried.

We were told to come back the next day. They had to take the remains of tuppence from Denise's womb. Denise was 18 week into her pregnancy and Tuppence would have been more than just a foetus.

This operation was awful for Denise. She had wanted tuppence so much. We were both certain the baby was a girl. Even now we always talk of her. We asked the doctors if they could tell us the sex of the baby. They said it was impossible to say. We couldn't understand why, but perhaps it's better not to know.

This was a massive blow for both of us. Everything had been going so well. I was getting back on my feet and we were going to have our final child, hopefully a girl.

I had to be strong for Denise, but losing Tuppence weighed heavily on me too. I could not jeopardise our future so had to keep going through what was the final part of the course.

It was not easy but I got through. It was hard enough writing about theories that were ridiculous, developed by academics who had never translated their own thoughts into practice. It was doubly so in these circumstances.

Towards the end of the course, Alun Connick asked us to prepare letters of application for his company, Mid Glamorgan Careers Ltd. He collected them and presumably took them in.

A couple of weeks before the last term ended, students were offered interviews. Everyone except me. I wondered why. Perhaps I was too old. Perhaps it was because I did not have a degree. There were others of my age in the group. But everyone else had a degree.

I think that is probably what it was. Nowadays it is impossible to get an interview in the Welsh Careers Service unless you have a degree. I have suggested to interviewees with a lifetime of relevant experience that they apply to become a Careers Adviser. The service will interview a 24 year old graduate with no real experience and reject an older applicant.

I don't suggest it anymore because I don't like to set anyone up to fail.

If I was to apply for my job in today's career service, I would not even get a preliminary interview.

Others from the course were meeting up in the student bar to celebrate having been offered jobs with Mid Glamorgan Careers Ltd. Mark had gone for Gwent and got a job too. I was pleased for them, but annoyed for myself.

I expressed my displeasure to Alun Connick. He came back to me the next day and said I had an interview. I was pleased, but sceptical.

Like the others I was required to make a presentation followed by a panel interview. My presentation was good, though I say so myself. I stressed my experience, especially in interviewing and working with employers. I know they were keen to build relationships with local employers for things like work experience.

Of course, the usual problems were still there. Floating faces, distant words. I had become used to it. This was my normal now. I still thought I had done well.

I then had to face the panel interview. In charge was Mr. Wayne Feldon, the current CEO of Mid Glamorgan Careers Ltd. Alun Connick was there and a couple of other managers, notably a Ms Sue Phillips who was going to feature large in my life further down the road.

The panel interview did not last long. The questions were superficial. I would have asked far more searching questions. I would have been deciding whether to put the interviewee forward for consideration. I was not sure if these people were actually considering me at all.

The course ended and the graduation date was set. I went to hire my robes for the event. Denise came with me. I don't know which of us was more pleased.

Before that day came, I received a letter from Mid Glamorgan Careers Ltd. Not unexpectedly, It began 'We regret to inform you'...... It went on to tell me what an excellent presentation I had given blah blah blah.

I was about to screw it up and throw it in the bin when I noticed some spidery writing at the top of the letter, just to the side of the letterhead. It just said Call Me - Wayne Feldon. There was a number scribbled alongside this short note.

I'd had the phone disconnected because I could not afford to pay the bill. So I took the letter and headed for the public phone box at the top of the hill behind our house.

I had a pocket full of change. I dialled the number on the letter. Wayne Feldon answered the phone. This was his direct line. I told him who I was and why I was calling. He told me that although he could not offer me a contract to complete part 2 of my Dip CG, he had another idea in mind. He started to go on about the company's contract to deliver work experience for all the schools in it's area.

Wayne liked to talk. I had to keep sticking change into the slot. I didn't want to interrupt the CEO whilst he was in full flow. However as I was about to run out of money I had to tell him and I asked him to call me back.

He did so and must have realised he had been going on a bit. He got to the point. He said that he was impressed by my experience working with employers.

He told me that he needed someone to deliver the work experience contract in the Caerphilly area. There was one person currently doing that job, but it was too much for her to handle alone.

He wanted to offer me a job as a work experience assistant. Not really what I wanted after a year studying to become a Careers Adviser. However I needed a job and anything was better than going back on the dole.

I asked him how much he would be paying me. £10,000 pa he told me. About half what I was earning 10 years earlier. A quarter of my income in 1986, my first year of self employment. 'Yes please' I said gratefully.

I started working for Mid Glamorgan Careers Ltd. in September 1995. I will never forget that date because my annual leave entitlement commences at the end of September every year. Everyone's leave year starts at the end of the month in which they joined the company. I have no idea why.

Over the years, there have been many occasions when some management decisions have made little sense to me. That was one of the reasons I was glad to get out of the Civil Service in England. Nonetheless I will always be grateful to them for rescuing me from the slippery slope I was on.

My first day with the company was very strange. It was that very day that the Caerphilly branch was moving from its current location in Ystrad Mynach to new offices in Caerphilly, a couple of miles away. The office was situated over the local registrars, across from the Castle and surrounding park. It was a lovely location with great views.

When I joined the Careers Service was in transition from council ownership to commercial status. Council employees think very differently than those from the private sector. Processes are slow and ponderous. Systems are paramount. Most of the current Careers Wales management originate from council backgrounds.

For my first few days I was involved in the physical moving of premises. Once we were settled into the new office, I began my training. The woman I was working with was called Sarah Boone. I will never forget her as she was very strange. I was not the only one to say so. I am a bit odd myself, so maybe we made a good team.

Sarah informed me that she was my manager. I was never sure about this as she had nothing to do with my supervision or appraisal, which was carried out by the Operations Co-ordinator. I can't remember who that was at the time.

I just got on with my job, which I found very easy. It was like being back in Harwell working as a Clerical Officer. Once I had mastered the system which took about an afternoon, I began looking for ways to improve it.

The aim of the job was simple. At that time every school throughout Wales was obliged to send its year 10 pupils out on Work Experience. At least one week working out in the real world, ideally doing something relevant to the career they wanted to follow. I always thought this was an excellent scheme. An insight into the world of work was almost always useful to the individual pupil.

Our job was to make the arrangements to place each school's year 10 pupils on their work experience. Every school went out at different times of the year. All of them going out at once would have been impossible.

I had the dates for the year. I also had a database of employers who were happy to take pupils on their work experience. This database was a set of cards with the contact details and information of placements the employer could offer. It was kept in alphabetical order.

Every year group had broadly similar requirements. Teachers, plumbers, office workers, computer technicians and so on. The first change I made was to reorder the database according to employment sector. All the local primary schools for potential teachers etc. This made more sense to me than an alphabetical index.

Throughout the year we would contact employers, starting about a month before that particular school was due to go out. I would phone up a particular employer and ask if they could possibly take a pupil for their work experience. I tried to convince them to take several to make my life easier.

I was amazed at the generosity of the local employers. Most agreed to take on a pupil or two, despite almost always having had bad experiences in the past. There were always students who would take the opportunity of escaping school for a week to play up. Sometimes they learnt that it was not wise to behave that way in the workplace, which was a valuable lesson in itself.

Sarah Boone was a bit disorganised as well as more than a bit odd. On several occasions I heard her asking an employer for a placement and that employer saying no, not his time. A while later she would phone the same employer for a second time. 'Could you take a pupil for their work experience please' she would say. I could hear the voice on the phone say 'I'm sorry, but as I told you before, I can't take anyone at the moment'

Sometime later, Sarah would make another call to that same employer. Same question. Normally there was a loud slam followed by a buzzing sound. She often looked up and said 'How rude'

After a while we moved offices again. This was getting like the relocation programme from dining room to lounge in my house in Ock Street. This time we moved to the centre of town. The new office was above an estate agents and a bank. It was on Caerphilly's main street, Cardiff Road.

The wall that faced the road was made almost entirely of glass. There was a panoramic view of the castle and moat. It was stunning. There was no better view anywhere in Caerphilly. It is now an Italian restaurant which has people fighting to get a window seat.

The office was mostly open plan. There was a separate office for the Co-ordinator. There was also a bigger room with a glass front that faced into the main office. That is where I was incarcerated with Ms Boone.

I was stuck in that glass box for a year. It was here that I witnessed the rude behaviour of our employers upon receiving their third request from my apparent boss. It was also here that I dreamt up my improvements to the process of finding placements for our youngsters.

It soon became evident to me that we were phoning the same people every time a school went out. I asked a couple of employers who took pupils throughout the year whether they would prefer to have the details of schools and the dates they would be going out for the whole year. All of them thought that would be a good idea. They would be able to plan things better.

From my point of view, all I had to do was fill the places. I would know how many students each employer was happy to take and plan accordingly.

I told Sarah about my idea. She didn't like it at all. 'We won't have enough to do," she said 'I could lose my job' It was like being with Big Brother in Harwell, all over again. 'I'm in charge', she said 'so you can't do it' Big Brother did have the authority to stop my plans. Sarah Boone did not.

I must admit I enjoyed working on the work experience contract. I really believed in it. Schools loved it too. It took out the whole year group for at least a week and the teaching staff didn't have to do anything.

There was a sales element to it, but it was by no means a hard sell. The only part of the job that could be a bit wearing at times was sharing a room with a slightly demented colleague. Like my bipolar it was an unavoidable nuisance that I became used to.

Regarding my 'condition' it had gone into some sort of remission. I still had some feelings of paranoia and displacement, but it was easily managed. This was a good time.

One day I was called into the Coordinators office. I was informed that it was felt there was only need for one person on the work experience contract, in Caerphilly. I thought I was going to be 'let go' Why had I made those improvements? I had done myself out of a job.

The Coordinator went on to say that because of this they wanted me to commence the second part of my DipCG. I was going to be a Careers Adviser. I had given up on that, feeling my year at University had been wasted. There was a period of time after which the academic part of the qualification became invalid. I did not know what it was, but my paranoia told me it was close, or I may even have passed it. The same as it told me I was about to lose my job when I walked into the Coordinators office.

This was the best news I'd had for a long time. When I got home I took Denise out for a meal on the strength of it. Perhaps the tough times were behind us.

I started my training to be a Careers Adviser in school. The specific school was Rhymney Comprehensive. I was told to meet up with Cathy Murphy who was a manager with the company. We met in the car park at the rear of the school. It was a fairly new and impressive looking building.

Cathy took me in to meet the teacher responsible for Careers Education. His name was Ron Vaughan. The same name as the older Vaughan brother who had eaten most of my birthday spread back in Sutton Courtenay.

We had a chat about the school. He took us to a small room in the middle of the school. There was a desk, two chairs and a filing cabinet. There was no room for much else. I was more than happy. This was to become my little kingdom for the next year.

Cathy said she was going to leave me to get on with things. She wondered whether there was anything I needed. I said no, I was ready to get started. So she left and so did Ron. He was off to take a lesson.

It was a Friday and I spent the rest of the day having a look around the school. I found the staff room. I poked my head round the door. There were a couple of teachers there taking a break between lessons. I have always admired teachers in secondary schools. How they can face a class of 30 hormonal teenagers on a daily basis is beyond me. I couldn't do it.

I did have to deliver groupworks to pupils, but not often. Even that could be exhausting. We had been given lectures on classroom management on the course, but like the theoretical models of guidance, the practical reality was totally different.

It was not easy to apply these management techniques to a year 9 pupil from one of the rougher Caerphilly schools who decided in the middle of a session on future career ideas to climb onto a desk and start playing air guitar.

I told him to sit down, but he just kept on playing. Eventually his classmates coaxed him down. I remember thinking even my behaviour in school was not that bad.

It wasn't just me. The Careers Teacher in the same school was Head of English and a very experienced teacher. She was also a lovely person who I had got to know well. One day during an ordinary English lesson, for no obvious reason, a year 11 boy had punched her full in the face. Of course he was expelled. Permanent exclusion it was called then.

That did not help that excellent teacher, who could not face her job any more and took early retirement. No, I could not be a teacher in a Secondary School. I salute them all.

Before going home, I introduced myself to some of the most important people in any school. The school secretary and reception staff. They could help or hinder you depending whether they liked you or not. I always tried to get them onside.

I told them who I was and that I would be the school's new Careers Adviser. I was proud of that then. I told them I would be in early on Monday. They explained the lesson timetable and where everything was. I thanked them very much and went to my car.

Rhymney Comprehensive was about 20 miles from my home in Pontypool. The hills that I travelled through going home might have been slag heaps according to the Irish man in the careers office in Pontypool, but they were still lovely to behold especially at sunrise or sunset. In the Spring early lambs would gambol around within touching distance in some parts of the journey.

On the Monday I undertook my first real interviews with real students. The ones at University were real, the circumstances weren't. Over twenty years and thousands of interviews later, I can't remember the details of those first interviews. I can't really remember much about the school, to be honest. I was very much left alone. Ron Vaughan rarely made an appearance.

After about a year at Rhymney Comp, I was asked to go to a school called Afon Taf. The Adviser in the school was leaving and for some reason they wanted me to take his place. The school was in a place called Troedyrhiw which, being English took me a long time to pronounce. It was in the Merthyr Tydfil office area.

I was told that I would need to move offices from Caerphilly to Merthyr. Both were the same distance from my home, so it made little difference. I was to get expenses for the inconvenience of being moved. A relocation allowance. This would be at the full mileage rate which was about 35p a mile, Wayne told me.

It was 20 miles from my house to the Merthyr office. That was £7 a day. £140 a month, roughly. Tax free, that was well worth having. Of course I said yes.

After I had been in the school for about two weeks, I had a letter from Sue Phillips, Corporate Services Manager, confirming my new role and my relocation allowance of 10p per mile.

Sue Phillips was the power behind the throne. Whenever Wayne Feldon made a mistake, she followed along and cleaned up. I have always believed his heart was in the right place, but he did make a lot of mistakes. He was wrong about the amount of relocation allowance I was going to get. There was no right of appeal. There never was with Sue Phillips.

I liked Wayne. He was Chief Executive of quite a sizable organization. Yet he knew everybody by name. That certainly can't be said of the Chief Executive today who only communicates via video clips. It's getting a bit like Big Brother in 1984. But it is Big Sister in 2021.

Wayne wanted to do the best for his staff. It was one of his boasts that he had never made anyone redundant. Those in power now certainly cannot make that claim.

The way he offered the work experience job to me was typical. I found out that he had decided to do that himself. No discussion with HR or even Sue Phillips. I was lucky Sue Phillips did not retract the offer. She would have done if she felt it necessary. Wayne would not have argued. He always deferred to her.

Luckily I was a nonentity as far as she was concerned. Like back in my school days, that was going to change. If she could have seen into the future Wayne would most certainly have not had his way and I would have remained unemployed.

I moved to the Merthyr office. I have found that Merthyr people are a race apart. They have their own way of speaking and their own approach to life. I liked them. However, I did not spend much time in the office. I had a large well appointed room in Afon Taf school. It was luxury after the pokey room I had in Rhymney Comp.

I set myself up for business and soon started to meet the pupils. In those days we saw everyone in the year 11 cohort. It was interesting as we would see all different sorts of students from potential Oxbridge applicants to plumbers. The latter were probably going to end up richer than the former.

On the first day, I had a visit from the deputy head teacher. She said she would like me to come to assembly on the following day, so the students could meet me. I said I would be happy to.

The next day, I was not sure what to do, so I went to my room. The deputy head was called Sue Thomas. She came to the room and told me that assembly was about to start. I followed her down the long corridor. At the end was a huge assembly hall.

She ushered me up the steps leading onto the stage. There were rows of chairs laid out ready. The back ones were full up with teachers and other staff. The head was sitting in the middle of the few chairs right at the front. Sue headed for one and pointed for me to sit beside her. I was centre stage and beginning to feel anxious.

I looked down at a sea of faces. The whole school was there plus a number of teaching staff to keep them in order. From the first row to the back was at least a couple of hundred metres.

The first two rows were taken up by the sixth form. They were difficult to distinguish from the teaching staff. They stared intently at the stage. It felt like they were looking directly at me. Maybe they were. I was the only person they did not know.

The Head stood up, said a few words and then led the school in prayer. Apparently that happens every morning. It might have been a legal requirement. I think I said earlier that I am not a particularly religious person. I stared at my shoes and mumbled.

The Head then issued a few statements. Praising some students for their achievements. Admonishing some others for their non achievements.

Heads of Department stood up one by one and gave information on various school activities that week.

Then Sue Thomas stood up. She reinforced the Head's messages and introduced a few of her own. Then she said 'Today we have a new member of staff' I thought that's nice, I am seen as a member of the team. I had been an outsider in my other schools. She then said ' His name is Mr. Hutt. I am sure you will give him a warm welcome' Now they definitely were all staring at me. Apart from those who had fallen asleep. She turned to me, ' Would you like to say a few words Mr. Hutt?'

'I would prefer not to, if you don't mind' I thought. I felt a huge panic attack starting to build. I tried to tell myself that everything was fine. I could do this. I knew my job. I'll tell them about that.

I stood up, my knees knocking. Well it felt like that. Someone started to speak. I realised it was me. The voice was telling everyone about the importance of thinking ahead and working out plans for their future. Apparently I could help them with that. I went on for some time.

When I had finished I looked out at the crowd. I was hoping for applause. Some acknowledgement of my great achievement. I was rewarded with silence. The sixth form looked at me with disinterest. Oh well, I had got through it at least.

Sue Thomas stood up and said 'Thank you. I think school should thank Mr. Hutt in the usual manner.' There was a faint ripple of applause. That was as good as it was going to get.

Afterwards Sue said 'Thanks for that. I thought it went well. Did you?' I said 'Yes. I hope I got my message across' Sue said that she thought I had. Maybe I could give the odd talk on different types of career in future assemblies. Hopefully, she will forget that one, I thought.

They always treated me as a part of the management team. I was often called into meetings with the Head, Deputies and sometimes the Heads of Department. I might have been seen as the Head of the Careers Department although it was a Department of one.

It really was a privilege to be treated this way. I felt respected, which was novel in this job. Careers Advisers were often seen as second class citizens in schools. It was a legal requirement for us to be there providing impartial advice and guidance. But we took up space that was in short supply and was needed for teaching staff.

We were often put into cupboards to do our work. In one school, the Adviser was based in a disused boys toilet. The urinals were still on the wall and the toilet was still in its original place. I know. I had to work in it once.

I enjoyed my time at Afon Taf school. There was even talk of them employing me as a Careers Teacher/Adviser. I had my eye on the unused caretakers bungalow in the school grounds. Unfortunately it came to nothing.

There are some pupils that stand out in my memory. Only in specific schools for some reason. I have mentioned the young pianist who told me my plastic prism was valuable. He definitely lives on in my mind.

There were a few in Afon Taf. One year 10 student had come in to talk to me about her work experience placement. Her family had recently relocated from England. They had been given a house on the Gurnos Estate. This was a notorious place, known across the whole of Wales, never mind just locally. It had a reputation for all sorts of unsavoury activities from drug dealing to murder.

She informed me that in fact most of the people there were normal, law abiding citizens. Like her family. There were just a few extremely bad families. They were best avoided, she told me. She then said something that I will always remember.

'Have you heard of daylight robbery?' she asked. 'Of course' I answered. 'I have actually seen it' she told me. She went on to tell me about a day when she was at home. It was around 2pm when a large van pulled up outside the house over the road from hers.

Several burly men got out and went up to the house. One of them kicked the door open. They all piled in and came out with TV's, tables, chairs. The whole contents of the house, in fact.

When the van was fully loaded, they drove off. The student told me this was why she could say she had witnessed daylight robbery. Of course, she said nothing about what she had witnessed at the time.

Another student I remember was a young man who had always wanted to become an RAF pilot. He had been preparing for this since he was a small child. He was a very bright boy who achieved straight A grades in all of his GCSE subjects. For sixth form, he chose 4 A levels which included Maths and Physics. These are not prerequisites for pilot entry, but they are preferred.

He had been taking his private pilots licence and was close to qualified when he entered sixth form. Many people joining the RAF as a pilot do so as a stepping stone to becoming a commercial airline pilot. Self funding the training is extremely expensive so this is a less costly route.

That was not the case with this young man. He had always wanted to become a fast-jet pilot. He was very tall. On entry to sixth form he was six foot six inches tall.

He didn't find out until then that there was a height limit of six foot four inches because of the need to fit into a fighter jet cockpit. His ambition to become an RAF pilot was over because he was extremely tall. He could be a helicopter pilot, but that was of no interest to him.

I told him that with his ability he had many career options open to him. At the time he had no interest in anything else. I heard that he gained a place to study science at Oxford. I hope he found something to replace his ambition to become a fast-jet pilot.

One day I was sitting in my room catching up on some paperwork. There was a knock at the door. In walked Shirley, the work experience manager. She told me that because of all the changes taking place in work experience, she no longer wanted to be the manager. Mostly the changes were about Health and Safety.

She was going back to being a Careers Adviser. She wondered whether I might want to apply for her job. I loved being a Careers Adviser but had alway enjoyed work experience. This position would be a first foot on the management ladder. It also paid more.

I said that I would be very interested. She then told me that a senior manager would be in touch in the next 2 days to set up interviews. All jobs had to be offered throughout the company as a matter of policy. I would be in competition with anyone else that might be interested.

It turned out that there was one other person interested in the position. This person had no experience of working on the contract, other than the normal involvement that any Careers Adviser had, so I was confident that I could convince Wayne that I was the man for the job.

The senior manager that Shirley had mentioned called me the next day and told me that the interviews would take place the following Wednesday. She told me that she would be in touch later. I wondered why.

On the day before the interviews were to take place, I had a call from the manager who had arranged them. The reason I have not mentioned the name of this manager is that the call was to give me the questions that I would be asked the next day.

I wrote them down as she gave them. I wasn't bothered that this was going to give me an unfair advantage over the other applicant. I had decided that I wanted this job. I asked the senior manager what the answers were. She laughed and told me I would have to find that out for myself. God loves a trier.

I read up on the answers and was well prepared the next day. The other applicant was sitting outside the CEOs office when I arrived. He looked at me and smiled. I realised I knew him. He was a decent guy. I felt a bit sorry for him, but not a lot. I still wanted the job. He was called in first. 'Good luck' I said to him. 'And you' he replied

I went in next. Wayne smiled at me and said for me to sit down. He told me he was going to ask me 4 questions. He started with the first. I gave what I knew to be exactly the right answer. 'Excellent' he said.

When the interview was over he told me I would hear before the end of the next day. I don't think he knew that I had been given the questions by the senior manager although he did know her very well. If he did, he was a very good actor. Actually he was, as anyone who worked for the company in those days would testify.

I am on my way I thought. I left Afon Taf school with some regret. I liked the senior management team there and always enjoyed being treated as part of that team. However, I owed it to myself and my family to take this first step onto the management ladder.

I was given my own room in the Merthyr office. Before that I had a desk in an open plan office which I struggled with. A major symptom of bipolar is an intolerance of noise. I try to explain to those who say you should just block it out, that this is not possible.

In fact it is the opposite. I automatically focus on noise, so I can suffer in the quietest of rooms. When I have to tolerate the cacophony of a group of Careers Advisers who are often not the quietest of people it is unbearable.

So I was very happy to have my own room. As the work experience manager or co-ordinator as it was called, I headed up a team of half a dozen assistants, doing the job I had started out with. I knew the job well, which is always an advantage for a manager. It was difficult for anyone to pull the wool over my eyes.

Part of my job was to travel around the company area, talking to my colleagues and carrying out appraisals. I have always had the opinion that I am as good as anybody but no better than anyone. I treated every one of my colleagues as equals. I just happened to be the co-ordinator. We all seemed to get on well. One of them went on to become a Careers Adviser and told me that I was a good manager. That pleased me.

There was obviously more to the job than that, but it was the bit that I enjoyed. What my manager had not told me was that apart from being coordinator, I had to place all of the Merthyr schools myself. That was a mammoth task in itself.

After about a year doing the job, I was told that I had been signed up to do a two week course at Glamorgan University. It was the NEBOSH which is a Health & Safety qualification. The idea was that apart from everything else, I could carry out Health & Safety assessments throughout the company.

The course was intense. The first part was one week long. It was largely academic, looking at the legislation. There was a lot, much of it because of the plethora of rules coming out of Europe.

There was a one week break in which a number of assignments were to be completed. Then a final week, followed by a day of exams. Two 2 hour exams and a practical. It was hard going.

In the one week break, I was told to sort out the work experience placements for one of the Merthyr schools. I completed the assignments at home in the evenings and over the weekend before returning to University.

I managed to complete the course and the exams. Much later I received a certificate through the post. I had passed the NEBOSH with merit.

As an aside Sue Phillips had been studying NEBOSH for the past year on a part-time basis. She only achieved a pass. Apparently she wasn't very happy on hearing of my merit.

Around this time, I began to feel unwell. Denise told me I was beginning to act like I had in the bad old days. Bizarre behaviour. I began smoking. I hate smoking and can't stand the smell of cigarette smoke. When I am going manic, I invariably start smoking.

Work colleagues began to notice changes. One day Wayne said he wanted to take me somewhere in his company car. I had been in it before. It was more like a mobile skip. Wayne smoked and the ashtray was overflowing. It used to bother me, but not on this day.

Wayne just talked to me. I answered back. I don't know what I said. After a while Wayne said 'I see what they mean' Those were his exact words. He drove me back to headquarters and sent me home on indefinite leave.

At the time I was incapable of rational thought. After I had come through the dreadful period that was to come, I realised that this situation was entirely down to the company.

They had placed me under intolerable pressure and the extreme stress that ensued triggered a period of Mania. I had not experienced this before. I had an ongoing series of depression and hypomania in the past. This was a stand alone experience and stratospheric in its impact.

I totally lost the plot. Bipolar disorder took over. I began dismantling the house. Took out the gas fires for some reason known only to me. Denise had to get them capped off. I scrawled meaningless statements on the walls of the living room.

I dressed in strange garb. Had my ears pierced and began to wear earrings. Many men wear earrings. I wore hoops.

I must have been a laughing stock. My Father disowned me. Eventually even Denise had enough. She found a council flat in a nearby block and moved everyone out. She left Sandy the wolf dog. I would take him out for mammoth marches. He loved it.

I would go over and see Denise and the boys. She was always supportive and happy to see me. She could not live with me at that time, which I find understandable.

One evening I had gone to a local pub, dressed in floral shorts and a vest. I began talking to a couple of girls. They seemed OK with me. I was just making conversation, no more than that.

There were a couple of men glowering at me from across the room. After a couple of hours, I decided to leave and head for another pub nearer to my house. As I came out of the door, I noticed the two men sitting on a bench that was against the wall of the pub.

I didn't like the look of them, so I turned in the opposite direction and began walking off. Suddenly one of them jumped on my back, from behind. He pushed me to the floor. Then he proceeded to kick me in the head. I think his friend joined in.

I rolled into a ball, trying to protect my head. After an age it stopped. I sat up slowly, looking around to make sure they had gone.

I headed for home. My head was pounding, my face ached and all of my body hurt. I couldn't understand why that had just happened. I didn't go home. I kept walking and ended up at Denise's place.

When she saw me she was clearly shocked. I had not seen myself at that point. When I did I was shocked. I looked like the guy that Paddy had the altercation with on the day I moved into my new house in Ock Street.

Paddy had not jumped him from behind. He was not a coward. That seemed a lifetime ago.

Denise said I had to go to the police station. I said what was the point, they knew everyone in the pub. I was just a bizarre looking stranger. Nobody would back me up. She insisted and after she had cleaned me up, we went to the police station.

After quite a long wait, sitting amongst the dross of Pontypool, we were called in. The policeman was the one who had dragged me out of the house 7 years earlier. I'm not sure if he recognised me, but I definitely recognised him. He had a long scar down his face. We had already named him scarface.

I explained what had happened. He told me that the guy who attacked me was well known for it. Apparently he was a heavy drug user and when he was particularly high on drugs, he liked to beat people up. That's not what happened to us in the halcyon days of marijuana smoking. Quite the opposite. We loved everyone. Yeah man.

He went on to tell us that there was no point in the police trying to do anything about this. They had tried on a few occasions and the people who would have witnessed the incident always denied any knowledge. His advice was that I don't go in that pub again. Very helpful.

A few days later I was in the local working mens club, playing pool. I had quietened down my appearance, wearing jeans and t shirt. My face was still a mess though. I was trying to be less conspicuous. I might have been mad, but I was not stupid.

A man I did not know came over to my table. He said he would like a word. He told me that the person who had beaten me up was really sorry. That was OK then. He could have given me brain damage, maybe killed me. But he was sorry so everything was fine.

This guy said that my attacker would like me to go back to the pub so that he could apologise to me. 'The police have told me never to go in that pub again' I said. 'He can come here and apologise if he likes'. He didn't.

For some reason when I get manic, I become interested in the SAS. I think it originates from my conversation at the bus stop with my Uncle Philip, when he told me my Uncles were in some kind of special forces unit.

I now know differently, thanks to my cousin. However, not at that time. One day I went down to Pontypool Park, which I often did. There was always space to get away from everything. Except my head of course.

I sat down on the edge of a pond to look at the fish. A man appeared and sat nearby. He asked me if I lived in Rosser Street. I said yes, I did. He told me that a friend of his also lived in the street, at the other end from me. He said his name. He informed me that this guy used to be in the Regiment which is how members of the SAS term it, apparently.

He also told me that they had a mutual friend who lived in a house in the Black Mountains. He was currently serving and had been involved in many missions to the several conflicts at the time.

I was doubtful, even then. I realised when I got 'better' that this was another of my psychotic episodes. I have begun to realise that they seem to be some visible manifestation of my thoughts at the time.

One night I was carted off to Pontypool police station by Scarface. I can't even remember why. I was not unfamiliar with the insides of the police cells in Pontypool. I was probably drunk on that last occasion.

Every few years I have an enhanced DBS check because of my job. None of these visits has ever shown up, because no charges were ever made. I personally think Scarface had it in for me.

This particular visit resulted in an important discovery for me. In the morning, after a night in the cells, a psychiatrist was summoned. Presumably somebody had finally realised that I might be suffering from a mental health problem.

He was called Dr. Siddiqui. He turned out to be almost as mad as me. However after a brief talk, he pronounced that I had Bipolar Disorder. I had never heard of it and said so. It used to be called Manic Depression, he said.

I had heard of that. Pete Abbotts Mum's partner had it. He always seemed perfectly fine to me. I suppose I do except for when I am manic.

I wasn't sure I believed him. I had been trying to find out what was wrong with me for the past 15 years. I had seen countless doctors and psychiatrists over that period and none of them had come to this conclusion.

It turned out he was right. He told me that bipolar can be treated by the use of some Australian salts. I had no idea what he was on about. He arranged to come to my house to discuss things further.

I persuaded Denise to come to the house that day, as a witness. Again Dr. Siddiqui started talking about Australian salts. Neither of us knew what he was talking about. Eventually it came out that he was talking about Lithium.

Lithium is a naturally occuring mineral. Australia is one of the main places it is mined. It can be found in brine pools. Perhaps that is where he got it from. Why he didn't just call it Lithium I have no idea.

Dr. Siddiqui used to talk to Denise about his home life a lot. He told her that his wife liked gold and had many bracelets and bangles made of the stuff. Denise had no idea why. We decided he was a bit unhinged.

For many years after that I was sent to several different psychiatrists. Having read up on Lithium, I was not keen on its side effects. It could result in kidney failure, I was told. So I asked if I could try other medication. There are many for bipolar.

None of them were effective, but I only found out when I had another bout of mania.

It took months for this episode to pass completely. Towards the end I asked Denise to bring the family back home. Initially she would not. I reassured her that now we knew what the problem was, we could sort things out.

She came back a couple of weeks before the start of the new millennium. We celebrated it together. We both smoked and drank too much that night. After that I couldn't face cigarettes or alcohol for weeks. I haven't smoked since except for during manic episodes. I do like the odd glass of wine and the occasional pint of real ale.

I had been signed off work for months. I got in touch with Wayne and said I wanted to go back. Denise told me that he had been calling her over the time I was off to ask how I was. He really was a good bloke.

A meeting was arranged at HQ to discuss my return to work. It was held in the boardroom. When I was shown into the room, there was Wayne and Sue Phillips. Wayne smiled and said hello. Sue Phillips did most of the talking.

Mostly she told me that they weren't too sure what they would require me to do upon my return. She felt this meeting was necessary for her to explain the position. She was not sure that they could continue to employ me. They were going to come to a decision over the next week and would like to see me again. She specified a date.

I left in shock. Could she get rid of me for being ill? I believed it was her, not Wayne. I contacted the union rep and was put in touch with a UNISON official. His name was Steve Belcher. I can remember him clearly even though this meeting took place 21 years ago. I saw him on TV recently. He is now a very senior UNISON manager and was involved in negotiations with a major national employer.

He came to the meeting with me. Initially he said nothing, just sat at the end of the table and observed. Wayne had clearly been programmed to say a few words at the start and finish of the meeting. Once again Sue Phillips did most of the talking.

She told me that I could not return to my previous role. She went on to say that they would try to find me an administrative job to do, as I clearly could not be allowed to work one to one with clients.

At this point Steve interrupted. He sounded quite annoyed. 'What do you mean by that?' he enquired.

'The company cannot risk client safety by allowing Arthur to work on a one to one basis' Sue Phillips explained.

'Can you provide evidence of that? Arthur has had this illness all of the time he has worked for you. Why would he be a threat now?'

There was no answer to that and I was allowed to come back. Not as the work experience coordinator, but as an Adviser, which meant a pay cut. Being the work experience coordinator was too stressful for me apparently.

At the time I was just relieved to get back. It was not until some time later that I realised the reason I became ill was due to the unnecessary pressure the company had put me under. I felt I had been treated unfairly.

I told the company union representative that I felt cheated and wanted to seek reinstatement. She said forget it. I had no chance.

Not content with that, I contacted the UNISON branch office and was put in touch with Mr Billy Liddon who was the Assistant Branch Secretary. He said I was right. I had been unfairly treated and he would represent me.

He arranged a meeting with Sue Phillips and myself. He questioned her about the reason for my demotion. She explained from her point of view. He put a couple of possible scenarios to her. She insisted these did not apply. Billy painted her into a legal corner. I can't remember the exact details, and if I'm completely honest I didn't really understand at the time.

But eventually, he got her to a point where she had to admit that she had not acted legally and she would have to reinstate me.

The problem was that my job no longer existed. They had amalgamated it into some other employer related work and recruited someone from outside the company to fill the new position.

Billy made a suggestion. How about I continue to work as a Careers Adviser but be reinstated to my pay grade as a work experience coordinator. Sue Phillips had to agree. He further said that I should be repaid the money I had lost since demotion, in a lump sum.

I thought he was pushing it, but she agreed to that as well. It came to a tidy sum, which we made full use of. Peter got a new computer and Denise got a new wardrobe.

I couldn't stand living in Pontypool anymore. I felt I had burned my bridges in Abingdon. I wanted to set them alight in Pontypool. I put the house on the market after I had cleaned it up. I sold it for exactly the same amount I had paid for it 10 years earlier.

We went looking for a house away from Pontypool. I had been sent back to Caerphilly to work as a Careers Adviser, so we started looking there. The houses we saw were far too expensive.

Eventually we found a lovely little semi detached house in Blackwood where prices were much lower. It was a lot closer to Caerphilly than Pontypool.

We didn't have a lot of furniture and I didn't want to pay a removal company to take our few possessions from Pontypool to Blackwood. Colin's employer had a flatbed truck. He said we could use that.

We piled everything onto this truck and headed for Blackwood. We looked like the Clampetts from the Beverly Hillbillies as we pulled into the cul-de-sac where our new house was situated.

I don't know what our new neighbours made of us, but we were all very excited. I had taken on a mortgage to buy the place, but it was well worth it. It even had an en-suite in the main bedroom, albeit an extremely small one.

This all happened in the first year of the new millenium. I was given a new school on my return to work. It was St. Martin's school in Caerphilly. I was to work there for the next 6 years. The careers teacher was Lianne Page. She was without doubt the best teacher I ever worked with.

Lianne always supported me in all that I tried to do. We worked together on the mammoth logistical task of getting year 10 out on work experience. I liked talking with the pupils about where they would like to go. They all enjoyed it, even if it was only to get out of school for a week. I enjoyed it a lot more than having to actually arrange the placement.

The school was not as supportive however. I was given a careers room that had been a store cupboard for games equipment. It still smelt of leather and dubbin. That was not so bad. Not as bad as a boys urinal. It was very small and the back wall had the girls toilet behind it. It was a stud wall and not at all soundproof.

The school gym was directly in front of the careers room and could get extremely noisy. In summary, this was not a particularly peaceful place. Sometimes I could hardly hear the pupil in front of me.

I have explained my aversion to noise because of my bipolar. This was torture on a daily basis. I spent as much time out of the room as I could. Much of our work is interviewing so that wasn't much.

The ceiling was made of asbestos, which was damaged in places. I could see strands of asbestos hanging down from holes in the ceiling. It was obviously dangerous. I reported this to the school. Nothing happened.

I told my manager about it. He informed a senior manager who came out to discuss it with the deputy head. As a result of that meeting, nothing happened.

I contacted our health & safety team. They sent a health & safety officer to inspect the room. He put a comprehensive report together pointing out a number of faults. He recommended that the office not be used. Nothing happened.

I never escaped the room for the six years that I was at the school. Within a few months of my leaving St. Martins the new Adviser was given a brand new, purpose built office.

It was at St. Martins that I interviewed the talented pianist who intended becoming a world famous concert pianist.

There were quite a number of others I remember. A young girl who was also a talented musician. She played the trumpet. Her uncle was Andy Fairweather-Lowe who was the lead singer in Amen Corner, a famous pop group from the mid sixties.

An accomplished guitarist, he has worked with Eric Clapton, George Harrison and others. This girl had played with him and Eric Clapton. She seemed to think that was normal.

There was a young man who wanted to go to university and study law. He is now a successful criminal lawyer in London. His dad recently told me in Asda that he still remembers my encouragement in school.

Another young man wanted to study medicine. He is now a consultant at the Heath hospital in Cardiff.

I love to hear about the success of these former pupils. There have been many more over the years. I cannot claim responsibility for their successes, but hope that I might have made some small contribution.

As well as moving house and restarting my career, I thought it would be good to take my wife and youngest son on their first foreign holiday. I would use my share of that lump sum to part fund it.

We went to Thomas Cook in Caerphilly high street. We talked through all the various holidays on offer. Denise liked the look of a place called Olu Deniz in Turkey. Peter and I did too, so we booked it.

Before we were due to fly, Tony Blair sent our armed forces into Afghanistan. Denise decided Turkey was too close to Afghanistan and said she wanted to change the holiday.

We went back to Thomas Cook. I said I wanted to change the booking. I asked the rep if she had any ideas. She told us that they were just completing a new hotel on Zakynthos in Greece. Because it wasn't quite finished they were offering discounted holidays this year which would be the first year of operation.

She recommended it very highly, so we said yes.

Denise didn't much enjoy the flight. She still doesn't. Peter loved it. I bought him a model of a My Travel plane from the inflight magazine. I had to buy him one every time we flew from then on.

We landed on the island. As we stepped out of the cabin, we experienced the usual blast of hot air that greets you. I had experienced it before but they hadn't. They both gasped.

We got through customs and found the bus that was taking us to our hotel. It was called the Alykanas Beach. It was in a small village called Alykanas and backed onto a beautiful sandy beach.

As we travelled across the island to get to Alykanas we passed through a desolate looking landscape. Here and there were old rusty cars and various piles of junk. It didn't look like on the brochures.

Denise told me later she and Peter both wondered what kind of dump I had brought them to. But then the coach pulled up at the hotel. It was clearly brand new. It had a large, impressive marble entrance. Inside was air conditioned and massive with sofas and tables dotted around the reception area. There were a couple of bars that served snacks too.

I went up to the very long reception desk and was quickly served. I wasn't used to that in Greece. We gave over our passports and were given our room keys. We went through the back entrance and came out to a huge swimming pool. It was scorching hot and I wanted to dive straight in.

We found our room and went in. It was a lovely corner room. The large balcony faced out to sea. There was a bath and shower. Denise likes a bath, I prefer a shower. A lot of holiday places overseas do not have baths so this was ideal for her. Peter at that time would prefer neither, but we made him.

We had a magical holiday that year. We went back several times, but somehow it was never as good. I guess it was because it was our first overseas holiday together. Walking out across the grounds behind the hotel you passed another large swimming pool. The garden then sloped down to the beach.

The sea was nearly always calm in Greece as they have no tides. This year it was like a sheet of glass. The first time I went into the water, it felt like a warm bath. The water was so shallow it was only up to your knees one hundred yards out.

Peter wouldn't go in the sea, despite me walking out and showing him how shallow it was. Denise stayed out as well, to look after him. He was only 9 at the time.

We were self catering as the restaurant had not been built. I prefer to eat out in Greece anyway. We would walk down the main street in the evening, looking at menus and deciding where to eat. Invariably a waiter would come out and try to get you in. Sometimes they were insistent to the point of being rude. I would walk off at that point.

After a few nights, we had settled on a couple of tavernas we liked. From then we used the 'Sorry, I have eaten' technique to ward off unwanted waiters.

All too quickly the holiday was over and I was back in school. Everything went back to normal. My bipolar seemed to have gone, or maybe I had got used to it.

Chapter 28

Dads funeral and a major episode of mania

In 2006 my Dad died and everything changed massively. He knew that he was dying and had planned his own funeral. He had paid for everything too. He had booked a golf clubhouse for the reception. It was in a village near to where he lived in Caldicot, Wales. This clubhouse was an impressive place, but I was in no state to appreciate it at the time.

On the day of the funeral, Colin drove us to the church, which was just as well as it turned out. It was very strange. I was fine when we left home. We went into a pub near the church before the service. I had a few beers and smoked a cigar. Denise saw the signs, she told me after. By the time we got to the church I was in the early stages of mania.

The ceremony began. Dad's coffin was wheeled in. It had been parked outside for a while and I stood nearby smoking with my nephew Anthony, Tims' son. Anthony had been diagnosed as a paranoid schizophrenic a while ago, so we were able to share our madness over a cigarette or three.

After the usual hymns, my brother gave the eulogy. He was standing on some kind of a stage rather than at a lectern. He put on a good act. I realised during this speech that some of it was like the one he gave at my Mum's funeral. He said that he had been looking through Dad's things after his death and had found some papers setting out his wishes.

I thought that's not true. My Dad had made a will and lodged it with a local solicitor. He told me so himself. Would a man so organised as to arrange his own funeral and wake not make a will? Dad had told me the contents of that will, which included a bequest to myself. I never saw anything.

My brother had said exactly the same thing at Mum's funeral. I knew she had been paying a monthly sum towards her funeral costs for years. She might have stopped paying of course, but that is not clear. Should I have given my brother £1,000 the day of Mum's funeral? Probably not.

I have never been that bothered about money. If I have it, I'll spend it. If I haven't I can't. It's not the money that I might have been left, it's the fact that my parent's last wishes may have been ignored because of the avarice of people who don't need the money.

All through his speech my brother referred to Audrey as his Mother. He said it many times. I said each time 'she's not your mother'. All of Dad's brothers were at the funeral. They had hired a minibus to bring them from Reading. They planned to have a good drink at my Dad's expense. A few around me heard what I was saying. They seemed to agree.

After the service we went to the golf club. I was fairly bonkers by this time. My cousin Nigel had taken over the family business. Uncle Les had retired. Nigel had a pen stuck behind his ear. I asked him what it was for. He said 'you never know when some business might come up' I thought probably not at my Dad's funeral you stupid (expletive). I still can't believe that.

For some reason I had brought some old black and white photos I had found. They showed my Mum and Dad on holiday on the Isle of Wight. They both looked really happy. There were a number of photos of Hutt family members including long dead relatives. My Nan was there and Poppy. Jeff, an Uncle who had learning disabilities and had died a long time back.

I went round showing these to my Uncles. They were all interested. They had not seen them before. My Uncles used to call my Dad Ticker. He used to like to dismantle clocks when he was a child. He couldn't put them back together again.

There were comments like 'There's Ticker with Nettie. Don't they look happy?' The wicked stepmother was nearby, seething. She was angry with me for even being there, let alone reminding my Uncles that she was actually nothing to do with my family. She had always hated his nickname, Ticker

Denise told me much later that she had said she didn't know why I was so upset, I didn't care about my Dad.

After the funeral I went home and became increasingly crazy. In 2004 we had moved into a brand new detached house on a small estate above Blackwood. It was built off plan. I liked to go up and see it being built. I found out later that Denise had cried as we left our little semi detached. She didn't want to move.

I loved the house. It was roomy and the main bedroom was big with a large en-suite. When we first moved in we had a lovely neighbour named Phil. We helped each other out. There was a shared driveway separating the two houses.

In 2005 Phil sold the house to a couple from hell. I won't go into detail but they were always causing trouble for us. There were disputes over parking in the shared driveway.

Denise had started a childminding business which was going OK. The wife called the council accusing her of abusing the kids in her care.

The husband got me sectioned. He might have inadvertently done me a favour there.

So, we went home after the funeral. I continued to act like an idiot. I couldn't help it of course. Every other time, I had come out of my manic phases relatively unscathed. Not this time.

I have no idea how it happened but I teamed up with some guy called Mark. He used to take me drinking. I met some of his girlfriends. I spent lots of time with them all. Denise tried to warn me, but to no avail.

I should have been suspicious when I went to a party around one of their houses and saw boxes of new TVs, computers and other things which practically filled a spare room.

Meanwhile, I would smoke cigars in my bedroom and flick the butts into my neighbour's garden. It amused me, but not them. They would challenge me and I would give a suitable reply.

One day, I decided to buy a Porsche. I had always wanted one. I had seen one in a garage near Usk. I went over and bought it. The salesman looked at me and thought I was a timewaster. The deal went through however and I drove off in my bright yellow Porsche Boxter S.

In time I realised I didn't need the car and sold it to a garage in Bridgend. I got the same for it as it had cost me, so I only lost the insurance money I had paid out. I'd had my Porsche, if only for a brief time.

Chapter 29

Sectioned

I had decided to give the back garden a makeover. I was out there turning it into a fairground when some guy came through the gate. He told me he had been contacted because someone was concerned about me. Next thing I knew he was joined by several others. He was a psychiatrist, there was a social worker and I could work out the others as they were dressed in police uniforms.

I was taken to the front of our house where I saw a police car parked next to mine. Denise and Peter were in the doorway. Denise was in tears.

I was put into the police car. The police were pleasant enough. There was no rough stuff. As we drove off, I saw our next door neighbours waving and laughing from inside their bay window.

Denise thinks I blame her for calling this team. The man next door worked for Mind, which is incredible. He knew how to arrange this type of thing. I am certain it was him.

I was taken to a place called Ty Sirhowy. The local nut house I would have called it. Or the loony bin. I was there for about three months. Some had been there for years, so I didn't do too bad.

It was quite a pleasant place, although it was full of odd characters. I eventually accepted I was one of them. I do remember the food was excellent. I had a full English every day and delicious curries, pies and all sorts for dinner. I could have got fat, but luckily mania keeps the weight down.

Every evening we had to line up for our drugs. A nurse measured out whatever was your particular cocktail and made sure you took it. Denise told me that for the first few weeks I was a zombie.

Denise carried on as she always did, looking after me, at a distance if necessary. She came with Peter every day. She walked over a mile each time. She would stay with me for as long as was permitted.

Peter hated being there. Many weirdos would accost him. I told Denise she should not come, but she did. Every day. She kept me sane. Almost.

There were some fascinating characters. One guy claimed to have visited the Dalai Lama in a cave in Tibet. He said that when you met him, you had to bring a gift and he would then impart some wisdom to you. Really? I thought. Perhaps I should have done that outside the Swan.

Of course, there is always someone who was in the SAS. They say that it is the biggest regiment in the British Army. There is at least one SAS soldier in every pub in Wales.

There was one man who I was never sure whether to believe or not. He was always smartly dressed. He expressed himself well, with a refined accent that was not faked. He told me that he was a Sales Director with a well known brewery that I can't remember. He told me that he had introduced Kopparberg Cider to the UK.

This was such a specific and plausible claim that I am not sure whether it was true or not. I guess even high flyers lose the plot. Bipolar certainly shot me down whilst I was flying high.

I can't say that my stay in Ty Sirhowy was all bad. At the end I had got through the mania. But this time it was not without damage.

I soon found out that I was massively in debt. I had no idea how and still don't. Apart from the Porsche, I did nothing extravagant. As I said I didn't lose much on that deal.

The only answer is that Mark person. I didn't hear from him again. I did have a phone call from some stranger who knew I was financially in trouble. Mark had told him. He was prepared to offer me next to nothing for my new house. Thanks, but I'll pass on that one.

Finally, it worked out to about £50,000. I sold the house and we moved into a terraced ex-miners cottage as the estate agents euphemistically called it. This enabled me to clear the debt, leaving a deposit for this place.

We were happy enough. Denise wasn't bothered at all. She didn't like the detached house. I had always wanted a detached house and a Porsche. Like the cocaine back in Abingdon with Peter. I had tried them all once, and so was content.

Chapter 30

Back to work

This time I went back to work and there was no question from the management about my fitness to do my job.

I was put into another school which was probably just as well. I had roared into St. Martins in my yellow Porsche, narrowly missing a couple of pupils. Roy the caretaker came out to admire the car. He found my unannounced arrival amusing.

I thought it was probably best to steer clear of St. Martins. Having said that, I did go back as part of a team delivering group sessions. Lianne came over and had a chat. She seemed pleased to see me. I was certainly pleased to see her. Maybe there was no issue. I can never tell.

I was only at this new school for a couple of terms. I was approached and asked to work with adults. There was a need for an experienced adviser to deliver some Welsh Government contracts and Wayne had apparently decided with my background I was an ideal candidate. Perhaps I was back in his good books. Maybe I was never out of them.

I did not want to work with adults. I enjoyed school work. Always had. But in the end it was an order.

The contract is called ReAct and it still exists. It is a grant for people who have been made redundant. The idea is to help them get back into employment as soon as possible. It is and always has been an excellent project which has had many successes.

I found that I enjoyed it from the start. I came to the realisation that I am an adult, so why should I be concerned about working with adults? I should be able to better understand them than school kids, who were often a complete mystery to me.

With no disrespect to school based Advisers, this work has far more impact with the client and can therefore be far more rewarding. I can help someone make a major change in their circumstances.

There was one client I remember who came to see me. He seemed very unhappy. He had his wife with him. She told me he had been clinically depressed for some time and was on medication. He had a responsible job running a nearby food processing factory.

He had done this job for many years but had begun to hate it a few years ago. He now dreaded going into work. He had negotiated a voluntary redundancy deal with his employers. He had no idea what to do next.

We had a long talk about all sorts of things. With many adult clients it is necessary to just let them talk with the odd interjection. Models of Guidance go out the window.

Throughout our conversation, we talked about his hobbies. The thing he most liked doing was working in his garden. He had a large garden that took a lot of maintenance. He became most animated when this subject came up. It was clearly something he loved to do.

I asked him if he had considered working in grounds maintenance. He said no he hadn't even thought of it. We talked more specifically now. What jobs were there locally. What training would he need to do. Would the ReAct grant fund it.

He decided why not? Rather than type up a report of our meeting in a couple of days then post it to him which is what we were doing at the time, I took the Judith Evans route. I wrote down several bullet pointed actions for him to take.

He came back the next day. He wanted to get going straight away. He had found the courses he wanted to do having discussed his plans with a local college that could provide the training. We completed the paperwork and off he went.

He contacted me a few months later. He had got a job with an agency. He was maintaining grounds for CADW. He has kept in touch. The last time we talked he had set up his own business, maintaining a few private gardens. He wasn't making a lot of money, but it was enough, he said. He would not be rich but he was very happy.

Over the years there have been many such cases.

Chapter 31

Final Major Madness (hopefully)

Following my 2006 manic episode, I was seeing the psychiatrist who had sectioned me on an outpatient basis. He told me that I must take Lithium. I was still totally against the idea. I don't know why. In fact I refused any medication because I was feeling OK.

He told me that if I didn't take the Lithium, I would have another manic episode by the time of the upcoming Olympic Games in London in 2012

I actually had it in 2011. I am hoping that it was my last major episode. There is a suggestion that these manic episodes are caused by extreme stress. This one occurred when I was back in Zakynthos. I had agreed to a three week break with my employers. We were part way through when I once again started to behave in a bizarre fashion. Staying up all night, smoking, drinking constantly.

I saw an advert on a telegraph pole. It said nightclub for sale. I decided I wanted to buy it. I got someone I knew to take me to the nightclub. I had a chat with the owner who for some reason took me seriously. It was on for two million euros. No problem affording that on a Careers Advisers salary.

The lunacy continued. I was going to buy a hotel at one point. The time came for our departure. I had hired a car to continue to pursue my various deals. I took Denise to the airport. I said I had to stay on and conclude my business ventures.

She begged me to get on the plane with her. I wouldn't. Even now I feel dreadful about this. She had looked after me so often, but I abandoned her to fly home on her own. She never flies without me.

She phoned David from the airport and asked him to go to Gatwick and meet her. He did.

One day I was walking from Alykanas to the next village, Alikes. There is a small canal that runs between the two villages and I have often walked along it. I saw a group of people in the distance, heading in my direction.

As they got closer I realised it was David with his wife and William his youngest son.

David told me he had come to take me home. Of course I refused. He stayed as long as was necessary to make me agree. His wife and William went back long before then.

Eventually he got me onto a plane to Gatwick. When we arrived there, Peter was waiting. They piled me into the back of Peter's car, wedging me between two suitcases to stop me doing anything stupid.

We got back to Blackwood. They took me straight to Ty Sirhowy where they had arranged for me to be accommodated for the next couple of months. Again Denise came to see me every day.

That was the last time I was in that place. I won't be going back because they have flattened it and built offices on the site. I won't be going to its replacement in a nearby hospital either.

I went to see the psychiatrist again. He more or less said 'I told you so' I asked to be put on Lithium. He wrote the prescription out.

Once again I returned to work. The lithium put me into a semi coma for a couple of weeks. I struggled but I think I managed to hide it. I did feel quite dreadful, but it got better. I still take it every day.

I was afraid of kidney problems. That was what had been putting me off. Now I get my blood tested frequently which checks on the level of lithium in my blood. I am confident that my kidneys will be OK. My only regret is that I didn't start taking the stuff years ago.

Chapter 32

Safe at last

Unfortunately Denise had finally had enough. I can't blame her. She divorced me in 2016. I actually moved out of the miners cottage in 2011, when I got out of Ty Sirhowy. I rented a flat in Caerphilly. I have now managed to buy a little one bed flat.

I've cleared the mortgage so I no longer worry about ending up in a shop doorway. I really did think I would become a tramp. They have to come from somewhere.

Denise and I are the best of friends. I see her several times a week. We enjoy each other's company far better this way. Can't live with her, can't live without her, to coin a phrase. I know she could quite easily live without me, but for some inexplicable reason she sticks by me.

We go on holiday together every year. We haven't been back to Zakynthos. I don't like going back to places I have been crazy in.

Since 2011 I have not had a major manic episode. That's down to lithium. I was told when I started it that it wouldn't necessarily stop the mania, but it would reduce its effect considerably.

I have always been a creative person. The trouble with Bipolar is that during the depressive times, I don't have the energy or even ability to be creative. It's all I can do to keep going. When I enter into a manic phase, I get creative in so many ways that it all gets totally muddled up.

I try to paint, draw and write all at the same time. The result is a mess. I believe this is because after ages laying dormant, the creative urge is like a dam bursting and everything comes out at once.

I have always wanted to write a story about my life and experiences. I have only ever attempted it whilst manic and when I come out of the mania it makes no sense.

I have now been on lithium for over ten years. Denise told me a few weeks ago that she thought I was going manic. I wasn't smoking or wearing hoop earrings. I wasn't behaving particularly strangely. I was talking too much however. She knows me much better than I do. She was right. As the psychiatrist predicted, I have had a much less devastating episode. The flow of creativity has been controlled, like the weirs in Sutton Courtenay that control the Thames as it passes from the river to the pools below.

Without the weirs the water would cascade down, out of control and quickly overwhelm the lower levels. This new manic phase has given me the urge to be creative but in a far more controlled and productive way.

I have always been afraid that I would soon have another manic experience. I have never seen them coming and never accepted there was anything wrong when they did. It was only afterwards when I had to clear up the debris that I realised it had happened again.

Things would have been different now if I had been diagnosed with bipolar when I had that first attack in 1985 and if I had been prescribed lithium. But I wasn't and probably wouldn't have taken the medication if I was.

I don't believe in looking back with regret and wishing things could be different. At least Bipolar has taught me to live for today.

My Mum used to say 'If wishes were horses, beggars would ride' I think I know what she meant.

She also said 'Little things please little minds. little trousers fit little behinds'

Love you Mum

Printed in Great Britain
by Amazon